Bilbury Times

Vernon Coleman

Books by Vernon Coleman include:

Medical
The Medicine Men
Paper Doctors
Everything You Want To Know About Ageing
The Home Pharmacy
Aspirin or Ambulance
Face Values
Stress and Your Stomach
A Guide to Child Health
Guilt
The Good Medicine Guide
An A to Z of Women's Problems
Bodypower
Bodysense
Taking Care of Your Skin
Life without Tranquillisers
High Blood Pressure
Diabetes
Arthritis
Eczema and Dermatitis
The Story of Medicine
Natural Pain Control
Mindpower
Addicts and Addictions
Dr Vernon Coleman's Guide to Alternative Medicine
Stress Management Techniques
Overcoming Stress
The Health Scandal
The 20 Minute Health Check
Sex for Everyone
Mind over Body
Eat Green Lose Weight
Why Doctors Do More Harm Than Good
The Drugs Myth

Complete Guide to Sex
How to Conquer Backache
How to Conquer Pain
Betrayal of Trust
Know Your Drugs
Food for Thought
The Traditional Home Doctor
Relief from IBS
The Parent's Handbook
Men in Bras, Panties and Dresses
Power over Cancer
How to Conquer Arthritis
How to Stop Your Doctor Killing You
Superbody
Stomach Problems – Relief at Last
How to Overcome Guilt
How to Live Longer
Coleman's Laws
Millions of Alzheimer Patients Have Been Misdiagnosed
Climbing Trees at 112
Is Your Health Written in the Stars?
The Kick-Ass A–Z for over 60s
Briefs Encounter
The Benzos Story
Dementia Myth
What Doctors Won't Tell You About Chemotherapy

Psychology/Sociology
Stress Control
How to Overcome Toxic Stress
Know Yourself (1988)
Stress and Relaxation
People Watching
Spiritpower
Toxic Stress
I Hope Your Penis Shrivels Up
Oral Sex: Bad Taste and Hard To Swallow
Other People's Problems

The 100 Sexiest, Craziest, Most Outrageous Agony Column Questions (and Answers) Of All Time
How to Relax and Overcome Stress
Too Sexy To Print
Psychiatry
Are You Living With a Psychopath?

Politics and General
England Our England
Rogue Nation
Confronting the Global Bully
Saving England
Why Everything Is Going To Get Worse Before It Gets Better
The Truth They Won't Tell You...About The EU
Living In a Fascist Country
How to Protect & Preserve Your Freedom, Identity & Privacy
Oil Apocalypse
Gordon is a Moron
The OFPIS File
What Happens Next?
Bloodless Revolution
2020
Stuffed
The Shocking History of the EU
Coming Apocalypse
Covid-19: The Greatest Hoax in History
Old Man in a Chair
Endgame
Proof that Masks do more harm than Good
Covid-19: The Fraud Continues
Covid-19: Exposing the Lies
Social Credit: Nightmare on Your Street
NHS: What's wrong and how to put it right
They want your money and your life.
Their Terrifying Plan

Diaries and Autobiographies
Diary of a Disgruntled Man

Just another Bloody Year
Bugger off and Leave Me Alone
Return of the Disgruntled Man
Life on the Edge
The Game's Afoot
Tickety Tonk
Memories 1
Memories 2
Memories 3
My Favourite Books
Truth Teller: The Price

Animals
Why Animal Experiments Must Stop
Fighting For Animals
Alice and Other Friends
Animal Rights – Human Wrongs
Animal Experiments – Simple Truths

General Non Fiction
How to Publish Your Own Book
How to Make Money While Watching TV
Strange but True
Daily Inspirations
Why Is Public Hair Curly
People Push Bottles Up Peaceniks
Secrets of Paris
Moneypower
101 Things I Have Learned
100 Greatest Englishmen and Englishwomen
Cheese Rolling, Shin Kicking and Ugly Tattoos
One Thing after Another
Vernon Coleman's Dictionary of Old English Words and Phrases
Old Man in an Old Car
Vernon Coleman's Commonplace Book

Novels (General)
Mrs Caldicot's Cabbage War

Mrs Caldicot's Knickerbocker Glory
Mrs Caldicot's Oyster Parade
Mrs Caldicot's Turkish Delight
Deadline
Second Chance
Tunnel
Mr Henry Mulligan
The Truth Kills
Revolt
My Secret Years with Elvis
Balancing the Books
Doctor in Paris
Stories with a Twist in the Tale (short stories)
Dr Bullock's Annals
The Awakening of Dr Amelia Leighton
A Needle for a Needle (novella)

The Young Country Doctor Series
Book 1   Bilbury Chronicles
Book 2   Bilbury Grange
Book 3   Bilbury Revels
Book 4   Bilbury Country
Book 5   Bilbury Village
Book 6   Bilbury Pie (short stories)
Book 7   Bilbury Pudding (short stories)
Book 8   Bilbury Tonic
Book 9   Bilbury Relish
Book 10 Bilbury Mixture
Book 11 Bilbury Delights
Book 12 Bilbury Joys
Book 13 Bilbury Tales
Book 14 Bilbury Days
Book 15 Bilbury Memories
Book 16 Bilbury Times

Novels (Sport)
Thomas Winsden's Cricketing Almanack
Diary of a Cricket Lover

The Village Cricket Tour
The Man Who Inherited a Golf Course
Around the Wicket
Too Many Clubs and Not Enough Balls

Cat books
Alice's Diary
Alice's Adventures
We Love Cats
Cats Own Annual
The Secret Lives of Cats
Cat Basket
The Cataholics' Handbook
Cat Fables
Cat Tales
Catoons from Catland

As Edward Vernon
Practice Makes Perfect
Practise What You Preach
Getting Into Practice
Aphrodisiacs – An Owner's Manual
The Complete Guide to Life

Play
Mrs Caldicot's Cabbage War

Written with Donna Antoinette Coleman
How to Conquer Health Problems between Ages 50 & 120
Health Secrets Doctors Share With Their Families
Animal Miscellany
England's Glory
Wisdom of Animals

Another collection of memories from the English village of Bilbury.

Copyright Vernon Coleman 2025
The right of Vernon Coleman to be identified as the author of this work has been asserted in accordance with the Copyright, Designs and Patents Act 1988. All rights reserved. No part of the work may be reproduced, stored or distributed in any new form without permission. To reproduce material all enquiries should be addressed to the author.

**Dedicated to my beautiful and brilliant Antoinette,
with all my love**

There's a weariness touching my soul
And a weariness deep in my bones
The strength to continue, my love
Comes from your presence deep in my heart
Thank you for being you, and for everything you do.

Contents
Introduction
Bodley Hall
The Campers
Alarums, Excursions and Confessions
Uncle Charlie
A Hard Night, a Long Engagement and Gilly's Rock Cakes
The Student
Evening Surgery
A Miracle in a Stable
Chase Anderson
The Mystery Illness
Thinking about the Future

Appendix One
Appendix Two
Appendix Three
Appendix Four

Introduction
The Young Country Doctor series

It is apparently seven years or so since the last Bilbury book appeared. My excuse is that strange things have happened in the outside world and have caused some disruption to all our lives. This is the 16th book in this series and so, if I have done my sums right, there are probably around fifteen other books describing the Devon village of Bilbury and its inhabitants. All the books in the series are available as paperbacks and as e-books on Amazon. A few hardback editions of the first seven books were self-published in modest runs but these are all now out of print. Some of the books are available in large print versions and some are available as audio books. The first few books are sequential but after about the third book you can read them in any order you like without getting into a tangle. Bilbury and its residents are, of course, still firmly and comfortably ensconced in the 1970s and will doubtless remain there indefinitely. In the world about which I write here, the mobile phone does not exist and nor does social media. Poor reception means that not even the television has made a mark on life in Bilbury. And so, as you can see, the world of Bilbury is, indeed, very different to the world we know today.

    There are two main ways to begin an autobiography. The first way, the traditional way, is to begin with the protagonist's childhood and to describe his school days and early memories of his parents, aunts, siblings and playmates. The disadvantage with this approach is that it is inevitably as dull and worthy and predictable as a royal Christmas broadcast. The reader will struggle and probably give up before Chapter Two. The second way is to begin with an account of some event for which the subject is best known – an in-depth account of how he won his Olympic medal, how he won his Oscar or how he prepared for his streak across Lord's cricket ground in London. The snag with this approach is that Chapter Two will have to flash back to the subject's tediously predictable childhood. And, of course, the reader will have nothing to look forward to because they will have already devoured the juicy bits.

My approach in writing about my life in Bilbury has been quite different. I have eschewed all memory of my childhood, and since my life contains no high points I have found it easy to avoid the second technique too. Instead I have chosen to describe my experiences in an episodic way, describing my experience with my wife, my friends, my patients, my home and my practice.

It seems fair to say that this technique has served me well enough since this is the 16th volume of my reminiscences, and I commend the method to all those who feel themselves unable to resist the temptation to describe their lives on paper and who wish to avoid the two deadly ways of doing this which I have described above.

As usual, the names and details of individuals, animals and establishments, except the Duck and Puddle (recently described in print as 'the most authentic and most welcoming inn in England) and Peter Marshall's shop (described in print as 'famous for overpriced tat and food that is long past its sell by date), have been altered to protect the author from lawsuits launched by both the innocent and the guilty. The stories in this book are all set in the 1970s when life was very different in a multitude of ways. The author makes some predictions in this book and you can judge for yourself whether you think they were well-based and accurate or bizarre and completely off the wall. If you ever feel that the world is sometimes strange, difficult, frightening or alien in some ways, please consider yourself a citizen of Bilbury where trust, respect and dignity are still in vogue. You will always be welcome to enjoy a pint and one of Gilly's rock cakes at the Duck and Puddle. And if you're passing Bilbury Grange and need to have your verruca pared or your stitches removed do pop in. The magazines in the waiting room are changed every six months. The place where you feel safest and most comfortable is your home. If it helps, please think of Bilbury as your 'safe' place; your refuge at all times, and please think of the Doc, Patsy, Thumper, Patchy, Frank and Gilly, etc., as your friends. Living in Bilbury means you never have to be alone.

Whether you are a resident, a regular visitor or someone wandering into the village for the first time, I bid you welcome and thank you for sharing my life and my memories. Kind readers sometimes ask if the Bilbury stories are real. It's a fair and reasonable question and one which I have asked myself more than once. There is one thing we can agree on: there is no village with the name of Bilbury. No real village with that name exists. We know this because if we look up 'Bilbury' in a Gazetteer or a map of Devon, we won't find it. We will end up in a place called Bibury, which is in Gloucestershire and has nothing to do with Bilbury, or we will end up with a reference to one of the Bilbury books which means that we have ended up back where we started and are absolutely no further forward. So, that much we know: the name 'Bilbury' is fake. I admit it: I made it up. But that doesn't mean that the village doesn't exist. It just means that if it does exist then it must be called something else. And you have to make your own mind up about just how true the stories are and, indeed, whether I exist or am a figment of my own imagination. My only hope is that you will enjoy reading these tales. After all, that's what really matters. Isn't it?

Welcome to Bilbury. And welcome to my world.

Vernon Coleman, Bilbury,
January 2025

Bodley Hall

Bodley Hall is one of the largest houses in the village of Bilbury, and it stands on the outskirts of the village.

The previous owners, Mr and Mrs Wilkes, were amateur developers, both in their 40s, who had spent the previous 15 years buying up derelict houses described as 'in need of care and attention' (estate agent's parlance for 'there are holes in the roof, the kitchen dates back to the 1920s and there is little or no indoor plumbing') or advertised as 'an attractive property which needs a little updating' (estate agent's parlance for 'the kitchen dates back to the 1930s, the solitary bathroom contains a cracked iron bath and the only heating in the house is a hearth in the middle of the drawing room which the sellers jocularly refer to as an early example of central heating') doing them up, in a superficial sort of way (painting over the woodworm and the subsidence cracks in the walls), and then selling the property to a gullible purchaser, usually making a substantial profit.

The Wilkes were referred to locally as 'amateur developers' because they had no regular jobs and no other source of income, but moved regularly and made their living from the houses they lived in. They had renovated a number of houses in the South of England. They had two huge advantages over professional developers. First, in Britain, house owners do not have to pay capital gains tax if they make a profit out of selling their home. And second, in the 1970s the British tax laws provided big tax breaks for home owners who wanted to borrow money to purchase or improve their private property. These two fiscal treats meant that 'amateur developers' had a huge advantage over professional property developers.

Sadly, for the Wilkes this particular project had failed. They had completely under-estimated the cost of renovating Bodley Hall and after eighteen months of hard work, they had run out of money and, since there was no happy end in sight, the bank which had loaned them the money to buy the house had refused to lend them any more money and had pulled the plug on their enterprise. They had left quite quickly, leaving much of the work half done, and, it was reputed, had moved to Scotland where they had bought a castle with 500 acres of forest and rough land, together with an island and loch fishing for the sort of money that a Londoner would expect to pay for a small, semi-detached house in a rather gloomy suburb. The word was that they had found a bank prepared to lend them 110% of the purchase price.

The Hall had been empty for two years, and the regular North Devon gales had taken the fabric's condition back to where it had been before the Wilkes had worked on it, and so I was more than slightly surprised when at the end of my morning surgery my loyal and long-serving receptionist Miss Johnson (whom I had inherited, together with my car and the property which became the Bilbury Hospital, from Dr Brownlow) told me that I had a telephone call asking me to visit. 'They're new patients and they'd like to join the practice. They said it's not urgent,' said Miss Johnson, 'but if you could visit sometime this week they'd be very grateful.' She hesitated. 'I did tell them that they're actually nearer to the practice in West Parracombe, but they said they had asked around and they'd rather be registered as patients with you.' Having told me this, Miss Johnson paused and lowered her voice. 'I'm not surprised,' she whispered, though there was no one around to overhear. 'I've heard terrible things about that practice. The doctors there allow their receptionist to decide whether patients receive a home visit and sometimes they won't visit at all.' She looked at me sternly. 'I don't agree with that, doctor,' she said sternly. 'Don't you get any ideas of asking me to start quizzing the patients about their symptoms. That's not my place.'

I promised her that I wouldn't. Miss Johnson sometimes acts like a sergeant major, welcoming a bunch of new recruits to the parade ground but underneath the surface she is a big softy and has a heart of gold.

Apart from the transparent flattery, the message told me one thing: the callers were new to the village and had probably come from a town or city where patients have to wait a week or more to see a doctor.

'I'll call in before lunch,' I told her, looking at the very short list of patients asking to be visited at home before picking up my black bag and heading out to the car.

It is my experience, having visited a good many of them, that large country houses often look much better from a good distance and, preferably, from a distance of at least half a mile. The older the house the more likely this is to be true. The closer you get to one of these ancient piles, the more likely you are to see the crumbling stonework, the blistered remains of paint on doorways and window frames, the cracked window panes, the missing bits of guttering and downpipes and the weather-disfigured, carved stone gargoyles.

Repairing one of these huge, old houses can cost vast sums, especially since those houses in England which are considered to be of historic importance are often put on a list of properties worthy of special attention, and consequently every minor repair must first be approved by teams of fussy bureaucrats who, it is widely believed, are driven more by envy and spite than any genuine concern for history or architecture.

The drive to the house was at least half a mile long. The first 400 yards ran as straight as a die between rows of Lime trees. After that the driveway wriggled a bit, clearly designed so that visitors could better view the house ahead of them and be impressed by the owner's taste and wealth. I am constantly surprised by the number of large houses in North Devon, and even more surprised at the size of the largest of them.

Landscape gardeners who were hired to plan the grounds of large houses always tried to impress visitors as much as possible. And their determination to do so is understandable. What's the point of owning a huge park and a massive pile in the country if visitors aren't impressed?

The fields on either side of the driveway contained deer, which were kept in place by a metal fence which must have cost a fortune to erect and another fortune to keep painted. Sadly, no painting had been done for some years and the fencing was mostly the colour of rust. The fence was nowhere near high enough to keep the deer in place. Deer can leap fences with the greatest of ease.

I parked the Rolls alongside a dark blue Range Rover which was itself parked alongside a grey Bentley Continental. Also, parked in the gravel area in front of the house, but a little way distant, were a Maserati, a BMW and a lorry full of building equipment.

'Rolls Royce 20/25,' said a slim, young man who was wearing jeans and a scruffy jumper and who had appeared through the front door. His light brown, streakily sun bleached hair was just short of shoulder length and he wore an impressive Zapata style moustache that was clearly his pride and joy, and on which he undoubtedly spent much effort and time. Indeed it looked more like a hobby than a moustache. He had the easy, innocent smile of a man who has had things easy and doesn't yet understand why so many people find life a trial. It was the smile usually seen on the faces of young men who have come into a good deal of money or who have fathers who are dukes, inordinately rich or in some way influential. He was carrying a large sized Filofax which was bulging with loose pieces of paper. His comment was a statement not a question but I replied, nevertheless.

'It is.'

'1933?' This time it was a question.

'Close, but out by a year. It was built in 1934. They brought the model in as a smaller and cheaper version of the Silver Ghost. It was the cheapest Rolls Royce of its time.'

'But still a Rolls Royce.'

'Yes, still a Rolls Royce.'

The young man walked around the car, examining it carefully from every angle. 'Who did the bodywork?'

'Thrupp and Maberley.'

'Four litre engine?'

'A bit less, it's 3675cc. They only ever built 3824 of them.'

He nodded. 'Lovely car. Do you use it every day?'

'Yes.'

'Bit big for the lanes around here, I'd have thought.'

'It's OK.'

'Reliable?

'The local garage looks after it for me. It runs very well. I had to have a stainless steel exhaust system put in because all the stopping and starting on short trips to patients meant that the exhaust never heated up properly and went rusty. And the short trips are a strain on the battery so I connect it to the mains occasionally and give it a good feed of electricity.'

'I love old cars. If you're interested I'll show you round the barn some time where they're all stored. They're old, little known British made cars. There's an Armstrong Siddeley 20/25 saloon, an Alvis speed 20 drop head coupe, a British Salmson 14 hp saloon, a

Humber Snipe sports saloon, a Frazer-Nash TT, a Siddeley special touring limousine and a Daimler Light Straight Eight.' He recited the names without hesitation. The moustache was clearly not his only hobby.

I was impressed and said so. Some of the cars I'd never heard of, let alone seen. For a few seconds I was even slightly envious and then I remembered that the more stuff you have the less time you have for fun, the more insurance you need and the more reasons you will have to worry.

'You'll be the doctor,' he said. 'I saw you coming up the drive. Thank you for coming out so quickly.'

A young woman, about the same age as the man in jeans, hurried out to join us. She too was dressed in jeans and a scruffy looking sweater. But whereas he wore what used to be called pumps she wore knee length, black boots. Her blonde hair, swept back in a pony-tail, shone in the sunshine.

'Hello, thank you for coming so quickly,' she said. 'Before we go any further, may we join your list of patients? Is that how it works? I suppose I must be registered with a doctor somewhere but I can't remember who or where. Are you private or part of the National Health Service?'

'I'm a very small, tucked away part of the NHS and yes, that's how it works,' I said. 'Every GP has a list of patients he looks after. The Government gives me around nine-pence a year to take responsibility for all your health needs for 24 hours a day and 365 days a year. But because my practice is inevitably small and intrinsically rural, they give me a small bonus on top of that.'

'And is it true that you don't have an appointments system? Patients just turn up at your surgery?'

'That's right, there's no appointments system. You just turn up to Bilbury Grange which is where I live and work. There are surgeries at 9 a.m. on every weekday morning and surgeries at 4 p.m. on Mondays, Tuesdays, Thursdays and Fridays. At the weekend and on bank holidays you have to telephone if you want to see me. If you need me at night or you need me to visit you just telephone and either speak to me or leave a message with my wife or my receptionist. I'd give you a little card with the phone number on but I never got round to having any printed so I haven't got any little cards. The phone number, however, is in the phone book.'

'Under your name?'

'Under my name. And talking of names, I'll need yours. And I'll need your national insurance numbers. Eventually your old medical records will come to me. Even if the medical records only have to travel two miles that will usually take six months or so because there are a lot of bureaucrats involved and they like to stretch things out as much as they can. Meanwhile, tell me if you have any health problems I should know about or if you're taking any regular medication.'

'I'm Dick,' said the young man. 'We've just bought this place.'

'His real name is Marmaduke,' said the blonde who, since she was wearing a wedding ring and an engagement ring with a huge diamond fixed into a gold claw was, I assumed, his wife. 'He was a spotty kid and they called him Dick. You know what boys are like. As far as we know we're both healthy and neither of us takes any medication.'

I must have looked puzzled.

'Spotted dick, the pudding.'

'Ah, yes.'

'I like to tell people that they called me Dick because of Dick Barton – the detective series on the radio,' said Dick. 'My surname is Barton.' He sighed. I gathered that he preferred the thought that he was named after Dick Barton, rather than a sponge pudding. 'Either way I prefer Dick to Marmaduke or Hildebrand – which are my official Christian names.'

'But officially you're still Marmaduke Hildebrand Barton?' I said, taking out a notebook and making a note of his name.'

'Unfortunately, yes, I keep meaning to change my name legally but I haven't got round to it. And strictly speaking the name is Barton-Hennessy. It's one of those daft double barrelled names. I only use the Hennessy bit for passports and bank accounts. I prefer to stick to just Barton if that's allowed.'

'That's fine with me.' I made a note of the name and looked at the woman whom I assumed was Mrs Barton.

'Emily Barton. I was christened Emily and I've been Emily ever since. My mum was a fan of the Bronte sisters. My full name is now Emily Anne Charlotte Barton would you believe it.'

'This is becoming quite a literary village. I have a patient called Byron Shelley. Do you by any chance have a brother called

Branwell?'

'No I actually have two brothers. But my father insisted on naming them. He was a huge cricket fan. One is called Denis and the other is called Jack.'

'After Denis Compton and Jack Hobbs?'

'Exactly,' she smiled. 'Unfortunately, they both hate cricket. And I can't stand the Bronte sisters I'm afraid.'

'And we can come onto your list?' said Mr Barton.

'Yes, that's fine. But if you're well enough to move around I prefer it if you come to the surgery if you need anything.'

'Yes, of course. We do actually need you to look at someone who is rather poorly – not poorly enough to need an ambulance but too poorly to leave the house. She's upstairs. She doesn't actually live here, she lives in London, and obviously we can't call her doctor from London.'

I got my black bag out of the car and followed them into the house and up a ridiculously grand staircase. Two men, standing on planks suspended between two stepladders, were removing a false ceiling in the house's entrance hall.

'The previous owners put horrid false ceilings in a lot of the rooms in order to cut the heating bills!' said Mrs Barton. 'But we're having it all ripped out. The original ceilings are wonderful. 'I'm tempted to have a stair-lift put on one of the staircases,' said Mr Barton. 'These ceilings are so high that the stairs go on for ever.'

'Or we could put in a proper lift,' said Mrs Barton. 'I think having our own lift would be rather nice. We could hire a chap to stand in the lift and press the buttons so that we didn't have to. He could tell us which floor we were on and what to expect.'

'Going down, third floor, bedding, soft furnishings, second floor, ladies underwear, that sort of thing,' grinned her husband.

I wasn't entirely sure that they were joking. Rich people often do strange things.

At the top of the grand staircase, I turned left and followed them along a grand corridor, about as wide as a motorway and decorated with lots of gilt framed old paintings. We passed half a dozen doors before Mrs Barton stopped, knocked, turned a huge brass doorknob and opened a huge door.

'I'll go downstairs and see how the builders and architects are doing,' said Mr Barton tactfully. 'They're around somewhere but I haven't seen them for an hour.'

I followed Mrs Barton into what turned out to be a vast bedroom which contained little more than a very large four poster bed, a bedside table, a wardrobe and an assortment of chairs which were sprinkled around the room, looking rather lost. In the bed lay a young woman who was obviously related to Mrs Barton.

'This is my sister Sabrina,' said Mrs Barton, who then introduced me and explained why I was there.

I put my black bag down on the floor, sat down on a chair which had been conveniently placed beside the bed and looked at Sabrina. 'Tell me what's wrong.'

'I don't know,' said Sabrina. 'That's what I want you to tell me.'

I began again. 'What symptoms do you have? When did they start?'

'I woke up yesterday morning and I was paralysed. I couldn't move my arms or legs. It was terrifying.'

'But the paralysis wore off quite quickly,' said her sister, trying to offer comfort.

'Yes, but it was bloody terrifying when it happened. I didn't know where I was or what was happening.'

'She has also had bouts of fainting,' said Mrs Barton. 'She's had hallucinations and been unconscious several times.'

'And I was sick too. And I had diarrhoea. If I get out of bed I feel faint and wobbly.'

I was beginning to feel overwhelmed with all these symptoms. Nothing made much sense.

'The symptoms seem to change and they come and go,' said Mrs Barton.

'May I examine you?' I asked, hoping that I might find more useful clues that way.

Sabrina threw back the bedclothes and undid the buttons of her pyjama jacket. I opened my black bag and took out my stethoscope and sphygmomanometer. After a fairly extensive examination all I could find was that her heart beat was very slow – only 46 beats a minute.

'Are you an athlete?' I asked her. 'Your heart is unusually slow.'

Mrs Barton laughed lightly. 'No! She certainly isn't an athlete.'

'I used to play tennis,' said Sabrina, defensively.

'You haven't played tennis since you were 16!'

There was a pause.

'No, I don't suppose I have.'

'Do you take any prescribed drugs?'

'No. Nothing at all. I was on the contraceptive pill for a year or two but my boyfriend and I split up so I stopped taking it.'

'Don't be offended,' I said, 'but have you taken any other drugs?'

She looked at me, apparently puzzled.

'Cannabis? Anything stronger? I'm not proposing to be judgemental and I obviously wouldn't report anything you tell me but I need to know.'

'No, no. Nothing like that. I don't even smoke cigarettes.' She shook her head. I believed her.

'How much alcohol do you drink?'

'I don't drink much alcohol – just a glass of champagne at weddings and so on. I'm very particular about what I put in my body. I'm vegan and I only eat really healthy foods.'

'What do you think it is, doctor?' asked Mrs Barton.

For a moment I didn't say anything. I was nonplussed. If it hadn't been for the slow heart rate, which was very real, I might have suspected some sort of psychosomatic problem. Sabrina wasn't obviously depressed or anxious, other than about her curious symptoms, and she was alert and clearly desperate for a solution. And the curious thing that I couldn't get out of my head was that the symptoms came and went and came and went. This sort of episodic change made everything even more difficult to understand.

'You're vegan?' I said to Sabrina.

'Yes. I've been vegan for seven or eight years.'

'Have you eaten anything unusual recently? Has your diet changed? Have you picked any mushrooms for example?'

'No. And I wouldn't pick wild mushrooms. I don't know enough about them to feel safe eating mushrooms I've picked myself.'

'Have you been abroad?'

'The three of us travelled a good deal before we bought this house,' said Mrs Barton. 'We went to China, Thailand and India for three months though Sabrina stayed on for another month after Dick and I came home. But we stayed in very good hotels and we were careful about what we ate.'

'Were any of you ill while you were away?'

'I had an upset tummy for a couple of days,' said Sabrina. 'I vomited and I had terrible diarrhoea and felt incredibly disorientated. I had hallucinations too, but I thought everything was due to the fact that I was feeling weak after the vomiting and diarrhoea.'

'Were you or your husband ill?' I asked Mrs Barton.

'No, we were home by then. This was while Sabrina was on her own.'

'Do you know why you were ill? Could that have been something you ate or drank?'

'I don't think so. I was staying in a hotel in India. They served mostly Western food to be honest and when I went out for the day I prepared my own food. As I said, I'm very careful about what I eat. At lunchtime I mostly ate sandwiches which I prepared myself in my rooms. I know it might sound odd but none of us is particularly keen on curries and spicy foods. We all went to India because we find the culture fascinating.'

'Can you remember what you had eaten before you were ill?'

'Nothing out of the ordinary. I had the usual breakfast and dinner in the hotel and took sandwiches with me for lunch.'

'What did you have on the sandwiches?'

'Don't laugh. I had Marmite sometimes and sometimes I had honey. I bought tiny pots of both in a shop near the hotel. I made my own sandwiches and there wasn't much left in the little pots so I threw them away each time I'd used one.'

'When did all your current symptoms start?' I asked Sabrina, deciding to go back to the start in case I had missed something.

'I actually started to get some of the symptoms about three days ago.'

'Had you been gardening? Could you have been in contact with any unusual plants?'

'No, I don't go out of the house much,' said Sabrina. 'When I got here my sister asked me to offer some design ideas for the house so I've hardly been out at all.'

'You haven't been scraping off paint or anything like that?'

Sabrina and Mrs Barton both laughed and shook their heads.

'Tell me exactly what your diet consists of.'

'I have toast in the morning, pasta and salad at lunchtime and I usually have rice with nuts and vegetables in the evening. I drink green tea and bottled spring water.'

I scratched my head. 'It really sounds as if you're being poisoned by something,' I told Sabrina. 'All I can think of is that it's something you've eaten. Have you eaten anything unusual or new in the last week or two?'

Sabrina and Mrs Barton both thought for a while.

'Let's work our way through the day. What do you put on your toast at breakfast?'

'Honey. Nearly always honey.'

'Where do you get the honey from?'

'Oh, all over the place. I buy different honeys. I did open a new jar a week or so ago. It was something I brought back from Nepal. I had some once and rather liked it so I brought back a jar.'

'Was that by any chance the same honey that you used to make your sandwiches before you were ill?'

'Actually, yes, come to think of it was. I liked the honey so on my way back to the hotel I bought a large pot of it and brought it back with me.'

'Are you the only one who's eaten that honey?'

'Yes. My sister never eats honey and Dick says this particular honey is too bitter for him. It's an unusual colour and, I suppose, rather an acquired taste.'

'What colour is it?'

'It's redder than usual honey. It was terribly expensive. Apparently it's something of a speciality in Nepal.'

'So, you were ill after you'd eaten a sandwich you'd made with this honey when you were in India, and you've been ill, with similar symptoms, after eating the same honey for breakfast?'

'It's the honey!' said both Sabrina and her sister simultaneously.

'Until proved otherwise. Could I see the jar, please?'

Mrs Barton disappeared and returned four or five minutes later with the jar of honey. She was breathless. 'The kitchen is miles away from here!'

I took the jar from her and looked at the label. There was a brand name and underneath the name ''rhododendron luteum' which was, I assumed the name of the bush from which the bees collected the honey in the jar. I wrote the name down in my notebook. 'May I borrow your telephone?'

Mrs Barton led me downstairs to their solitary telephone and I rang my friend Will, a GP who is now also a Professor at the medical school where we both qualified.

'Do you know anyone who is an expert on different types of honey – and the problems they can cause?' I asked him.

It seemed such an esoteric request that he laughed.

I explained that I wanted to know whether rhododendron luteum had ever been known to cause any health problems.

'Give me two minutes,' said Will. 'There's a toxicologist working in the pathology department. I'll ask him.'

'Do you really think the honey could cause all Sabrina's problems?' asked Mrs Barton.

'We'll know in a moment,' I replied.

And we did.

'Have you got a patient who's been eating honey made with bees who fed on pollen from rhododendron luteum or rhododendron ponticum?'

'Yes. rhododendron luteum.'

'It's known as 'mad honey',' said Will. 'Those two types of rhododendron contain a neurotoxin called grayanotoxin. It can be nasty stuff which causes temporary paralysis, hallucinations, unconsciousness, disorientation, bradycardia and intestinal upsets – vomiting and diarrhoea.'

'Do you happen to know if the effects are transient or permanent?'

'Our guy says they're temporary. Stop eating the honey and the symptoms disappear. It's mainly sold in Nepal apparently.'

'That's where my patient got it.'

'Our toxicologist is quite excited. Apparently one of Socrates' students described how a company of Greek soldiers ate honey which they stole from beehives in Turkey. They were disorientated and had vomiting and diarrhoea for a day. But as soon as they stopped eating the honey they were fine. And there's also a story that Pompey the Great led his army into a genuine honeytrap. The locals put honey on the route, knowing that the soldiers would steal it and eat it, and then when the intoxicated soldiers were temporarily hors de combat they killed them all.'

'Thank you! I owe you.'

'You can pay the debt straight away if you like.'

'How?'

'Is there any of the honey left?'

'Yes, half a potful.'

'Send it to me to give to the toxicology guy. He's quite excited about it. He wants to do some tests with it. He reckons he can get a couple of scientific papers out of it.'

I turned to Mrs Barton and Sabrina and explained that the honey was definitely the cause of the problem. 'Would you let me have the honey so that I can send it off to the toxicologist who's just confirmed that it is the culprit?'

'Definitely!' said Sabrina. She gave me the pot of honey. 'Please take it away!' she said. 'I never want to see it again.'

I put my stethoscope and sphygmomanometer away in my bag and added what was left of the pot of honey – carefully wrapped in an old piece of cloth that Mrs Barton gave me for that purpose.

And then Mrs Barton led me back downstairs.

'How long have you been living here?' I asked her.

'We bought the place three months ago but only started moving in a week ago. It needs a lot of work. The previous owners hacked it around a good deal but most of what they did was done on the cheap and it shows. We're going to have to tear out most of their improvements. It's a huge place but we plan to use it all. According to the estate agent's particulars, there's a billiard room, a library, a smoking room, a music room, a butler's pantry, a flower room, a gun room, a fish room, and a walk-in strong-room for the silver and glassware. We haven't found all the rooms yet. Heaven knows where the fish room is. We own a lovely cottage a field and a half away and apparently we sort of own most of a village a few miles to the West. We went looking for it but got completely lost and just kept driving past a pub called 'The Duck and something'. We've got a muniments room and a map room too. The map room is full of maps showing the estate's boundaries. We're lucky the previous owners didn't throw them out or sell them. If you know anyone who is looking for a cottage to rent please ask them to get in touch. It's an awful shame to see it empty.'

'What is a muniments room?'

'Oh, sorry, I had to look it up too. Apparently it's a room in which all the title deeds are kept. Most of the stuff our solicitor didn't have was in there – all packed away in tin trunks.'

'Are you doing all the restoration yourselves?'

'Good heavens no,' laughed Mrs Barton. 'Dick wouldn't know which end of a hammer to hold and he's a real wimp. The first time he hit himself on the thumb he'd give up. We've got a series of builders and architects coming in to give us quotes. There are two architects in the house at the moment. The builders are just pulling down our predecessor's improvements. We're both a bit scruffy because we've been trying to unpack some of our stuff and settle into a couple of rooms that we can make liveable.'

As we approached the ground floor, Mr Barton came up to us. We stood for a while in the spacious reception hall.

'The doctor has found the reason for Sabrina's problem!' said Mrs Barton.

'That's brilliant. What was it?'

Mrs Sabrina explained about the honey. I added that the diagnosis was made with the help of a university toxicologist.

We carried on walking towards the entrance.

'We thought about finding somewhere to rent while we had this place renovated,' said Mr Barton. 'But a couple of friends who've done up an old house told us that the only way to do it is to live in the house. If you let the builders do things while you're not there you'll find that they've taken over.'

'One couple we know had builders who, entirely off their own bat, put false plaster board ceilings throughout the ground floor,' said Mrs Barton. 'Our friends had to sack the builders and hire new ones to take down the ceilings. Builders seem to like putting in false ceilings.'

'And the builders had poured waste oil and dirty diesel into the septic tank,' added Mr Barton. 'You'd think they'd know, wouldn't you?'

I nodded understanding. 'The same thing happened to us when we moved into Bilbury Grange.'

'The decor is absolutely awful,' said Mrs Barton, as I looked around the reception hall.

There seemed to be no pattern to the renovations except bad taste. The huge hall was full of large oil paintings of people who looked like someone's ancestors. They were imprisoned in huge gilt frames and stared down at all interlopers with that haughty, superior air which seems common among such portraits. I wondered, as I had done before, if the people being painted assumed the standard expression while sitting for the painter or if the painter added the look for no extra cost.

'The previous people bought all these pictures for peanuts at auction,' explained Mr Barton. 'We have no idea who any of them are but they're a pretty miserable looking bunch.' He stopped in front of a painting of a man with a huge black beard. 'We'll keep this one. We call him Great Uncle Esmond and rather like to think he was a pirate. We're probably going to have to pay a dealer to take the rest away. No one has walls big enough for paintings as big as these. Do you happen to know of any reliable antique dealer?'

I gave them Patchy Fogg's name and details. They thanked me. 'Can we mention your name?' he asked me. I said they could.

'The previous owners partly furnished some of the rooms with real rubbish. You saw the stuff in Sabrina's room. Most of it looks as they'd been bought wholesale from a landfill site. I think they were planning to take in paying guests or open the house to the public though I can't imagine why they thought that would have worked.'

'They were going to do weddings as well,' added Mrs Barton. 'Almost all old houses do weddings these days. The banqueting hall is usually big enough for the reception and the bedrooms are good to house all the relatives.'

'Doing this place up is going to cost a fortune!' I said, looking around the great reception hall, which looked big enough for five a side football.

'Money is actually the least of our problems,' said Mr Barton. 'I made my money out of a piece of software I wrote when I was 20. I wrote it thinking it would make a good game but I used an agent who sold it for £73 million to an American software company and the software company then sold it to a large American bank. They used what I'd written to help them create some sort of complex financial product which I don't begin to understand. These days I never gamble, I never bet because I reckon I've used up all the luck God gave me. Three days after the bank had bought my software, they bought another bank which was already using something similar so they dumped what I'd done and used that one.'

'You don't mind that they dumped your software?'

'Not in the slightest. I get to keep the £73 million, which is mostly invested in gold and some really boring bonds and stocks, and I've retired,' said Mr Barton. 'Restoring an old house is far more fun. Now I get to learn the meaning of words such as 'curtilage', 'ha-ha' and 'demesne'.'

'This place was built in the 1720s and we've got around 200 acres of parkland, woods and gardens,' said Mrs Barton. It wasn't said in a boastful way but more in a sense of surprise and mild awe. 'The house is crenelated, as you'll have noticed, a bit like a castle, and it is known as a calendar house.' I thought she sounded a little like one of those guides who escort paying visitors around stately homes. It was warming to see someone enjoying their good fortune. I wondered if they had been married before Mr Barton had become a multi-millionaire.

'I know what crenelated means but you'll have to remind me – what's a calendar house?

'Oh, sorry, it's a house that has 365 leaded windows, 52 rather ornate chimneys, 12 turrets and seven staircases. I don't really understand why anyone should build a house to remind them of the number of days in a year or the number of weeks in a year since it would probably be cheaper to buy a calendar or some sort of almanac but in times when cost was never regarded as a factor when designing a house they did things like that. Can you imagine how easy it is to get lost when you're living in a house that has got seven staircases? We've had to stick numbers at the top and bottom of each staircase so that we don't keep getting lost.'

'But there's no moat,' said Mr Barton. He sounded rather disappointed.

'So the little boy has to have one made!' said Mrs Barton with a rather proud smile. 'We're negotiating with the historic houses people, and I think they might let us put in a drawbridge. We'll have three huge JCB diggers creating a massive ditch and then we'll use the earth to make a hill that we don't need. We'll need to take down a pile of topiary but I hate topiary. It's all made up of yew trees carved into fancy shapes and I feel embarrassed for them. We'll move the trees somewhere else and let them do whatever they want to do. And we have to move a grave near to the shrubbery and an early 19th century cess pit by the back door. There's a stone marked with dates and the name Bernie. We can just make out some words in Latin which Sabrina translated as 'The rabbits are safe now'. We're not entirely sure whether Bernie was a person or a dog but since the grave is right by the very old cess pit, we rather think that either way he wasn't very popular.'

'We're' going to put up a sign saying 'Trespassers will be shot and buried and we're going to put a folly on top of the hill,' said Mr Barton. 'Every old house should have a folly. We could plant the yew trees round the folly, and maybe we could hire a hermit to live in it. The moat is for security, by the way. We'll raise the drawbridge at night and any burglars who want to try their luck will have to swim, or bring a boat with them.'

'We haven't got anything a burglar might want to steal.'

'We've got Great Uncle Esmond. I'd be heart-broken if we lost him. And people might think we've got valuables.'

'If we have a moat built they'll think we must be rich and worth burgling.'

'The moat is going to be a circular swimming pool, too. We'll line it and put filters in so that the water is clean.'

'We looked at a house in Wiltshire which had a folly built a mile from the house. The folly consisted of a church spire without a church. The spire was built behind a hill so that the man who built it could just see the spire from his bedroom. He also had a huge stone wall around his entire estate and a stone mausoleum based on the design of one of the pyramids.'

'And a monument to some knight who died in 1755 as a result of having been kicked in a vital organ by a chambermaid to whom he was paying his obviously unwanted addresses.'

'I wonder which organ she kicked. It would be useful to know.'

'I fancy a folly based on the Parthenon, but perhaps just half size.'

I was quietly amused by the way the two made their plans. And if they really did have £73 million or so sitting in the bank then they probably would do all the things they had mentioned and bring quite a bit of business to local builders, carpenters, electricians and plumbers.

People who have old money, inherited wealth, are nervous about losing it because they didn't make it and know that if they lose it they will be reduced to being poor people, a prospect which fills them with quiet terror. On the other hand, people who have made their own money are often much more confident and free and easy with it – ready to spend what they have. They made their money all by themselves and, generally speaking, are confident that if they lose it all they're pretty sure they will find a way to make some more.

One thing was for sure: Bodley Hall was going to keep them busy for quite a while.

I was home late for lunch that day.

Patsy greeted me at the door with a big smile.

'Mrs Trelawney came round this morning,' she said. 'She knows how much you love home-made honey and she's brought you three pots of her very latest.'

I looked at her, slightly startled. 'She doesn't have any rhododendron bushes in her garden, does she?'

Now it was Patsy's turn to look surprised. She frowned. 'I don't think so, it's a traditional cottage garden. But why…?'

I explained.

The Campers

It was 6.30 a.m. on a beautiful June morning. The finches, the tits, the robins and the blackbirds were singing and chattering endlessly, constantly searching for food to supply to their noisy and demanding chicks; the sky was that wonderful blue that artists struggle to capture, and it looked as if was destined to be another beautiful summer day. Our resident family of ravens, croaking away in their unmistakeable way, were as always a comfort. Contrary to legend, ravens make loving parents. Ours always make a terrific racket if another bird dares to go too near to their young. At the Tower of London, where there is always a raven called Grip (named after the series of ravens who lived with Charles Dickens) it is feared that if the last raven leaves the Tower then England will fall. I feel the same way about our ravens.

As far as the weather was concerned, we'd had a couple of bad years in Bilbury, and the weather had hardly seemed to vary from season to season. We'd had too many dull days, grey skies, merciless winds and showers that turned into storms, turned back into showers and never seemed to end, but this was turning out to be the very best of summers – one of those seemingly endless summers we remember from childhood.

And considering that I have never been a person who much enjoys being out and about so early in the morning, I was feeling surprisingly good and at peace with the world. An hour or two earlier I had been called out to see Mrs Mayberry's 14-year-old daughter, Hettie, who had been having a bad asthma attack, almost certainly triggered by her hay fever. She suffered from awful bouts of sneezing and wheezing triggered by summer pollen and had been alarmingly close to status asthmaticus when I'd arrived. Her inhaler hadn't worked. However, an intravenous injection of hydrocortisone had done the trick and within minutes the wheezing, the struggling for every breath, had been banished and replaced with a big smile of comfort and relief.

Generally speaking, few things are as easy or as quick to deal with as night time asthma attacks and few things give more simple satisfaction to the doctor on the other end of the syringe.

I'd looked at my watch as I'd turned into the drive of Bilbury Grange, wondering if it was worth going back to bed or if I should have an early breakfast. I settled on making a quick breakfast: a cup of Earl Grey with a slice of lemon, a long glass of grapefruit juice and a couple of thick slices of wholemeal toast, generously smothered with home-made marmalade. I found myself wondering why marmalade tastes so much better on toast than on untoasted bread. And who first thought of toasting bread anyway. On a winter evening I liked to make my toast with an extendable brass toasting fork, holding the bread in front of a blazing log fire. Toast tastes (and smells) even better that way.

I'd just decided on the early breakfast, and could almost taste the toast, when Patsy, my wife, came running out of the house. She was still in her nightie, and had, more out of habit than any sense of decorum, put a thin, summer dressing gown around her shoulders. It was untied and trailing behind her as she ran, or rather half hopped and half limped across the gravel to the car. She had lost a slipper and was waving a piece of paper. She had obviously been waiting for me to arrive home.

'Don't get out of the car,' she said, as I was about to do just that. I turned the window winder and lowered the window of the 20/25. They hadn't put electric windows in motor cars in the 1930s, not even in the vehicles made by Rolls Royce. I'd inherited the 20/25 from Dr Brownlow, my predecessor in my medical practice, and it was a link with the past, a daily reminder of the days when motor cars had dignity and presence.

'Audrey Futtock telephoned ten minutes ago,' explained Patsy, rather breathlessly. 'I'm sorry but you need to go out again. I rang the Mayberrys but you'd just left. What was wrong?'

'Hettie had a bad asthma attack.'

'Is she OK?'

'She's fine and dandy. I think she probably left her bedroom window open again and spent the night breathing in pollen. I've told her and told her mum about shutting the window but they either forget or don't take any notice. Anyway, she's OK now. What's wrong with the Futtocks?'

'There isn't anything wrong with the Futtocks but Darren Futtock was out in one of his fields checking on a ewe that was a little lame yesterday when he saw two tents. He went over because he doesn't like campers just putting up tents in fields where there are animals. Anyway, to cut a long story short he found four young men in the two tents. They were unconscious. At first he thought they were all dead but Audrey says he doesn't think they are quite dead but in his words 'they aren't far off'. Audrey said could you get there as soon as you can if you don't mind because, in her words, 'my Darren isn't one to exaggerate or make a mountain out of a molehill'. And you know how Audrey is. If her house were on fire she'd apologise before asking you for a bucket of water.

'Which field?' I asked.

This wasn't as daft a question as it might sound. It's not widely known but nearly all fields in the English countryside have names though, as a rule, only the locals know them. Some of the fields in Bilbury have bizarre and surprising names. There are, for example, two fields near to Bilbury Grange called 'Well's Big Bottom' and 'Well's Small Bottom'. These fields, which are towards the base of a small hill (there are no big hills in Bilbury) used to belong to a man called Walter Wells. He owned a number of fields and these two fields were originally known as 'Well's Big Bottom Field' and 'Well's Small bottom Field'. Over time the word 'field' was discarded as unnecessary. When I first started work as a young GP in Bilbury, the doctor I was working for (a wonderful old gentleman called Dr Brownlow, the doctor who taught me everything I know about general practice and the previous owner of my 20/25) gave me a hand-drawn map on which he had sketched all the fields in the village. He'd written the names on each field. Like all doctors he had squiggly handwriting, of course, but after years of reading the medical notes he'd written I was still able to read most of his notes quite easily. Although I knew the names of most of the fields in the village, the map was still one of my most valuable and useful professional possessions, and when it had begun to fall apart I'd had copies made by a print shop in Barnstaple. I kept one copy in the house and one in the car. When I had a call to visit a farm, a house or a cottage that I hadn't visited for years or couldn't quite place, I'd just ask what fields were nearby.

'The one they call Timpson's Folly,' replied Patsy. 'It used to be called Seven Acre Field and then someone measured it and found it was only five acres. They then renamed it Timpson's Folly because Bert Timpson was the one who bought it thinking it was seven acres.'

I put my head out of the window, gave Patsy a peck on the cheek and just about remembered to pull my head back in before I put the Rolls into gear and set off again.

Ten minutes later I found Darren Futtock standing in the gateway leading into Timpson's Folly (nee Seven Acre Field). Well over six feet in height and almost as wide as he was tall, he had a permanently sad countenance which made him look as if someone had just run over his working sheepdog, and today was no different. He had a long thin nose which could have been used to open envelopes, eyes of an astonishing blue and ears which stuck out like the proverbial jug handles. His wife had, for years, wanted him to have surgery to have them pinned back but he had refused to do anything quite so 'soft' as to accept cosmetic surgery. Despite the nose, the eyes and the ears he looked as hard and as tough as he was, though he looked as though, in the battle with life, he always managed to be on the losing side. Despite all this I always found him friendly enough and never a man to turn down a neighbour's request for help. He had once helped me sort out our drains. He'd been passing, saw me struggling and stopped to help. I had worn rubber gauntlets and a mask to filter the smell. He'd just used his bare hands. I'm proud of the fact that I found the strength to shake his hand when I thanked him.

I drove a few yards into the field and Mr Darren shut the gate behind me, for there were several dozen sheep gathered at the far end of the field. I got out of the car and he led me along a hedgerow and stopped just short of a huge, spreading oak tree under which two tents were pitched.

'I don't think as how they're quite dead,' said Darren. 'Not all of them anyhow. But they aren't what I'd call well-looking.'

The flaps to both of the tents had been untied and I knelt down and peered inside the tent which was nearest.

Two young men were lying in the tent, fully clothed and seemingly asleep on top of their sleeping bags. They both looked to be in their late teens. My first thought, I confess, was that they were drugged and my initial assumption was that they'd taken something illegal. Both were barely breathing but clearly still alive.

I backed out and hurried to the second tent where, once again, there were two young men, of roughly the same age, lying, fully clothed, on top of their sleeping bags.

'We're going to need two ambulances,' I told Darren Futtock. 'Would you go back home, ring 999 and ask them to send two ambulances to your address. Then stay there and when the ambulances arrive bring them down here.' It was my experience that ambulance drivers, however good they were at their job, often got lost in the North Devon lanes and if they were given the name of a field as a destination they would be likely to become hysterical.

When Darren had gone, I crept back into the second tent and eventually, after shouting for a while, and shaking him a little, I succeeded in waking one of the boys enough to question him. I still suspected that the four boys had either taken an illegal drug or, perhaps, all eaten some toxic fruits or fungi which they'd picked. I couldn't think of another reason why four boys should collapse all at the same time. If they'd been in a caravan or motor home I might have suspected that they'd been overwhelmed by leaking carbon monoxide from a faulty heater or cooker but they were in tents so this was clearly impossible.

'What have you taken?' I asked the boy, as he gradually came awake a little.

'I haven't taken anything,' he said, defensively.

'I need to know so that I can help you,' I told him.

It took me nearly ten minutes of slow, determined questioning to find out what had happened. And it was one of the oddest stories I'd ever heard.

I never fail to be surprised by the people I meet in general practice, and some of the things they do to themselves. Every day brings something new, something you would never read about in the medical textbooks or the medical journals.

Almost (but patently not) unbelievably, it seemed that the four boys had decided to have a competition to see which of them could produce the darkest coloured urine. For three days they had, therefore, stopped drinking any fluids whatsoever as they attempted to produce darker and darker urine. It had, of course, been an immensely, unbelievably stupid idea (and the sort of thing only a group of youths would contemplate – I hate to appear sexist but I cannot for a moment imagine a group of similarly aged young girls doing anything similar) but their reckless sense of competitiveness kept them going, even as they began to show serious signs of dehydration. They were, indeed, in serious danger and urgently needed to be rehydrated.

A moment after I'd found out what had happened, Darren came running into the field, calling my name.

'They say they can't send an ambulance,' he said, between gasps and wheezes. He was a fit man in many ways but not a man for whom jogging or running were a part of his daily life.

'Not one?'

'No. There's been a big crash on the Exeter road. A coach overturned. All the ambulances are there.'

'Did they say how long before they can send us an ambulance?'

'They didn't know but they said they thought it would be several hours.'

And so, since there was no alternative, I decided that we had to take the four young men to the tiny, cottage hospital in Bilbury. It wasn't the first time that I gave thanks for the fact that the village had its own small hospital.

For many years, the tendency in Britain, and in many other countries, has been to close small, local hospitals (traditionally in England they are often known as 'cottage hospitals' though that is perhaps a little patronising since they were and are run along very professional lines) and to put all the available resources into enlarging and staffing huge hospitals designed to provide routine and emergency services for all the patients within a large catchment area. The financial reason for this is that it is supposed to be cheaper to run a few very large hospitals rather than a traditional mixture of large and small hospitals spread out geographically.

Unfortunately, the evidence suggests that closing down small hospitals and building up massive hospitals is neither efficient nor financially wise. Big hospitals accumulate huge numbers of administrative staff (there are often more clerks than nurses in a large hospital) and so patient care suffers. The evidence clearly shows that a decent number of well-distributed small hospitals will provide much better health care than a small number of huge hospitals located in big cities.

And there is another problem, because huge numbers of people are now up to an hour away from their only 'local' hospital and, with public transport often poor or non-existent, people simply cannot get to a hospital at all. An overworked and patchy ambulance service means that patients are often stuck without any effective hospital service. It had often occurred to me that if GPs ever stopped providing night time and weekend care for patients then the whole National Health Service would quickly collapse with the pressure on the ambulance service and on accident and emergency departments quickly resulting in disaster.

In Bilbury we are lucky because, thanks to the generosity of my predecessor, Dr Brownlow, we had our own private cottage hospital. When he died, Dr Brownlow had left his large house and most of his money for the development and maintenance of the Bilbury hospital. Just about every penny raised for charity in the village went to the upkeep of the hospital which had only one full-time member of staff but which was kept going by a number of willing and enthusiastic volunteers.

As the only doctor in the village I was the medical superintendent, the chief doctor, the visiting physician, the attendant surgeon, the house officer and just about everything else. If there were bottles to be washed and a shortage of bottle washers, I would have happily taken on that chore too. I also sometimes helped out by sitting on Dr Brownlow's old ride-on mower and cutting the lawns around the hospital. Occasionally, villagers would be surprised to see me cutting grass but I found this a pleasant, peaceful, relaxing and simple task with a low level of responsibility and a high level of reward. I particularly liked the fact that you can immediately see the results of your labour, though I readily admit that I wouldn't have enjoyed the lawn cutting if I'd had to do it with a push mower or a scythe.

'I need to find some way to get these four into the Bilbury hospital,' I told Darren. 'And I can't get them all into my car.'

'My tractor and trailer are just over here,' said the farmer. 'We could put them on the trailer. It's a bit mucky but...'

'We'll put them on the trailer,' I said, without hesitation.

And that's exactly what we did.

One by one Mr Futtock and I lifted the boys (for I had by now stopped thinking of them as 'young men' and started thinking of them as 'boys') onto the trailer. We fitted them on rather like sardines in a tin. Mr Futtock then slowly drove his tractor to the Bilbury hospital. I shut the farm gate and followed him in my car.

Fortunately, since it was summer time, the hospital was almost empty and there was no problem in finding four beds for them. Darren promised that he would call back at the field, collect the tents and rucksacks and store them in one of his barns.

Mr Bradshaw (known to everyone as simply 'Bradshaw') had been Dr Brownlow's butler, receptionist, nurse and odd job man, and he now looked after the hospital. He didn't look a day older than he had when I'd first met him for he seemed to have somehow succeeded in persuading time to stand still. He helped me to undress the four new patients. Without any further delay, I then put up drips so that I could rehydrate them. This wasn't an easy task since their veins had collapsed. I failed completely to get a needle into the usual veins for two of them. For one of those I had to put the needle into a vein near his ankle. And for the other I had to put the needle into the long saphenous vein in his thigh. This involved making a small incision in the skin. I didn't bother with a local anaesthetic since he was plainly unconscious. Eventually, Bradshaw and I managed to get fluid flowing into the venous systems of all four boys.

Within a remarkably short time, the four boys all started to show signs of improvement and by the following day, when they could drink and rehydrate themselves, I took out the drips, called the ambulance service and sent all four over to Barnstaple so that they could be examined, completely rehydrated and checked to make sure that no permanent damage had been done.

A day later I spoke to a house physician at the hospital who told me, to my relief, that all four had completely recovered without any long-term damage. The four had been collected by their parents and driven home. Indeed, the young doctor told me that his consultant had wanted to know why four apparently healthy boys had been admitted to his ward.

There is a rather sad and annoying addendum to this story.

A month later, I received one of those unpleasant letters which solicitors send out with such enthusiasm. This one, rather more threatening than most, claimed that Darren Futtock and I should have taken the tents down at the time when we had removed the boys from the field. The complaint was that two of the tents had been badly damaged by sheep, as had some of the contents of the four rucksacks. The lawyer demanded substantial reparations and damages.

The case dragged on for some weeks, as these things often do, and eventually Darren's solicitor, who handled the case for both of us, managed to get the demands dismissed by pointing out that the boys had camped illegally and that considerable damage had been done both to the field itself and to Mr Futtock's livestock. Mr Futtock's solicitor, a feisty fellow, who was genuinely angered at what had happened, even included a demand for £50 for the cost of transporting the boys on the farmer's trailer to the Bilbury hospital. And to his, and my, surprise a month later he received a cheque for the £50 and his legal costs.

The Dinner Party

Patsy and I have dinner parties about as often as there is a blue moon in the sky but to celebrate their anniversary we invited Patchy Fogg and his wife Adrienne to a meal. Adrienne is Patsy's sister.

When Adrienne and Patchy got married, everyone had been surprised and not a few people in the village had intimated that they did not think it was a marriage made to last. But the doubters had, I'm pleased to say, been proved wrong. Patchy and Adrienne may be very different people but somehow they seem perfectly suited to each other.

Partly because it was her sister and her brother-in-law who were the guests, and partly in deference to the nature of the occasion, Patsy had spent days designing the menu and doing everything possible to ensure that the evening would be a huge success. Patsy is the sort of person who would have gone to a lot of trouble whoever the guests might have been but this, we both agreed, was a very special occasion. For my part I tried to make sure, as far as was humanly possible, that everyone in the village who was likely to need medical help was unlikely to telephone at an inopportune moment. On the afternoon of the meal, I visited no fewer than eleven of my oldest and frailest patients to make sure that they were 'as well as could be expected' and to be certain that they were well supplied with their usual medication. I didn't want someone ringing me at 9.00 p.m. to ask me to go round with a packet of their usual painkillers. One of the few disadvantages of running a dispensing practice is that patients know that any drugs they might need are stored at Bilbury Grange, rather than a pharmacy in Barnstaple. I was once rung at 3.00 a.m. by a young girl who was going on holiday and who demanded that I deliver the supply of oral contraceptives which she had forgotten to obtain.

The menu Patsy had planned was impressive to say the least and to accompany the meal (vol au vents filled with a vegetarian pate, a vegetarian casserole to be served with two types of potato, beans, carrots, leaks and kale and two types of fruit pie). I had two good bottles of claret and two bottles of Peter Marshall's best champagne to drink. Patsy had also made sure that we had a sufficient supply of gin, whisky and brandy. Patchy and Adrienne were staying the night in our spare bedroom, so that there would be no need for them to drive home.

The disaster struck about fifteen minutes before our guests were due to arrive.

'The cooker has broken again!' cried Patsy.

I was in the cellar picking up the wine we had selected and I knew immediately that what had happened was not the cooker's fault. Patsy thought the cooker had suddenly stopped working – as it did all too frequently – and she cannot be blamed for suspecting that this was the problem.

Twice recently we'd had an expert in from Barnstaple to look at the cooker which was, admittedly, rather long in the tooth. I can't remember the expert's name but everyone called him Dundee because he was, in his own words 'considered a bit of a fruit cake'. He rode everywhere on a small 50 cc Honda moped with all his tools stashed in a little trolley which he towed behind him. The Honda's engine wasn't quite strong enough to pull the trolley up the modest inclines which are an integral part of North Devon's countryside, and so Dundee spent much of his time walking alongside his machine. Whatever the weather he wore khaki shorts, a Hawaiian short sleeved shirt, short white socks and the sort of black plimsolls that school children wore in the 1950s. Instead of a helmet he wore a woolly hat. Prior to specialising in repairing ovens, Dundee had had a catholic job history. For a while he had worked in Bath in a small factory where they made glass eyes. Dundee who reckoned he must have blown at least 5,000 glass eyes said he had once made a bloodshot glass eye for a man who drank a good deal and claimed that he needed a bloodshot eye for the 'mornings after' which were a big part of his life ('He said that a glass eye with a lovely white conjunctiva looked strange alongside his bloodshot real eye.'). He also told us that he had once made a hollow glass eye for a diamond smuggler. The smuggler had used the prosthesis to smuggle diamonds through customs' posts all around Europe. Dundee's life as a glass eye blower had come to an end when Chinese companies started producing glass eyes by machine. 'They weren't anywhere near as convincing as my bespoke eyes,' said Dundee with genuine regret. 'And I bet the Chinese never made a bloodshot glass eye.'

Dundee's advice to us had been quite direct if not particularly welcome: buy a new cooker and dump the one we've got. 'It'll be cheaper in the long run,' he told us. I had no idea exactly how old the cooker was. We'd bought it second hand when we'd first moved into Bilbury Grange at the start of our marriage

Dundee, who lived in an old caravan in Bilbury, had a reputation for honesty and had, not surprisingly perhaps, known just where we could buy a new cooker at a very reasonable price. He told us that he would receive £20 in commission if we bought our new cooker through him but that he could get us a £30 discount from the retailer. The perhaps surprising thing was that we felt certain that we could trust him. Sadly, however, at the time we couldn't afford to take advantage of his expertise. (We also had an old AGA in the kitchen but that had for a long time been nothing but a large ornament and was far too expensive for us to repair. Patsy used the twin AGA ovens as a storage space for her saucepans.)

My experience in the cellar meant that I had inside knowledge and knew that this time the cooker hadn't stopped working because it had broken down. The cooker had stopped working because there was no electricity. Just as Patsy had called out, I had suddenly been plunged into darkness and I was thanking the fact that, as I always do, I had a small torch in my trouser pocket. My definition of an optimist is someone who lives in the countryside, with their electricity supplied by overhead wires, and who doesn't carry a small torch with them at all times.

'Everything will be ruined!' she cried, as I gave her a hug and tried, unsuccessfully, to comfort her. It was clear that a hug, although welcome, doesn't quite cut the mustard when you're trying to make sure that all the various ingredients are ready at the same time, and when you're preparing for your first dinner party for three years. I know nothing about cooking but I know that preparing all the ingredients for a meal so that they are all ready to eat at the same time is like conducting an orchestra. The carrots need to be ready just as the potatoes are ready and the potatoes have to be ready to eat at the exact moment the kale reaches perfection.

'The cooker has decided to break down just when I need it to be reliable!' Patsy announced, not realising yet that the cooker had not given up the ghost of its own volition but had stopped working because it wasn't being fed its life-giving electricity. How old is it now?'

'The cooker is too old,' I told her. 'We definitely need a new one. But it isn't the cooker that's broken.'

'Can we get Dundee out to look at it? Isn't there some sort of warranty on it?'

'There's no guarantee,' I told her. 'There may have been something when we bought it, though I doubt it, but any warranty undoubtedly expired long ago.' I tried to tell her again that it wasn't the cooker's fault.

'It doesn't matter,' said Patsy, trying hard not to cry. 'Whatever insurance or guarantee you have on any household appliance will always be a waste of money because the part which goes wrong will always be excluded from the insurance in a clause on page 43 of the agreement.' All this came out in a rush.

I put my arm around her. 'It's not the…'

'Can we afford a new cooker?' she interrupted.

'It isn't the cooker,' I managed to tell her at last. 'We do need a new cooker but this time it isn't the cooker's fault. We'll save up. I'll try to get a contract to write a new book so that we can buy a new cooker, but it isn't the cooker that has broken this time.'

We didn't spend any of our money on fripperies. We'd never been on holiday. We drove a 40-year-old car which we'd been left by its previous owner. We had no television set. We were as happy as anyone I knew but we were as near to broke as you can get without having the bailiffs at the door. Our life was rich in joys but a trifle on the poor side as far as hard cash was concerned. The basic trouble was, as it always had been, that I had too few patients for the practice to be viable. And it was impossible to expand the size of the practice because I couldn't take on any patients who lived more than a few miles from where we lived. As a GP I was responsible for my patients for 24 hours a day and 365 days a year.

'If it isn't the cooker,' she said, hopefully, 'what's wrong?'

'The lights are out in the cellar.' I moved across to the light switch and turned on the overhead kitchen lights. Or at least I played with the light switch which controlled the overhead lights. Nothing happened. 'We've got no electricity. Maybe it's a circuit breaker!' I suggested, hopefully. With my torch as my guiding light I made my way into the butler's pantry where we keep what I still think of as our fuse boxes, but what the electricians tell me are now known as circuit breakers. The circuit breakers are kept in a neat little box inconveniently out of reach of anyone under eight feet tall. I stood on the stool we keep for the purpose, reached up so that I could open the little wooden door that hides the box from sight and examined the switches. None of them had been tripped into the off position.

'I'm afraid it isn't a breaker,' I told her. I looked out of the window. It is usually possible to see lights in a couple of distant farmhouses. There were no lights anywhere. 'I'd better ring the electricity board.'

Because my dispensary contains a fridge in which I store essential medicines which have to be stored at low temperatures I have a priority number to call. I rang the number.

'Sorry, doctor,' said a cheery voice at the other end. 'I'm afraid an electrical supply line to Bilbury is down. A tree fell and brought down a pole and the power line half a mile away from you.'

'How long will it take to mend it?'

'I don't think we'll get it mended tonight,' he said. 'The line that's down is partly in a field and partly in the river. We'll have to call in a specialist team. We've turned off the power until we can get a new pole up and the line reinstated. Do you have a back-up supply?'

I admitted that although we had talked many times about having a generator fitted we hadn't got round to it. Or, rather, that although we had once had a generator we hadn't got round to replacing it when it had given up the ghost.

'Best advice I can give you is to keep the refrigerator door shut,' said the voice.

Just then the doorbell rang.

'Maybe that's the electricity back on!' said Patsy, full of hope.

'I'm afraid not,' I told her. 'The doorbell is operated with batteries.'

'I'm so glad we're eating with you!' said Adrienne, when I opened the front door. She was wearing what I think is known as a party frock. Patchy was wearing a pin striped suit with a dress shirt and a poorly knotted tie and looked terribly uncomfortable in it all. I was wearing my old, faithful sports jacket, which has frayed cuffs and worn elbows, and a pair of grey flannels which I call my best trousers but which have baggy knees and a shiny seat.

'Our electricity is off so we wouldn't have been able to cook anything,' Adrienne added. 'We'd have been reduced to toast and marmalade.'

'Bread and marmalade,' said Patchy, correcting her. 'The toaster won't work without electricity.'

'Oh no, of course it wouldn't,' said Adrienne. 'But it doesn't matter because we're eating here. How romantic of you to turn off the lights. Do you have some candles?'

'Our power is off,' said Patsy, coming out of the kitchen and hugging her sister. 'Everything is ruined. Everything is all half cooked. It will all have to be thrown away.' And then she burst into tears.

'I'm so sorry!' said Adrienne who always bounces back quickly. 'But it doesn't matter. We'll sort something out. And we'll still have a wonderful time.'

'Do you have candles?' asked Patchy. 'Might be a good idea to light some before one of us trips over and breaks a leg.'

'Tons of them,' I replied.

This was no stroke of good fortune. Everyone who lives in the countryside and who relies on an overhead power supply doesn't just have a torch in their pocket; they always have a large supply of candles and a decent assortment of candle holders.

While Adrienne comforted Patsy in the kitchen, Patchy and I set about lighting candles, fitting them into candle holders and distributing them around downstairs rooms of the house so that we could at least see what we were doing and where we were. For a couple of minutes our dogs, usually well behaved, for they had acquired a certain gentility with age, ran round and round, sniffing and barking at the candles. Once bored and exhausted by this activity they found comfortable spots near to the fire and went to sleep.

'These are rather nice,' said Patchy, holding up two old and grubby looking candle holders, which had their own snuffers attached to the handles. 'They're solid silver, did you know?'

'I bought them from a shop in South Moulton,' I told him. 'They were in an oddments box outside the front door.'

'How much did you pay for them?'

'A quid for the pair, I think. No more than that. I bought them to use during power cuts. These are nice because they have the snuffers attached to them but I only bought them because they were so cheap. They're so discoloured that it never occurred to me that they might be silver. I keep meaning to clean them up.'

'Oh, they're silver all right,' said Patchy. He pointed out the silver hallmarks on each candle holder. There were even hallmarks on the two small snuffers. 'Did you get them from the antique shop next door to that café that serves huge and wonderful toasted tea cakes?'

'That's the one.'

'The guy who owned that went bust and I'm not surprised,' said Patchy, examining the candle holders. 'Underneath years of accumulated grime these are solid silver and they're George III. Look after them. Individually, they're worth about £400, together you'd pay £1,000 for the pair.'

I think my mouth fell open.

'They're really rather nice. Let me know if you ever decide to sell them.'

'I'll talk to Patsy. But I think we just decided to sell them!'

It looked as though our financial problems might be over for a while.

I was so startled I didn't say anything.

If there hadn't been a power cut I wouldn't have needed to fish out the candle sticks and the two solid silver George III candle holders would have remained in a cardboard box in the cupboard under the stairs. And if Patchy hadn't been our guest I would have never been any the wiser about their value.

'Good thing booze doesn't need an electricity supply,' said Patchy, wandering over to the old wooden trolley on which we keep our wine and spirits. There were glasses there too, all neatly laid out and sparkling in the candlelight.

'What do you fancy?' I asked him.

'Is the champagne for opening or for show?'

I opened a bottle of champagne and filled four glasses. Patchy and I took two glasses each and took them into the kitchen. We then handed glasses to our respective wives.

'Happy anniversary!' said Patsy, toasting her sister and brother-in-law. 'We've got a present for you, but first what are we going to do about food?'

I too wished our guests happy anniversary and we all took sips from our champagne.

'I forgot to put it into the fridge,' I said, apologising.

'But the fridge isn't working anyway,' laughed Patsy.

'We'll drink it before it gets warm,' said Patchy.

'The house is going to get cold soon,' said Patsy. 'Now that the AGA doesn't work we rely on a couple of electric fires.'

'No one in Bilbury has gas heating,' said Patchy. 'And neither gas nor oil heating systems work without electricity. They need power for the pumps to work.'

'I've got a fire laid in the sitting room,' I said. 'It'll take only a minute to light it. And I brought in a pile of decent, dry logs that'll easily last the night.'

I found a box of matches and lit the fire and then pushed the sofa and two arm chairs closer to the hearth. Patchy, trying to help by rearranging one of the logs, was hit by a spark which landed on the trousers of his smart pin striped suit.

'Thank heavens for that!' he said, examining the small hole that had been burnt in his trousers. 'I hate clothes that look brand new. It's not my style at all.' He seemed genuinely pleased to have scarred his trousers. For as long as I've known him Patchy has regarded sartorial elegance as a sign of weakness and considers men who spend too much time and money on their appearance as rather suspect. 'They look as if they belong to me now!'

'You could get the burn mark repaired,' I felt obliged to point out. 'They do marvellous invisible mending these days. There's a shop in…'

'Don't want it mending! Every time I look at the hole I'll remember our anniversary party.'

'Well, we might be hungry but we'll be warm and tipsy,' said Adrienne, coming into the room and sitting on the floor immediately in front of the fire with her back resting on the sofa and then suddenly jumping up and disappearing back into the kitchen in response to a call for help from Patsy.

'There must be some way to cook something,' I suggested, as the fire began to light up the room. 'We used to have a small camping stove but I have no idea where it is and I'm pretty damned sure we don't have any gas cartridges for it.'

'You've got a barbecue in the garden haven't you?'

'Yes. A huge brick one, which Thumper and I built. But it's

raining and the barbecue site is completely unsheltered. Even if we could get the charcoal going we'd be soaked within a minute.'

We sat and stared at the fire.

'We've got cheese and biscuits,' said Patsy coming into the sitting room with Adrienne behind her. They were both carrying large platters laden with different cheeses and different types of biscuit.

'You've burned your trousers,' said Adrienne.

Patchy agreed with his wife's observations.

'That must be a record,' she said. 'It's the first time you've worn that suit. Still, the burn mark adds a touch of je ne sais pas.'

'I'm an idiot,' I said suddenly.

Everyone looked at me. Patsy said I wasn't, Adrienne raised a well-manicured eyebrow but didn't say anything and Patchy said he wouldn't argue with me and didn't know of anyone who would and it was nice to hear me say it myself.

'We can cook in here!' I suddenly said. 'We have a fire. We have a couple of trivets and a frying pan. We have a decent supply of eggs, hash browns, onion rings, mushrooms and everything else we need. We can cook an all day brunch. And we've got two extendable brass toasting forks so we can make heaps of toast too.'

'It's not quite what I'd planned,' said Patsy, rather sadly.

But it was all we had.

And it is surprising how many types of food can be cooked, and well-cooked, on an open, indoor log fire.

Within very little time we had a feast prepared.

'I love picnics!' said Patchy, putting a slice of bread onto one of the toasting forks.

'Do you remember that picnic we had on Hangman's Hill at Combe Martin?' asked Adrienne.

Patchy thought, nodded and laughed. 'It was a lovely day so we took a picnic to eat on the cliffs. I packed what I thought were two hard boiled eggs but I took the wrong eggs – eggs which were raw. Unfortunately Adrienne and I both cracked the shells of our eggs at the same time. Thinking the eggs were hard boiled we gave them quite a crack and so a second later we were both were covered in egg.'

This time there were no problems with the eggs and the four of us had great fun cooking and eating our impromptu anniversary meal.

Afterwards, Patsy raided the pantry and found a spotted dick pudding, a Christmas pudding and a treacle pudding. We heated them all in pans balanced on the trivets and then we ate them all. Patsy even managed to make custard. I opened a bottle of 25-year-old port which I'd been keeping for a special occasion.

'This is good stuff!' said Patchy. 'Business must be looking up.'

'All our booze comes from patients,' said Patsy. 'We never have to buy any alcohol.'

'Patients give you presents?' said Patchy, sounding shocked.

'We get a constant stream of vegetables, jars of home-made jam, pickled beetroot and walnuts in kilner jars.'

'How wonderful! There's a good incentive not to kill too many patients.'

'The booze tends to last because I never dare drink much,' I said. 'In case I have to go out on a call.'

'There aren't any police cars around here,' Adrienne pointed out.

'There'll be one hiding behind a tree on the night when I go out after a few drinks. And I don't want to try delivering a baby if I can't see straight.'

'If you were seeing double you'd probably end up telling the lucky mother she'd got twins.'

'And when she discovered there was only one baby she'd spend hours looking round the bedroom to try to find the other.'

'Surely if the police caught you and breathalysed you, they'd let you off?'

'Afraid not,' said Patsy. 'A doctor we know was off duty for the evening when one of his partners – the one who was on call – was taken ill. Our friend said he'd take over the night duty but he'd already drunk several glasses of whisky. He was called out and stopped by the police. A month or two later the General Medical Council struck him off – took away his licence. The police apparently tell the GMC if they arrest a doctor for anything.'

'That's surely not true…'

'It is. The poor fellow was thrown out by his partners. He ended up working as a doctor in a large hotel in Paris that catered for English speaking tourists.'

'And he discovered that he was also looking after the girls working in the brothel next door.'

'Sounds like a bit of a result to me,' said Patchy laughing.

At midnight the electricity came back on.

As always happens, lights suddenly appeared and we could hear the fridge turn itself back on. The electricity supply company had worked hard in the dark and the rain.

'Shall I blow out the candles?' I asked.

'No!' was the response from three voices. 'Turn out the lights and leave the candles on.'

We piled another huge log onto the fire and belatedly Patsy remembered the anniversary gift she had so carefully chosen and wrapped. It was an oil painting of Patchy and Adrienne's home which Patsy had commissioned from a wonderful artist who signed her work just DAC. The artist had painted from her own photographs of the Fogg home, and Patsy and I had supplied photos of Patchy and Adrienne. The result was that the finished picture showed the front of the house with the Foggs standing in front of it. It looked rather good and Patchy and Adrienne were both delighted with the gift. Adrienne cried a little but I was relieved that Patchy didn't.

'And we can afford a new cooker,' I told Patsy as I poured out the remains of the port.

Surprised but delighted she looked at me. 'How?'

I stood up, walked across the room to where the two George III candle holders were sitting on a window sill and picked them up. Patchy and Adrienne watched me. One of them smiled knowingly. The other was as puzzled as Patsy was.

'Tell her, Patchy,' I said.

Patchy told her.

'How much?'

'I can get you at least £1000 for the pair.'

'How much is a new cooker?' Patsy asked me.

'Nowhere near that much. We'd have a little cash left over.'

The next morning, with the electricity back on, we had another brunch. Prepared on the cooker it was an excellent meal, and there were nowhere near as many burnt bits, but somehow it didn't have the magic of the impromptu brunch we'd cooked over the log fire.

When Patchy and Adrienne left, I gave Patchy the two silver candle holders to sell. He said he'd take them to Exeter that morning. Patsy and I insisted that he took 10% of the price as commission, pointing out that if it hadn't been for him, and the anniversary dinner, we'd have never known that they were valuable.

And after our visitors had left, Patsy telephoned Dundee to fix a date for him to bring us a brand new cooker and to take away the old one.

Alarums, Excursions and Modest Confessions

On some days the patients I see all have simple, uncomplicated symptoms which lead quickly to a simple, uncomplicated diagnosis and from there, directly, to a simple, uncomplicated treatment regime – often no more than a bottle or packet of some suitable medication from my dispensary.

Like other family doctors practising miles from a commercial pharmacy, I dispense as well as diagnose and prescribe. At the end of a consultation I do not give my patients a piece of paper which they must take to a commercial pharmacy to exchange for the medication they need, instead I go into my dispensary, pick out what they need, put it into a small, white paper bag and hand it to them there and then. If I didn't do this many of my patients would find it impossible to acquire the medication they needed or there would, at the very least, be a long delay in their starting treatment.

During one morning surgery early in autumn, I saw 17 patients who had just two diseases between them. Twelve of the patients had symptoms of the flu and the other five had musculoskeletal problems that needed nothing more than rest and a fairly simple analgesic and anti-inflammatory drug. I could have treated everyone I saw with just one drug in the dispensary: common or garden aspirin.

Aspirin, in my view still the best drug in the world for treating most simple cases of back or neck pain and most cases of arthritis is also one of the cheapest and safest pharmaceutical products around. Aspirin, acetylsalicylic acid, traditionally born of the willow tree, is a well-tried, much trusted and wildly maligned drug which has excellent anti-inflammatory, analgesic and anti-pyretic properties. It'll take away inflammation, deal with pain and reduce a temperature. It is one of the oldest drugs in the world and we know more about how to use it, and how to use it safely, than almost any other drug.

I usually prescribe aspirin in a soluble version because I believe it is safer than the other kind. If you swallow an aspirin tablet whole then it lands on your stomach lining and gradually dissolves. As it does so there is a risk that it will burn a hole in the mucosa and cause stomach bleeding. I believe that a soluble aspirin tablet, dissolved in a glass of water, is far less likely to cause problems of that or any other type.

Drug companies have for years done their best to dismiss and demonise aspirin as a dangerous drug because there is hardly any profit to be made from selling it, and sadly they have convinced many doctors to follow the drug company line, and to prescribe expensive and dangerous alternatives. Aspirin has for years been a generic product, costing only pennies, whereas branded drugs with a similar range of uses may cost several hundred times as much – and, ironically, prove to be far more dangerous than aspirin.

One trick commonly used by drug companies when testing a new competitor for aspirin is to test their drug against ordinary aspirin rather than soluble aspirin. And they usually test against far too high a dose of the non-soluble aspirin. The results usually show that the new product appears safer, in the short term at least, than the high dose of the non-soluble aspirin. But, far too often, the new drug, heavily promoted to doctors, will in a year or two's time turn out to be far more dangerous, far more lethal, than aspirin.

So, I often find that several of the patients I see need nothing more powerful than traditional aspirin to soothe their symptoms. Aspirin may not provide a long term cure but it can provide short and medium term relief.

And then there are the days when I find myself facing problems which are medically and morally unique, which don't necessarily offer much of a challenge in diagnostic terms, but which raise questions and concerns which were certainly never covered by the lecturers at medical school, or mentioned in the medical textbooks or journals. On those occasions it is my belief that it is the GP's job to offer care which is probably as much spiritual as clinical, and after being a country GP, or family doctor, for a while I have grown steadily to believe that the country GP's job is truly pastoral, both in the sense of providing care for the general well-being of his patients and in the sense of providing a rural service which would have been typical in the countryside of a century ago. I sometimes wonder how long this sort of practice will survive. I prefer the phrase 'family doctor', rather than GP, because it gives more accurately a sense of the responsibility which is inherent in the job.

Doctors like myself, who have been in practice for a few years and who feel a strong sense of vocation are, I fear, in danger of becoming dinosaurs; not out of date, I hope, but definitely out of their time. I honestly cannot see doctors in the 21st century being prepared to be available for their patients for 24 hours a day, every day of the year. In towns and cities, where people live close to hospitals, this may not be such a problem but just what will happen to people living in the countryside is, I fear, a serious worry. Moreover, there are moves afoot to close down more and more small hospitals, leaving only the huge metropolitan hospitals. Maybe part of the plan is to move people out of villages and hamlets and to force them to move into towns and cities. Whatever the intention might be, things are moving frighteningly quickly and as 1980 approaches I feel a sense of wariness, even fear, about the future. I think I was lucky to have qualified when I did, and I'm glad I started in general practice at the start of the 1970s. Even in the comparatively few years which have taken place since I started in general practice, the changes have been extraordinary. Furthermore, it is quite clear that the changes which have taken place will never be reversed.

As I write this I can't help wondering how tomorrow's GPs will deal with the flurry of problems I face quite regularly.

On the day I've begun to describe, after an intellectually undemanding morning surgery, I found myself dealing with some unusual medical dilemmas.

I suspect that all the following incidents could only have occurred to a country GP, practising alone and far away from the various influence of modern civilisation.

Bilbury, as you may know, is a small, rather isolated community which exists without much contact with the rest of the world. In winter, if it snows, the village can be cut off for quite long periods of time and when it is cut off we have to be thoroughly self-sufficient. I suspect that it is knowing that this can happen which encourages us to be far more independent and self-reliant than most city dwellers, who have immediate access to a reliable range of services.

If there is a small crisis in a town or a city, inhabitants are all too frequently inclined to lunge straight from complacency into panic.

But in a village which sits miles from the facilities accepted as standard in urban life (there are elderly residents in Bilbury who have never seen traffic lights, parking meters or pedestrian crossings) the capacity for simply dealing with things, sometimes by lateral thinking, is stronger because it is necessary.

And what I think I am perhaps trying to say, in a rather polite and roundabout way, is that as a country doctor, I am more inclined than a city doctor to bend the rules a little occasionally. After all, if you aren't prepared to bend the rules a little then you must live your life according to the rule-makers who have probably no experience of the situation you face.

There are times when we need to ignore the rules which the bureaucrats and apparatchiks have created. Rules which might seem sound and well based when dreamt up in an air conditioned office on the 14th floor of an office block somewhere hundreds of miles away might seem absurd, irrelevant, intrusive and unreasonable when applied in a small rural community.

My first call that day took place late in the morning. I always try to do my home visits after I have finished the morning surgery, signed a few prescriptions, dealt with the mail and kept my drug books up to date in the dispensary. If I haven't finished the visits by 1.30 p.m. or so, and don't think I will be able to complete them in the next half an hour, I go back to Bilbury Grange for lunch. If Patsy is out somewhere, I have my lunch at the Duck and Puddle, knowing that Miss Johnson, my long-serving receptionist, will telephone me there if a patient needs me. It is an understatement to say that I've never been terribly good at cooking and to be honest I am usually pretty tired by lunchtime and the last thing I feel like doing is fishing out a saucepan, deciding on something to make and then preparing it. Please don't tell anyone but if I have to feed myself I usually end up having a couple of slices of toast and marmalade or a bowl of soup.

Anyway, on the day I'm describing I'd spent quite a while dealing with the mail (there was a letter from the taxman, one from a publisher, and several from the hospital about patients of mine whom I had referred for further diagnosis and treatment) and by the time I got into the car and out on the road it was half past twelve. I decided I'd probably just have time to do one visit before I had a break for lunch.

The house I was visiting was one of a pair of semi-detached Victorian cottages about two miles away from Bilbury Grange, near to the Eastern boundary of the village. The cottages had been built for farm labourers but I don't think farm labourers had occupied them for thirty or forty years. They were owned by a landlord who lived in London and rented them both out. I suspect that the rent he was now receiving gave him a good return on his investment.

The woman living in the left hand cottage, who had telephoned for a visit at home, was a villager called Zahlia Butterbury whom I knew reasonably well but had not seen very often as a patient. In her late 60s, she was an assistant stage manager for the dramatic society's bi-annual productions, secretary of the village vegetable show and the driving force behind a campaign to halt a development of mobile homes planned for an area just a mile or two outside Bilbury. She was also a member of the St John's Ambulance, and I'd met her when I'd conducted rather informal tests of young volunteers wanting to join that organisation.

Prior to her retirement, Miss Butterbury had worked for the latter decades of her life as a sales assistant for a jeweller in Barnstaple. Before that she'd worked for the Drivers and Vehicles Licensing Authority in Swansea. As I say, I had, however hardly ever seen her professionally. My medical records told me that I'd treated her only twice. Once when she'd had an eye infection which had responded quickly to suitable eye drops and once when I'd called to see her and she had been complaining of backache. Her pains, all muscular, had started after she'd spent three days trying to dig, drag and pull the stump of a young but surprisingly stubborn self-seeded sycamore tree out of her front garden. Her symptoms had disappeared after she'd taken aspirin for a few days, had a few long, hot baths and paid a local farmer a crisp £20 note to use his backhoe to dig out the unwanted tree stump. Her brother worked in the local garage and helped look after my elderly Rolls Royce 20/25 whenever it needed a little loving care and attention. It was because of her brother that she had moved to Bilbury. Every year her brother gave her one of the oil company advertising calendars he received. Garages always seem to receive a supply of this particular calendar which consisted of twelve pages, each one illustrated with a photograph of a young woman who had forgotten to dress completely, and whose photograph was used to promote the company's product more astutely. This year's contribution I had noticed when I had visited had been hanging on the living room wall, turned to December.

'Why is your calendar showing December?' I'd asked.

'It's the only month for which the young lady in the picture is wearing any clothes,' she replied, blushing lightly. The model was dressed as Santa Claus, wearing a short red coat, black boots and a red hat with a white bobble. She didn't appear to be wearing anything else.

'My brother gave it to me for Christmas and so I like to keep it on display,' she explained in a whisper. 'It'll be useful when December comes round.'

When I arrived at Miss Butterbury's home this time I found that she wasn't the patient. She met me on the doorstep and seemed flustered.

'Mr Hodgson is a lodger,' she told me. 'He's been poorly for over a week. Would you have a look at him please? I'm very worried about him.'

She told me all this in a whisper, as though she felt guilty for some reason.

'I followed her up the steep, narrow stairs to a small bedroom at the back of her house. It was, I knew, usually her bedroom. A man I'd never seen before was lying in the bed. At first sight I thought he was dead. He had a round face which was ruddy and well weathered by sun and wind but he wasn't moving and he didn't seem to be breathing. He looked as if he was severely dehydrated. Suddenly he started coughing. He coughed quite violently for several minutes and then subsided again and reverted to looking more dead than alive.

I tried to ask him how long he had been ill but he started coughing again.

'Do you have pain?'

It took him a couple of minutes to reply. 'A nasty pain when I breathe.'

I unfastened his pyjama jacket and listened to his heart and lungs. When I asked him to sit up so that I could listen to his back he started coughing again. When the coughing stopped I asked him to take big breaths. He winced when he tried and I could hear the layers of the pleurae rubbing together – they made a rough sound that is pathognomonic of pleurisy.

'Is the pain sharp when you breathe?'

He nodded.

I checked his ribs but there were no signs that any of them were fractured.

When I took his temperature it was high. The list of possible diagnoses was long but the likelihood was that he had a chest infection and had developed pleurisy – a condition in which the membrane which lines the chest cavity and surrounds the lungs becomes inflamed. The pleurisy was almost certainly caused by an underlying chest infection. His condition was exacerbated by the fact that he had clearly become quite severely dehydrated.

'When did he last eat?' I asked Miss Butterbury.

'Three or four days ago,' she replied. 'I've tried to tempt him with the things he usually likes but he hasn't been hungry.'

'When did he last have something to drink?'

'Not in the last 24 hours, maybe longer.'

I turned to Mr Hodgson. 'You need to drink,' I told him. 'Will you do that for me?'

'It hurts to breathe,' he said.

'I understand. But you need to drink. You are dehydrated.'

'I do not feel much like drinking.'

'If you don't drink I will have to send you into hospital so that they can put up a drip and rehydrate you that way.'

'I don't want to go to hospital.'

'And you need to try to take deeper breaths. Do it gently now.'

Slowly, tentatively, he took a deeper breath. There were no signs of a bacterial infection and I didn't think he needed an antibiotic.

'What do you like to drink?' I asked him.

'Beer.'

'What do you like other than beer?'

'Orange juice with water.'

I turned to Miss Butterbury.

'I'll get a jug full of orange juice,' she promised.

I gave Mr Hodgson some aspirin to control the pain and to reduce the inflammation inside his chest cavity and from my car fetched a bottle of a codeine based cough syrup to control his cough. I told Miss Butterbury to call me if his symptoms got any worse. And I told Mr Hodgson that he might feel a little more comfortable if he lay not on his back but, paradoxically perhaps, on the painful side of his chest.

'Why didn't you call me sooner?' I asked Miss Butterbury.

'I didn't like to bother you,' she said.

I didn't say anything but just looked at her. I knew she wasn't quite telling me the whole truth but I didn't know what she was trying to hide.

'He's foreign,' she said in a whisper. 'Italian. He works in Ilfracombe. He's a waiter. I was worried that you might have to tell the police.'

I just looked at her and raised an eyebrow in disbelief. She knew that even if the man wasn't here legally I would not inform on him.

'He's been paying me rent,' she said. 'He's been here for nine months and I haven't told the tax people. I suppose I should have done. Will I get into trouble?' She paused. 'He doesn't pay me rent now. He stopped a month or so ago.'

'You won't get into trouble through me,' I promised her. I told her again how to look after her patient. And then I suddenly realised that I had left my sphygmomanometer in the bedroom. Leaving Miss Butterbury standing in the hall, I went back up the stairs to fetch it.

And when I walked into the bedroom I suddenly realised why she had really been so reluctant to telephone me and why she was acting so strangely. Her agitation had nothing to do with him being Italian. It was nothing to do with him paying her rent (if he did or ever had).

I noticed, for the first time, that there were two pairs of bedroom slippers beside the bed: Miss Butterbury's dainty pink pair and her lodger's large, sensible, leather slippers. And on the back of the bedroom door, Miss Butterbury's floral dressing gown was hanging next to Mr Hodgson's very masculine dark blue dressing gown. Miss Butterbury was worried that people would find out that she had acquired a lover. And it was modesty which very nearly led to tragedy.

When I got back downstairs, Mrs Butterbury understood that I had managed to put two and two together and get an answer approximating four. She was blushing. She looked at me and blushed a little more.

'Will he be all right, doctor?' she asked.

'He looks a strong man,' I told her. 'He'll be fine. Ring me if you're worried but I'll be back tomorrow after the morning surgery.'

'We're going to get married after Christmas,' she whispered. She was crying.

I put my arm around her and congratulated her. 'Make sure he drinks plenty of fluids, and ring me if there's any change.'

Since none of the other visits seemed urgent I went home and had my lunch with Patsy, and then sat for a few minutes with the latest edition of the British Medical Journal (the doctors' comic) and a cup of coffee. When I was in my twenties I drank coffee in the sort of quantities Balzac would have found agreeable but now that I am a little older I only ever drink one cup of coffee a day. I find that if I drink more I get palpitations. On the other hand, if I don't have the one cup of coffee I get headaches. I long ago realised that I'm mildly addicted to caffeine but I decided that if we give up everything to which we are addicted then there is a danger that life will become interminably dull.

While I drank my coffee I looked at the British Medical Journal for five minutes, found nothing in it of any interest and tossed it aside. Like just about all medical journals and magazines, the British Medical Journal, the official organ of the British Medical Association was always packed with drug company advertisements and I always worried how much influence the drug companies had over the content of the journal. I'm sure the BMA staff will say that drug companies have no influence but then, in the immortal words of Mandy Rice-Davies, 'they would say that, wouldn't they?' I then read a few pages of a cricket magazine which I had delivered every month. The cricket magazine was far more fun, and probably just as educational.

My first call after lunch was to see Paul Titmus.

Aged in his mid-40s, sharp featured, slightly built and usually seemingly shy, he worked in South Molton as an assistant in a small shop but, of course, when I was asked to visit him I was asked to see him at his home. Paul Titmus is a pernickety, careful sort of man who always seems slightly distrusting. I don't really know why but I have always thought that he was the sort of fellow who would add up a restaurant or café bill at least twice before paying what he was asked for.

The call had actually come through at lunchtime and although his wife, who had made the call, had insisted that it wasn't urgent, something about the call made me put it top of my visiting list for the afternoon.

Like most people in Bilbury, I knew Paul quite well by sight because every morning and evening, whatever the weather, he could be seen running around the lanes. He was something of an evangelist for running – constantly telling anyone who would listen that his daily runs kept him much fitter than other men his age. To be honest, he frightened me because the lanes of North Devon are narrow, and although it is usually possible to hear or see vehicles coming, a lone runner, always travelling silently, of course, can be invisible until you go round a bend and there they are. Believe it or not the lanes in North Devon are so narrow that there is barely room for a walker or runner to pass by if there is a motor car on the road. At least half of the Bilbury lanes have grass growing in the middle because no wheels ever run over that piece of roadway.

Paul was lying on the sofa in the sitting room of the cottage he shared with his wife, Peta who designs greeting cards for a living. Peta has her cards printed at a print shop in Barnstaple and sells them in several shops, including Peter Marshall's shop in Bilbury. I think she does quite well with them. Peter once told me that her cards, which are mostly watercolour paintings of scenes in North Devon, sell better than anyone else's though he didn't think she sold enough cards to live on the proceeds. He told me that she'd told him that she would have liked to paint in oils but that watercolour paints were far cheaper than oils. Moreover, she said that she could finish a watercolour painting in a day whereas an oil painting could easily take a month or more. When your livelihood depends upon your output it's essential to find a method that maximises your productivity.

Unless he was dressed for running, Paul always dressed conservatively and usually wore a sports coat and flannels. His wife, on the other hand, dressed like a hippie, in long, ankle length dresses which were very colourful and often lavishly embroidered. She always had several layers of coloured beads around her neck, and in the summer she usually had flowers in her hair. She had, for some reason of her own, shaved off her eyebrows and in their place painted replacement eyebrows in a way which made her look constantly surprised. Both of her arms were heavily tattooed with pictures of ferocious wild animals. She always wore open sandals instead of shoes and hardly ever left home except to visit the print shop in Barnstaple, or to go to Peter's shop to buy groceries and hand him another batch of her cards to sell. In recent months, Peter had started to act as a wholesaler for her, using one of the delivery drivers who brought groceries to his shop to distribute cards to shops outside North Devon. After Peter and the delivery driver had taken a percentage, there wasn't much left for Peta but I think she just liked people to buy her cards and even a couple of pence profit per card was a little more towards the household budget.

Peta was rather famous in Devon for a stunt she had pulled off at a local art gallery which had displayed some of her paintings. She described her style of painting as 'modern late 20th century realistic impressionism' but secretly I always suspected that the phrase was probably an excuse for the fact that she wasn't terribly good at painting and that her pictures were neither realistic nor imaginative. I admire many types of painting but I'm not terribly impressed by the sort of stuff the critics enthuse over these days. When Will and I were medical students, in the 1960s, we entered an art competition in Birmingham. We covered a piece of old hardboard with glue and then poured the contents of a waste bin onto the board. We entered the picture as 'Untitled' and didn't bother with a frame. The exhibition's organisers commended us, hung our artwork and sent us a very nice letter of praise. It was the highlight of our careers as artists and taught us a valuable lesson about modern art. At the end of the exhibition the organisers wrote and invited us to collect our work of art. We didn't bother. It didn't seem worth the effort or the bus fare.

Anxious for a little local publicity to draw attention to her work, Peta had asked two friends to throw a tin of tomatoes at one of her pictures to draw attention to something or other. (I cannot for the life of me remember the nature of the something or other. It was, however, definitely a protest.) They chose a tin of tomatoes apparently because they were the cheapest food they could find in the supermarket. In order to ensure that the stunt obtained a little publicity, Peta tipped off a friend who worked for a local paper as a journalist and photographer. The two faux vandals (or protestors, depending upon your point of view) wore masks so that they could not be identified.

Everything went as planned with the stunt. The only picture affected was one of Peta's, and since the watercolour was safe behind glass there was no serious damage. Peta and the gallery owner (who was in on the stunt) announced that they would not press charges and so the police rapidly lost interest. The press, however, was struggling with a quiet day or two and the story became far bigger than Peta had imagined. Peta herself was interviewed for two radio programmes and by reporters for two television stations. And best of all, from Peta's point of view, the owner of an art gallery in Taunton rang up wanting to put on a small solo exhibition of Peta's work to take advantage of the publicity. Peter Marshall told me that Peta had been working every day and every evening to produce the 24 paintings the gallery owner had requested.

When I arrived at their home, Paul, lying on the sofa, was still wearing his running gear which consisted of white shorts and a white singlet. Someone, presumably Peta, had lain a rug over him. He looked absolutely terrible. He was nearly as white as his running kit, he was sweating profusely and his circulation was so poor that his lips were frighteningly blue. To my surprise he was lying there quite alone. His wife, I could see through an open doorway, was in her studio working on one of her watercolours paintings.

When I first stood in the doorway and saw him on the couch in his running gear I had assumed, from a distance, that Paul must have pulled a muscle or injured a joint or done one of the myriad things which runners and joggers do to themselves. In my experience, running injuries occur with monotonous regularity. But as I stepped closer and saw his colour and general condition, I abandoned that tentative diagnosis. This, it was clear, was altogether more serious.

Mr Titmus was, of course, the last person you'd think of as a candidate for a heart attack. He ran every day and there didn't seem to be an ounce of fat on his body. He didn't smoke, he ate sparingly and he confined himself to foods generally regarded as healthy. He and his wife ate so many proprietary health foods that Peter Marshall, the village shopkeeper, introduced a line of products just for the Titmuses.

I listened to Mr Titmus's chest, took his blood pressure and felt his pulse and it didn't take more than two minutes to make the diagnosis. Paul had pains in his left arm and jaw (which were beginning to fade) and a pain in his chest (which was, he said, also less fierce than it had been when he had first returned home).

A quick listen to his chest confirmed that his problem wasn't anything to do with joints or muscles.

Paul had suffered a heart attack.

I checked that he wasn't allergic to it and then gave him an ordinary aspirin tablet to put under his tongue. Aspirin is more rapidly absorbed that way; it's much faster than swallowing it. I didn't give him the aspirin as a pain reliever (though aspirin does, of course, have excellent pain relieving qualities when given in the proper dose) but because it can help stop blood clotting – and thereby, hopefully, stop any more heart attacks.

'How on earth did you get home?' I asked him.

'He dragged himself home,' said Peta, emerging from her studio, where she had presumably been working on one of the paintings for her exhibition. 'He was half a mile away when he felt ill and he half crawled, half limped home. He's a fool. He could have made things far worse – and he probably has.' She sounded cross but it was pretty clear that her anger was born of fear.

'I wish you'd told me what had happened,' I said, cross that I hadn't been told of Paul's condition when Peta had telephoned me.

'I was in the middle of nowhere,' protested Paul. 'If I'd stayed where I was I'd probably still be there now.'

'He'll be fine after a little lie down,' said Peta. 'Won't he?'

I didn't say anything. I wasn't so sure that he would be fine after a little lie down, but I didn't want to scare them.

'What else could I do?' continued Paul, still responding to his wife. 'Hardly anyone uses that lane. If I'd stayed where I was when the pain started I might have been there for hours or even days.'

They were both right, of course, but Paul was more right. Not for the first time in my life I wished that someone would one day invent a portable telephone so that people could ring for help when they needed it.

'You need to be in hospital!' I told Paul. 'You've had a heart attack.'

'No, no!' I can't go to hospital, he insisted. Every word was clearly an effort for him. 'If I go to hospital everyone will know I've had a heart attack while out running.'

Puzzled, I looked at Peta for an explanation.

'He's president of his damned running club,' said Peta. 'They all tell everyone that running makes them fitter and stronger than anyone else. He's worried that if people know that he's had a heart attack he'll lose all credibility. And he thinks the other members of the club won't want to have anything to do with him.'

'Do you realise how serious this is?' I asked him.

'Can't you just say that I stepped in a pothole and twisted my ankle?' said Paul. It was obvious that the idea of being sent to hospital was distressing him.

It was such a comical request that I felt like laughing. 'You want me to send you to hospital but tell them you've twisted your ankle?'

I was actually quite cross with him for several reasons – not least for the fact that he wanted me to make myself look a fool so that he wouldn't be embarrassed.

'Yes, yes, please.'

'You don't think they might notice that you've had a heart attack?'

'Do I have to go into hospital?' he asked, rather pathetically.

No one ever wants to go into hospital (well, actually I suppose that isn't entirely true – there are some patients, hypochondriacs, drug addicts and individuals suffering from variations of Munchausen's Syndrome who do want to be admitted to hospital but they, thankfully, are pretty rare) and the reluctance to go into a hospital is entirely understandable. Hospitals can be frightening places and everyone knows someone who went into hospital and didn't come out alive. We have, I think, a cultural fear of hospital which dates back to the Middle Ages when hospitals were little more than charnel houses offering very little in the way of care or treatment and nothing in the way of hygiene. Patients slept on dirty straw and the medical staff had few treatments available to them. Sadly, some modern hospitals do not seem to be much of an improvement on those deadly institutions, where the most potent hope came from prayer rather than anything less spiritual.

I looked at him again and thought for a moment.

There had been times in the past when I had kept patients at home after they'd had heart attacks. Indeed, there is good evidence that for some patients staying at home can produce a better result than going into hospital. The ambulance journey from Bilbury to the hospital in Barnstaple can take the best part of an hour and once in hospital, in a specialist cardiac care unit with constant beeping warnings and flashing lights, and lots of tubes and scary looking equipment, patients can become enormously stressed. The medical and nursing staff sometimes become so devoted to taking readings and studying results that they forget that they are dealing with humans who need to be reassured and comforted and the trauma of going into hospital can exacerbate symptoms, create harmful stresses and actually kill people.

On the other hand, Paul Titmus had clearly had a serious heart attack and without the sort of equipment available in a specialist hospital unit I couldn't possibly tell how much damage had been done or begin to guess at the likelihood of him having another attack.

I thought for a moment about taking him into our local Bilbury cottage hospital but I quickly dismissed that idea. The hospital is set up to provide care for convalescent patients, and although I do occasionally have patients there who are seriously ill, the conditions are not ideal. The one full-time nurse used to work for my predecessor, Dr Brownlow, and although he is kind, caring and competent, he is elderly and cannot possibly provide 24 hour care for a heart attack patient.

There were, therefore, only two choices.

Either Mr Titmus went into hospital or he stayed at home to be looked after by his wife. And if he stayed at home, I'd have the responsibility of attending to him. Plus, of course, if things went badly and he died I'd have to explain to a coroner why I hadn't sent him into hospital.

'I'm not going into hospital,' said Mr Titmus with a firmness which rather surprised me. 'You can't force me to go. And I forbid you to mention my condition to anyone. If you send me into hospital I'll discharge myself straight away and make my way home.'

'I wouldn't dream of telling anyone anything about your health,' I assured him. Country doctors, living and working in small communities, are privy to an enormous number of secrets and learning to keep secrets is a vital part of the job. 'But if you stay at home then your wife is going to have to take on the responsibility of nursing you. I don't have a team of nurses whom I can send in to look after you. I'll call in regularly and I'll only be a phone call away but the two of you will have to take on some of the responsibility.'

'I'll look after him here,' said Peta. She spoke firmly and with certainty. 'But it would be easier if he was upstairs in the bedroom. The bathroom and our only loo are upstairs.'

'But you've got your exhibition to prepare for,' said Mr Titmus.

'I can set up an easel in the bedroom or perhaps in the spare bedroom just across the landing,' she said. 'I can keep an eye on you and if you need something all you have to do is call.'

'How is the pain at the moment?' I asked my patient.

'It's a lot easier,' he replied. 'The pains in my arm and jaw have completely gone and the pain in my chest is just more of an ache now.'

I listened to his chest again, took his pulse and checked his blood pressure. His colour was a lot better, his lips were now more pink than blue and the sweating had stopped.

And so Mrs Titmus and I put her husband onto a dining chair, tied him into position with a couple of dressing gown cords to make sure that he didn't fall off, and together we carried him up the stairs. Fortunately, being a runner he was thin and light; he didn't weigh more than a boy.

Once we'd got him upstairs, Mrs Titmus re-made their bed and we got him into it without any more alarums.

I told Mrs Titmus to give her husband soluble aspirin tablets every four hours. Since his pulse and blood pressure were fine I didn't give him anything else. I suspect that most doctors look down their noses at the idea of prescribing aspirin but in so many situations it is the drug of choice.

'Ring me if there are any problems,' I told Mrs Titmus. 'If you think it's urgent and you can't get me because I'm out on a call, ring 999 and ask for an ambulance. I'll be back tomorrow after my morning surgery.'

Finally, I told him that it was up to him and his wife to decide what they told relatives, friends and his employer. 'I don't have to tell anyone anything,' I assured him. 'And I won't.'

'I'm afraid I'll need a sick note for my boss,' said Mr Titmus.

I took out a pad of sick notes, wrote his name, scribbled something indecipherable and signed the note.

'What does it say?' asked Mr Titmus, scrutinising the sick note.

'Never you mind,' I smiled. 'It says whatever you want it to say.'

'Will you get into trouble for doing that?' asked Mrs Titmus.

'Probably,' I agreed. 'But I promise you that I shan't tell anyone what's wrong with you until or unless you give permission.' I have always felt that medical confidentiality takes precedence over whatever rules the bureaucrats might dream up.

And with that I packed my stuff into my black bag and set off to the next patient.

I suspect there are quite a few doctors who believe that I did the wrong thing. They may well be right. I'm not sure that there were 'right' and 'wrong' answers for a patient such as Mr Titmus. But faced with a patient who doesn't want to go into hospital, and who steadfastly refuses to go, life becomes very difficult. Theoretically, it is possible for a doctor to 'section' a patient and to send them into hospital against their will. But to do this I would have probably had to call in someone else, a social worker, a policemen or another doctor. And would that have been the right thing to do? I didn't think so at the time and I still don't think it would have been the correct thing to do. In the end it all comes down to making a judgement and being prepared to take responsibility.

My next patient, Byron Shelley, was several miles away and as I drove I couldn't help thinking about Mr and Mrs Titmus. The elderly Rolls Royce 20/25 which I inherited from Dr Brownlow has a surprising burst of speed when required but is a car well suited for meandering and, therefore, conducive to good thinking. I wondered if Mr Titmus would remain President of the running club. (I was assuming that he would survive his heart attack) And I realised that the next time I visited I would have to warn him to make some drastic changes to his exercise programme. There wouldn't be any long, competitive runs for quite a while, if ever. I would have to make it clear that I would not sanction him ever running with a number pinned to his vest. Even running for fun (something of an oxymoron for me, I'm afraid) would have to be strictly limited if not curtailed.

Whenever I go to see Byron Shelley I am always reminded of Mr Peggotty, the character invented by Charles Dickens for his autobiographical novel 'David Copperfield'.

Mr Peggotty, a fisherman who specialised in the sale of lobsters and crabs, lived in a converted boat on Yarmouth beach. Mr Shelley, on the other hand, lives in a converted boat which sits on the beach at Sawcliff Bay, just above the high water mark.

Carved on a flat piece of driftwood and attached to the side of the wheelhouse was a quotation from Cicero: 'It is not by muscle, speed or physical dexterity that great things are achieved, but by reflection, force of character and judgement; in these qualities old age is usually not poorer but richer.' I once asked him how long it had taken to carve the quote onto the driftwood. He said it took him most of the winter of 1959/60.

Mr Shelley had told me that his mother was a fan of the romantic poets. He said he thought that this explained why she had married a man called Shelley (who had stayed with her just long enough to assist in the production of a child, before disappearing long before Byron's birth).

'I don't think she realised just how romantic Byron really was,' said Mr Shelley ruefully. 'When I was at university the students' union wouldn't let me join after a cadre of aggressive feminists complained that Byron had regularly mistreated all the women in his life. They seemed to think that since I shared his name I was responsible for his peccadilloes.' He laughed. 'I once took off my shoes and showed them my perfectly healthy feet but it made no difference.'

To reach Mr Shelley's home I had to park my car at the top of the cliff and clamber down a long, steep and rather treacherous path to the beach. Holidaymakers never use the path, which looks and is dangerously narrow and precipitous and so the beach is always deserted. Not even local sea fishermen bother to scramble all that way down to the sea – there are much more accessible beaches nearby. Goats have a tippy-toe way of walking which doesn't produce wide paths. As Byron Shelley said, holiday-makers don't like to go onto a beach unless they're carrying a freezer box packed with sandwiches and fruit, a bag containing flasks and bottles, another bag containing swimming costumes, snorkels, masks and towels and yet another bag containing magazines, books, sun-cream, sunhats, spare sunglasses and other essentials. Those with babies or infants also need their pushchair. It's impossible to clamber down a steep goat track while carrying all those goodies. And hikers never go down the path because the path leads only to the beach and doesn't go anywhere else. Besides they always have heavy rucksacks on their backs and thumb sticks and map cases impeding their ability to balance themselves.

At the bottom of the goat track I had to pick my way across some huge boulders at the top of the beach (the residue of a long ago landslip) in order to reach Byron Shelley's boat, the 'Mary Jane'.

The 'Mary Jane' is the wind, rain and spray battered old boat that Byron has converted into a surprisingly comfortable home for a man and his dog. The boat had no mains electricity, no mains gas, no mains water and no mains anything. Naturally there is no telephone. Despite the absence of modern conveniences, Mr Shelley manages remarkably well and enjoys his isolation. He takes his drinking water from a sparkling stream that cascades down the cliff face, and he has a small windmill attached to the stern of his boat which provides him with the electricity he needs for a single 40 watt bulb. He has the lamp attached to a long trailing lead so that he can move the light wherever he wants it inside his boat. In the summer he cooks over a fire he builds with driftwood and in the winter he cooks with the aid of a small camping stove which runs on tiny gas cylinders. His loo is the chemical one inside his boat. I never asked him where he empties it but I very much doubt if he causes anywhere near as much pollution as a big city sewage facility emptying, by sanctioned overflows, into a nearby sea, estuary or river.

Mr Shelley is, as Alexander the Great was rumoured to be, one of those rare individuals who have a condition known as heterochromia iridum, which means that they have one blue eye and one brown eye. He is a self-contained man, now in his late seventies, who rarely has anything much wrong with him, despite his rather Spartan lifestyle. His medical records contained very little information except for the fact that when he was in his late twenties he had suffered from an acute attack of depression (the hinted reference in the medical notes suggested an unrequited love and a romantic betrayal) and had decided to kill himself by swimming out to sea and drowning. He had been living near Dover at the time and, by chance, picked the narrowest section of the English Channel. He had not, however, counted on his strength as a swimmer. He eventually found himself in sight of the French coast and had been greeted with some ceremony by French citizens who had seen him approaching. When he arrived in France, he was so delighted by his reception (which was heightened by the fact that he had arrived without advance notice or a support boat) that he regained his affection for life. He was, I suspect, the only individual to have swum the English Channel by accident. Nevertheless, he never again had any sort of romantic relationship, though whether this was due to lasting, unrequited love or to the fact that he had lost faith in women in general I never discovered.

When Mr Shelley needed help, he raised one of a variety of different signal flags on the mainmast of his boat. His one friend, Bromwell Clifford a former Chief Petty Office in the Royal Navy, watched for the flags and took whatever action he deemed necessary. Mr Clifford was writing a history of the North Devon coast. He was 84 and had been working on his book for eleven years. He had got as far as 1843 and told me once that the determination to finish the book helped keep him alive. He had a small, plastic device in one ear and a piece of wire from the device ended up in the top pocket of the jacket he always wore. It looked like a hearing aid but wasn't because the piece of plastic was a display model from a hearing aid manufacturer. Mr Clifford told me he wore the fake hearing aid in order to encourage people to speak more loudly and more clearly. He had retired to a former coastguard cottage at the top of the cliff, had a powerful telescope on a tripod in his small conservatory and used the telescope to help him keep an almost constant eye on the bay, the estuary beyond and Mr Shelley's home on the beach. For Mr Clifford it was a hobby that had become something of an obsession, but for holiday-makers and Byron Shelley it was a very healthy and practical life-saving obsession. Three times over the years, Mr Clifford had spotted small boats which had been clearly drifting aimlessly, their engines dead or their crew unable to manage their tiny craft for one reason or another, and once he'd helped direct the coastguard to a teenage boy who had drifted out to sea on an air bed.

In the summer, Mr Shelley operated a small, 16 foot fishing boat called 'The Pirate'. He would chug chug round to either Lynmouth or Combe Martin, put out a blackboard advertising fishing trips and trips around the bay and then wait for holiday makers or would-be fishermen to hire him for the morning, the afternoon or (his favourite commission, of course) the whole day. He had an excellent reputation as a boatman, and fishermen used to hire him regularly because of his skill at finding where fish could be caught. To help promote his services he always had a small Jolly Roger flying from a tiny flagpole at the prow of the boat. Since Byron Shelley had a large, grey beard and long, grey hair and wore an elderly, blue cap and an even older blue seaman's sweater he looked just like all the traditional pictures of a sailor and on fine, sunny days he was rarely short of customers. He was always paid in cash, of course, and with the money he made he would buy fuel, bait and whatever essential supplies he needed for himself. In the evening, Mr Shelley would chug back round to Sawcliff Bay, tie his boat up to a stanchion he had hammered into a huge and convenient rock, clamber ashore and go back to his home. Since Sawcliff Bay was small and had very little in the way of beach (and that impassable goat track) no tourists ever went there and Mr Shelley had the place to himself.

In the winter, of course, there was no call for his services as a boatman and so in the late autumn he dragged his boat onto the very small patch of gravel in the bay. He used wooden fence posts as rollers and a hand operated winch to haul the boat ashore. It was an exhausting business which used to take him much of the day. He'd then tie a tarpaulin cover over the boat and retire to his home until the spring. He spent the winter months sea fishing for food and attending to the fabric repairs which are required to keep even shore based vessels weatherproof. He was a keen reader too and had a remarkable library on board the boat that was his home, with a heavy emphasis on 19th century novelists such as Dickens, Thackeray and Collins from England and Tolstoy and Dostoevsky from Russia. He read every evening, with his tiny 40 watt bulb, and knew great chunks of both Dickens and Tolstoy by heart. 'Live your life as if it were an orange,' he once told me, 'squeeze all the goodness out of it until there's nothing left but the rind and the pith – and then you can leave happily.'

If he looked like running out of money he would make his way to the race course at either Exeter or Taunton where he would buy tickets for every horse in the first two races. He would throw away the tickets for all the losing horses and use the win tickets to convince punters that he was either a good tipster or having a lucky day. He would usually come away from a race meeting with £100 in his pocket. He wasn't a great man for paperwork and I doubt if Her Majesty's revenue men were aware of his activities. On the other hand he had, like so many country folk, never claimed a penny in benefits, social security or unemployment money. He was, like a number of my patients, someone who needed to live outside the system. I believe the modern term is 'off the grid'. Since, as far as Britain's National Health Service is concerned, he did not exist I didn't get paid for treating him. I didn't mind. My predecessor, Dr Brownlow, had practised before the National Health Service was founded in 1948 and he had charged his patients fees for his services. He had charged his richer patients £5 or £10 for a consultation and the poorer patients he had charged a shilling or half a crown. The richer patients paid more for the medicines they needed and if they needed an operation they paid notably more for that. The patients who couldn't afford a shilling Dr Brownlow had treated without charge, never even charging them for their medicines.

In those dark, off-season months, when he wanted fresh supplies of food, gas cylinders and other basic essentials, Mr Shelley would raise the blue and yellow K flag from the international seafaring code – that's the flag which is used to say: 'I wish to communicate with you'. He had a fixed shopping list of necessary supplies and Peter Marshall, who is, of course, the proprietor of Bilbury's only shop, would put the items into a basket and lower the basket down the cliff. The basket, suspended on a rope of precisely the right length was tied at the top end to a small, stout tree which clung rather precariously to the edge of the cliff.

When Peter arrived with Mr Shelley's order, he would haul up the empty basket, fill it and then lower it down to the beach. The empty basket always contained an empty coffee tin inside which there would be some money and a shopping list containing any special requests for the next delivery. Most of the food Peter delivered was in tins.

Mr Shelley lived largely on fish, lobsters and crabs which he caught himself. In the spring, summer and early autumn he caught these from his boat. In the winter he caught fish from the shore. When Peter sent down the full basket he would put the change in the coffee tin.

Peter can sometimes be a bit of a rogue (it is a well-known joke in Bilbury that Peter invented the promotional saying: 'Buy three, get two!', though Peter, of course, claims that this was the result of a printer's error) but he never cheated Mr Shelley. If there was ever any mail for Mr Shelley it either went to Peter Marshall at his shop or to his friend Bromwell Clifford in the old coast guard cottage.

Whenever he wants to see me, Byron Shelley flies the W flag (a blue square with a white square inside it and a small red square inside the white square) which ships send when they need medical assistance. Once Mr Clifford spots the flag, he telephones the surgery and asks me to visit. It is a system which sounds complicated but which works perfectly well. Mr Shelley doesn't routinely take any medicines and so doesn't need repeat prescriptions of anything. He deals with aches and pains and headaches and stomach upsets himself (which, basically, means that he just waited for the symptoms to disappear) and only ever calls me when he had a real problem of some kind.

I visit him at his boat because although I certainly find it difficult to clamber down the cliff to his boat, he would definitely find it infinitely more difficult to reach my surgery in Bilbury Grange. He has no car, no truck and no bicycle and even though there is still a bus stop just three miles away, there hasn't been a bus in his part of the world for longer than anyone could remember. Whenever I find myself stumbling as I scramble down the tiny cliff path (a path which is kept alive by the scrabbling hooves of the local goats who live on the cliff face) I remember that my predecessor Dr Brownlow had always visited Mr Shelley, even when he himself was frail. Once when his knee was giving him a lot of trouble, Dr Brownlow stopped on a ledge around 75 yards from the beach and shouted for Mr Shelley. Since Mr Shelley couldn't climb up the cliff and Dr Brownlow couldn't climb down, they then had a long-distance conversation during which Mr Shelley described the salient features of his symptoms, which consisted of a particularly virulent attack of haemorrhoids. Dr Brownlow decided that there was no need for a physical examination, and later that day Peter Marshall made a special delivery with the prescribed ointment which Dr Brownlow had dispensed.

Mr Shelley's basic health problem, and the main reason that he could not easily clamber up the cliff path, is that he has only one good leg. And in place of the missing leg (which had been amputated after an accident which occurred when he served in the Merchant Navy) he has a wooden peg leg – the sort made famous by Robert Louis Stevenson's character 'Long John Silver' and by Herman Melville's 'Captain Ahab' as well as just about every cartoonist who has ever drawn a pirate.

As my predecessor Dr Brownlow did frequently, I have tried to persuade Mr Shelley to have a proper prosthesis fitted but he has rejected the offer so often that I've stopped offering and have just told him that if he ever changes his mind then he should just let me know. His consistent explanation for refusing the offer of a modern prosthesis is that he just hates the idea of having to visit a hospital and talk to doctors and limb fitters. He is, he insists, comfortable with his wooden leg, which he finds tolerably comfortable. Although I understood his reluctance, I suspect that Mr Shelley is very well aware that a traditional wooden leg adds considerably to his piratical air. Visitors who want to hire a boat for a few hours love to have their picture taken with Byron Shelley because the wooden leg, the grey beard and the Jolly Roger flying on the prow of the boat all make their photographs look more authentic and even dashing. Indeed, a local wedding photographer will, on quiet and sunny days, hang around Mr Shelley's position near the harbour and offer to take professional pictures as souvenirs. He uses a large, colour Polaroid camera so that photos are printed without any delay. Together the pirate and the photographer do quite a good trade and visitors who don't want to go out in the boat will still pose for a picture. The photographer provides the camera and the film and the selling patter, collects the money and takes the pictures. Afterwards he gives Mr Shelley a flat 20% of his earnings – in cash, of course – for the loan of his body and accompanying wooden leg. Mr Shelley provides a smile or, if required, a fierce piratical look at no extra charge. Children either love him or cry and hide behind their mother's legs when they see him. Men envy him and spend the rest of the day stomping around as if they had a wooden leg. Women aren't quite sure what to make of him but usually decide they admire his rather sanitised version of piratical wildness.

On the day I am talking about, it took me longer than usual to pick my way down the path. Swallows were flying close to me, hovering and to catch the flies which I disturbed as I brushed against the few scraps of foliage that managed to survive on such inhospitable ground. I paused for a moment and watched a magpie and a pigeon squabbling over an abandoned rook's nest. Rather to my surprise, the pigeon eventually won and the disappointed magpie flew away with loud protestations. When I finally managed to scramble to the bottom of the cliff (relieved that it was summer and not raining nor even heavily overcast), and had made my way across the boulders to where Mr Shelley's home sat, partly on a small stretch of shingle and partly on a large flat rock (the boat, a 30 foot yacht that had once cruised the Mediterranean, was held upright by rows of wooden supporting stakes on each side) I called up to him to ask him to invite me aboard. Mr Shelley was quite old fashioned and would not allow visitors aboard his boat until the niceties had been observed.

Once he had acknowledged my presence (and I suspect I was the only visitor he ever had) he would toss a rather frayed and insecure looking rope ladder over the side of the boat and up I would climb, holding my black bag in one hand and trying to hold onto the ladder with the other. I had initially wondered what on earth would happen if Mr Shelley were too ill to throw over the rope ladder, but I had soon learned to suppress this particular anxiety partly since I couldn't think of a solution and partly because I realised that if Mr Shelley were too ill to throw over the rope ladder he would probably be too ill to run up the appropriate flag requesting my presence. As Colonel Rudolf Abel, the Russian spy, is supposed to have implied, worrying about something does not help bring about a satisfactory solution.

'I'm sorry to bother you, doctor,' said Mr Shelley. 'I didn't know who else to turn to.' He usually kept his boat and himself looking very shipshape but he looked more unkempt than I could ever remember seeing him. And the boat was untidy. It was as though he had somehow lost heart. I guessed these were probably symptoms of a depression. But, depressed or not, Mr Shelley had not lost his social graces. 'Gin or brandy?' he asked.

I thanked him and said I'd have a small brandy.

He filled half a tumbler with brandy and handed it to me. It was the sort of measure that Frank at the Duck and Puddle would have regarded as a healthy single but which anyone else would have measured as at least a quadruple. I looked at it and wondered how I could possibly drink it, climb back up the cliff, drive home and sober up enough for the evening surgery. I didn't like to tell him that I'm not very fond of brandy or gin. I surreptitiously glanced around, hoping that there might be a pot plant somewhere nearby. There wasn't. I took a sip of the brandy and waited for Mr Shelley to tell me his problem. The brandy made me cough.

'The council have decided that commercial boatmen have to have a licence,' he said.

'I think boatmen have needed licenses for some time,' I told him.

He looked genuinely surprised at this. 'First I've heard of it,' he said. 'Anyway, a young lad from the council's 'North Devon Small

Boat Licensing Authority and Directorate' came round when I was on the harbour wall in Lynmouth. He asked to see my licence. He said that if I want to carry members of the public in my boat then I have to have a licence. He wasn't more than a whipper-snapper but he had a suit and tie on and acted like he was the High Sherriff himself.'

'I think boatmen need a licence like taxi drivers,' I explained.

'The lad from the council said if I applied for a licence I'd fail because there's a medical examination which I wouldn't be able to pass. He gave me a form to fill in but said they'd fail me.'

'Did he say why?'

Mr Shelley tapped his wooden leg.

'You'd fail the medical because of your missing leg?'

'That's what he said.'

'How long have you been working on the sea?'

'Since I was 16.' He drank some of his brandy and I pretended to drink some of mine. 'That was 49 years ago. I've never known anything else.'

'And when did you lose your leg?'

'Twenty seven years ago.'

'May I look at the form he gave you?'

Mr Shelley stood up, walked over to a built-in desk and retrieved an official looking piece of paper from of one of the pigeon holes. He walked back to where we were sitting and handed me the form. As forms go it was surprisingly straightforward. I found the section dealing with medical requirements and sure enough there was a note there stating that applicants for a boat licence had to have all their limbs as well as good eyesight. I carried on reading the form. There was quite a lot of it.

'Is there anything you can do?' he asked.

'The medical requirements are quite clear,' I told him.

'Right,' he said, with a nod.

'But there's a clause here which says you can appoint a designated Mate to help you with the boat. The Mate doesn't need to be licensed – he can sail the boat on your licence. The licensee just has to give the name of his designated deputy.'

'I saw that,' said Mr Shelley. 'These people live in another world. I only just earn enough for me. I'd never be able to afford to pay someone else as well.'

'It also says that if you are prevented from taking your boat out then your designated Mate can take the boat out for you – and stand in for you in every way.'

'I don't see how that helps me,' said Mr Shelley.

'The Mate doesn't need to have a licence of his own and so he doesn't have to pass a medical. And it doesn't matter how many legs he has.'

Mr Shelley struggled to understand. 'I still don't see how that helps.'

'I think there's a loophole; a way round your problem,' I told him. 'If I take out a licence I can appoint you my Mate and substitute skipper.'

'But you don't want to be running a boat do you, doctor?'

'No, I don't. I couldn't do it anyway. I don't know how to find fish and I get seasick if my bathwater is too rough.'

'But will they give you a licence? Do you know about boats?'

'I know nothing about boats but it doesn't matter. They don't ask any questions about my boat handling skills. They just want to know that I don't have a prison record and that I've got four limbs.'

Mr Shelley still looked confused. 'How does this help?'

'I can easily get a licence as a boatman,' I explained. 'But I don't have to be on the boat at all. You can run the boat for me – using my licence as if it were yours.'

'And that'll work?'

'Yes. It's a bit sneaky, I suppose,' I admitted. 'But it's a stupid rule and this is just a way round it.'

Mr Shelley held his hand out to me. He grinned. We shook hands on the deal. There were tears in his eyes which he brushed away with the sleeve of his jacket.

'I'll fill in the form when I get home and post it off straight away,' I told him, standing up. 'You just carry on taking out your boat as usual. If anyone from the council asks to see your licence just tell them I'm the licence holder and you're my designated Mate.'

'Do you have to put my name on the form?' he asked. 'It might cause trouble if you do.'

'I don't think it would,' I assured him. 'But how about if I put you down as Edward Dempster?'

Mr Shelley recognised the name and grinned. 'The pirate?'

'Indeed, so. The pirate. The name fits your boat.'

And so Edward Dempster, a 17th century buccaneer and privateer, an associate of the notorious Henry Morgan, was to be reborn as my first and only mate.

Mr Shelley nodded his appreciation. 'If I can ever do anything for you, doctor, you've just got to say the word.'

'There is one thing you can do for me,' I said.

'Name it.'

'Finish that brandy for me!' I said, with a laugh. 'If I drink all that I'll never get back up the cliff.'

After clambering back up the cliff path (and giving thanks when I reached the top) I paused a few minutes admiring the view and getting my breath back, and headed just a quarter of a mile inland to visit Franklin and Doris Minton who still lived in the cottage where they had both lived all their married lives, and where Mrs Minton had lived since the day she'd been born 77 years earlier. Mrs Minton had, in fact, never slept anywhere other than in that cottage. I wonder how many people there are who can say the same.

Some couples grow apart as the years go by but some grow closer together with every passing page of the calendar. The Mintons had definitely grown closer and they had become one of those couples who, after living and working together for decades, end up thinking together. They no longer had to speak to each other to communicate. They scratched a bare living from the land and the countryside around but they never complained or seemed discontent.

Mr Minton had trained as a farrier but the number of people with horses in Bilbury had shrunk over the years and inevitably the need for his services had gradually diminished. He had tried chimney sweeping for a while but had abandoned that venture when a brush got stuck in one of those old-fashioned chimneys which, instead of going straight to the sky had an unforeseen right angle bend half way up. A chimney sweep from Exeter had to be called to extricate Mr Minton's brush from the chimney and that had been the end of the chimney sweeping business. Mr Minton hadn't been too sad about selling his brushes. He was an outdoors man through and through.

They kept chickens, of course. The hens were a success, and provided the Mintons with all the eggs they could eat (and a plentiful supply of poultry for Sunday dinners) but as a business venture, the hens were a failure. Attempts at selling eggs door to door had not produced the income they had hoped for since I doubt if there are more than half a dozen homes in Bilbury where there aren't chickens galore running around. At least half of the homes in the village have geese and ducks too.

Eventually, the two of them decided that they wanted a simpler, more reliable source of income and so they started collecting all the twigs and small branches on their five acre plot and selling bundles of kindling. They rightly guessed that there is, and always will be, a considerable demand for kindling in the countryside, where every house is equipped with a log fire or a log burner and where residents are happy to pay a few pence for someone else to collect their kindling for them.

Mr Minton built a trailer which could be towed behind a bicycle, and they bundled together the kindling they collected, tying each bundle of kindling with a length of orange binder twine, which they obtained free of charge from a friendly farmer who gave them the unwanted lengths of twine he'd previously used to tie up bundles of hay. The Mintons soon acquired a small but ample number of customers, and for years cycled round the village selling the kindling they had collected. When they ran out of the kindling they could collect on their own land, they asked permission from neighbouring landowners to collect their fallen branches and kindling. No one objected since none of the landowners they contacted had the time or inclination to wander through their woodlands picking up twigs. There wasn't a lot of money to be made from selling kindling but it was a cash business, and therefore exempt from paperwork and bad debts, and working together the Mintons made enough money to pay their living costs. They were, like many country folk, particularly those usually described as being 'of a certain age', far too proud to apply for or claim any of the State distributed benefits which are available to the poor and needy.

And then, slowly, a couple of years ago, it became clear that Mrs Minton's health was deteriorating. It was her mind, not her body, that was failing her. She began to forget the names of their customers and when she set out on the bicycle to make deliveries, she sometimes forgot where she was supposed to be going. For a while Mr Minton got round this by making all the deliveries himself and leaving his wife at home to parcel up the kindling they had collected. But eventually even this proved too much for her. He would arrive back home and find her sitting staring into space, not having done anything at all in the hours he had been away. Or, worse still by far, he would get back home and find her missing. He would then have to search for in the nearby lanes, fields and woods where he would find her hunting for something but not able to remember what it was that she was looking for. Eventually, of course, he found that he was spending more and more time looking after his wife and less and less time collecting, bundling and delivering kindling. And naturally, since they didn't earn any money when they weren't selling kindling, their income fell dramatically to pretty near nothing.

A friend, seeing their dire financial straits, suggested that Mr Minton, who was now his wife's full time carer, should apply for a 'carer's allowance' from one of the State's benefits schemes. For reasons which were never properly explained, the bureaucrats refused to give him a carer's allowance but the Mintons were given weekly benefits payments which helped to pay their bills. More importantly, the local council's taxes (by far their biggest outgoing) were paid on their behalf.

And then two months ago, an official employee from the council had turned up with paperwork, questions and judgements galore. She was one of those State employees who feels that it is their job to frighten the life out of people and to spread despair, depression and despondency as widely as they can. I had met this particular apparatchik before and had got the distinct impression that she was one of those individuals who always charges a high rate of emotional interest on her own perceived kindnesses or on those State provided favours which she found herself able to offer.

She began by telling Mr Minton that at their age they should both put their lives in order. Those were the words she employed. 'Put your lives in order'. Mr Minton didn't have the foggiest what she meant by this updated version of the previously popular 'put your affairs in order' (an exhortation which had attracted so many predictable jokes about 'Bill, John, David, Gilbert, Tom' or 'Hilda, Ethel, Heather, Gloria, Meg' that it had been abandoned) but the visitor, when pressed, explained that she meant that they should settle all their finances, make wills and sort through all their personal stuff. Mr Minton didn't have any financial affairs to sort out, had no money to leave and no one to leave it to anyway. Their cottage was rented at much the same peppercorn rent as had been paid for many decades and the furniture they possessed would have probably been turned down by a charity shop. Moreover, they had absolutely no desire to get rid of the few personal possessions which they owned, most of which would mean absolutely nothing to anyone else but which were full of singular memories for the Mintons. Franklin Minton was also well aware that if he threw out the few bits and pieces which they did own it would cause his wife great distress if she noticed that her familiar items were missing.

Mrs Minton, who was under the impression that the visitor from the council was her long-dead sister whom she had never liked, had said nothing whatsoever.

The council employee had then offered the usual advice which such people give to the elderly. Reading from a printed leaflet, which she had left with them when she left, she had advised them both to: 'Wrap up when it is cold'; 'be careful when the roads are slippery'; 'take an umbrella if it is raining'; 'make sure you drink plenty of fluids if the weather is hot' and so on and so on. Mr Minton, who had successfully navigated these potential hazards for many decades, had thanked her for these suggestions. In his place I would have been tempted to tell her that it was a wonder that I had got this far in life without having access to this fount of official wisdom. I found myself wondering what Thumper or Patchy would have said if advised to wrap up well in cold weather. I couldn't get past the exclamation: 'No shit, Sherlock!'

Finally, the council employee (who was registered as some sort of social worker) then told Mr and Mrs Minton that loneliness was as bad for them as smoking a pack of cigarettes a day, and offered to arrange for a volunteer worker to visit them once a week to provide them with conversation. Mr Minton had replied that he didn't smoke and was therefore already ahead of the game and was quite prepared to take his chances with loneliness if it ever troubled him which it had not done to date. Her visit, in short, gave Mr Minton nothing but worry which was, as it often is, nothing more than the interest payable on an un-payable debt.

To be fair, none of this had been much of a price to pay for the financial support which the Mintons had been given, and which had enabled them to keep a roof over their heads and to buy enough food to keep body and soul together. (They themselves looked after their need for heat by burning fallen branches which Franklin Minton still collected from the woods from whence he and Doris Minton had earned their living for so long.)

But then one day the social worker turned up with a list of questions designed to help her decide if either of the Mintons was suffering from dementia. It seemed that the council had for some reason decided that rooting out dementia would be its mission of the year, in the same way that repairing kerbs, installing new street lighting or turning perfectly decent thoroughfares into one way streets had been previous missions.

Mr Minton had no problem answering the questions which were asked but Mrs Minton was less able to produce the required answers, and the social worker had told Mr Minton that she would send a psychiatric social worker to conduct a formal assessment of Mrs Minton, with a view to moving her into a specialist home for the demented.

Mrs Minton might have wondered why her long dead and unloved sister was now visiting so frequently, but she had no idea of the significance of the questions that she was asked. Mr Minton, on the other hand, was desperately upset, indeed quite discombobulated and despairing, at the thought that his wife might be forcibly taken away from him and deposited in some sort of institution. He knew well that neither of them would survive the separation. The main problem was that if she was moved to a specialist institution in Barnstaple, or anywhere else, they would probably never see each other again. Mr Minton, who had once owned a small van, did not own any sort of motor vehicle, and had let his driving licence lapse because he could not afford the fees. He could walk or bicycle to Bilbury Grange but that was as far as he could travel under his own steam. And buses do not come to Bilbury.

Having locked their front and back doors, and pocketed the keys, to prevent his wife from wandering, he had come to see me one morning to ask if I could help. Two days later I had gone round to their home, taking with me a list of the questions which I knew the psychiatric social worker would ask so that together Mr Minton and I could train Mrs Minton to give the 'correct' answers.

And that, I'm afraid, is exactly what we did. I gave Mr Minton the list of questions which I knew his wife would be asked and we quite literally trained her to give answers which we knew would be acceptable.

I looked at my watch as I parked my car in the driveway to the Minton's cottage. The psychiatric social worker was twenty minutes late when she parked her Morris Minor behind my elderly Rolls Royce. She apologised, and explained that she'd got lost and had had to stop and ask for directions.

Everything then went quite smoothly. The psychiatric social worker asked her designated questions, just as expected, and Mrs Minton, thoroughly prepared, and with quite a good deal of subtle prompting from her husband, gave the required answers. 'My wife is a little hard of hearing,' explained Mr Minton, when providing answers for his wife.

There was only one small hitch.

'Are you an only child?' asked the social worker.

'Yes,' said Mrs Minton.

The social worker looked puzzled and studied her prepared notes. 'It says here that you have a sister.'

'Apart from the sister, of course,' I said quickly. I lowered my voice. 'Mrs Minton's sister died some years ago and she doesn't like to talk about her. Indeed she gets very upset if she is mentioned.'

'Oh I am sorry, I do understand,' whispered the social worker back.

And that was that.

Doris Minton was declared as sane and mentally capable as any of us, fit to sit on a jury, vote or form a government, and the threat of incarceration in some council run institution was lifted.

I had to stay behind for a few moments after the social worker had left since my car was blocked in by hers.

'Do you think that went well?' asked Mr Minton.

'It went splendidly,' I told him.

Before I left, he gave me an unexpected hug and I could see that there were tears in his eyes.

Finally, on my way home I made a small detour and called in at Miss Butterbury's home to check on what polite society would doubtless refer to as 'her gentleman friend'. I was relieved to see that he was already very slightly better, and Miss Butterbury was much more relaxed.

'I've had quite a morning,' I told Patsy, as we sat down to a rather late luncheon. 'If what had happened today became widely known I think I'd probably get struck off the medical register, condemned by the British Medical Association, criticised by the council and widely attacked in the media.'

'Do you wish you'd done anything differently?' asked Patsy.

'No,' I replied in an instant, with a grin.

And so those, dear reader, are my confessions.

I prithee, think not too badly of me.

Uncle Charlie

Being a single-handed GP in a remote country practice brings many quiet and often subtle satisfactions and there are endless challenges and surprises. I cannot think of any job which offers such an endless variety of responsibilities. The post is all consuming; it is more than an occupation, it is an integral part of my life.

But there is a downside.

I am on call for 24 hours a day, every day of the year. My wife, Patsy, accepts and shares the life we have chosen together. She knows that there will be times when I have patients who are seriously ill at home who will need extra care. Pregnant women tend to go into labour at unpredictable moments. Accidents and illnesses do not happen according to an agreeable schedule. But she agrees with me that we cannot think of any way of life which we would find more thoroughly satisfying and fulfilling. When I am out (and sometimes even when I am not) it is to Patsy to whom patients address their concerns and, as doctors' wives have done for decades, it is she who offers excellent advice. I wonder if doctors' husbands will do the same when there are more women doctors in practice.

But there is clearly no line between 'work' and 'life' and there is, on occasion, a painful price to pay. I was recently given a vivid and painful reminder of this.

We were having dinner one evening when the telephone went. It was a neighbour of my Uncle Charlie's. He'd found my phone number in Charlie's address book. As long as I'd known him he'd always been Charlie and never Charles.

I hadn't seen my Uncle Charlie much for most of my adult life, particularly since I had been living and working in Bilbury. Once, two years earlier, he and my Aunty Bertha had called in on their way to a holiday at a caravan site at Treyarnon Bay in Cornwall. They had stayed with us for a night on their way down and stayed again on their way back home a fortnight later. They had both seemed very old and frail, which indeed they were. Charlie still drove the same old 1930s Citroen Traction Avant which he'd owned when I was a boy. The car had been elderly then and it had done a huge mileage. It was the classic car of the type which I remember was later favoured by Chief Inspector Maigret in the television series which was so popular in the 1960s. That was the series in which Simenon's character was played by an actor called Rupert Davies.

I remember being shocked that Uncle Charlie never locked the car when he left it parked. 'Why would I lock it?' he asked me, genuinely puzzled. 'No one would steal it and if they do the insurance company will buy me a new one.'

When I was a boy, Uncle Charlie was the good uncle every small boy should have. He took me to my first football match, he bought me my first penknife (a Swiss Army knife with 12 blades of which only two were slightly broken), my first Montblanc pen (it had a crack in the case and the nib was slightly bent but I didn't care) and when we went away on holiday, he fed my pet cat and my goldfish. One year my goldfish died and Uncle Charlie spent four days visiting every pet shop in the area in the hope of finding a ringer to substitute for the deceased fish. When he failed he was distraught; far more upset, I fear, than I was. I had never really bonded with the goldfish. He bought me small, inexpensive toys which weren't toys at all. Most of them he picked up after rummaging around in local junk shops. He bought me a small brass compass in a leather case (it never worked very well but I didn't care), a small magnet and a set of darts in a little leather case. He made me my first bow and showed me how to make another, and made me all the arrows I needed. When I was 12 I began playing golf and he used to supply me with bags full of second-hand golf balls which he collected from the bushes bordering his nearest course. He collected plastic figures from his and the neighbours' cereal packets and gave me all the cigarette cards from his Woodbine cigarettes. When he found that I was collecting the cards, he persuaded his pals from the local pub's dart team to save their cigarette cards for me. He didn't have friends or acquaintances. He had pals.

Most people, especially writers, surround themselves with small artefacts which mean something and which hold memories, and many of the bits and pieces which adorn the shelves in my consulting room came to me from Uncle Charlie.

He was short, squat and solid and always reminded me of one of those concrete look-out block-houses which were built along the South Coast of England at the start of World War II. When I was small I thought he looked as if he had been put together by a whimsical, slightly tipsy angel on the first day of their apprenticeship, using mismatched parts and discarded seconds, the bits and pieces that all the other angels tasked with constructing human beings had rejected as barely suitable for human use. He had a huge head with twinkling eyes, a perennial smile and barely enough hair to fashion a pair of eyebrows for the average citizen. His hands were huge and gnarled and sun tanned, as though they had been carved out of ebony by a master sculptor. He always had balloons and marbles in his pockets and one Christmas he taught me how to make animals out of long thin balloons.

His wife, my Aunty Bertha, was a tiny thing, as quiet as a church mouse and one of those ladies who always greeted visitors (however transient) with a cup of tea and a slice of home-made cake. There were usually three varieties of cake to choose from. If the postman rang the doorbell to deliver a parcel, she would invite him in for a cup of tea and a slice of home-made cake. If a new neighbour called round to borrow a cup of sugar and a pint of milk, she would load them up with groceries and give them a home-made cake in a biscuit tin.

Charlie and Bertha lived in a small, well-built semi-detached house where they'd lived since the day they were married. It had been Bertha's parents' house but her mother and father had both died the month before she and Charlie married. I never knew what they died of, but it was family legend that the one who died second had died of a broken heart. The house had no central heating, of course, but they kept warm enough with a single coal fire in the living room, which they lit on the morning of the 1st November and allowed to go out on the evening of 31st March the following year. Uncle Charlie used to joke that their kitchen was so cold that when they wanted to warm something up they would put it into the fridge. He wasn't entirely joking. Uncle Charlie owned a World War II duffle coat, the really warm sort with horn toggles, the type which used to be worn by officers in the Navy, and when it was really cold he would sometimes wear the coat indoors. Aunty Bertha would wear a very old and rather threadbare fur coat which she was ashamed of and would never wear out of doors but which she used in the winter as a dressing gown. It had belonged to her mother and, before that, to her grandmother.

When she wasn't making cakes, Bertha embroidered antimacassars for the easy chairs and the sofa and collected black and white china dogs and soft toys, of which she had an abundance – all of them given names and personalities.

They had very little money but somehow they always managed to live like royalty. He liked Gentleman's Relish, Carr's Water Biscuits and Oxford Thick Cut Marmalade and she loved Jackson's Lapsang Souchong tea and Dundee Cake which, of course, she made herself. She made Christmas cakes all year round and iced them too. When they had visitors who were expected, she prepared cucumber sandwiches, cut into tiny fingers, and he always had a bottle of decent sherry and a bottle of Cockburn's port on the sideboard. She was a housewife, and proud of it and she was one of the best read people I'd ever known. They had no television but both read a great deal. He liked adventure and travel magazines and she preferred books, with a special interest in autobiographies. She loved reading about other people's lives. They had a sit up and beg piano which she played if they had persuasive visitors and she had drunk a schooner of dry sherry.

As a boy I never really understood what my Uncle Charlie did for a living. He had what is now known as a 'portfolio of jobs' and was always on the look-out for fresh employment possibilities. By the 1970s, the concept was well-known and popular but back in the 1950s it was pretty well unheard of and I like to think that if anyone invented the notion it was probably my Uncle Charlie. He cut lawns for people with an old-fashioned push mower which just fitted into the boot of the Citroen (he would tie the lid open with a piece of string, connecting the rear bumper to the boot handle). He had inherited the lawn mower from his own parents and maintained it himself. He loved to see lawns which had clean stripes on them. And he provided a cheap taxi service for folk who couldn't afford proper taxis. He never charged people if he thought they couldn't afford to pay anything. Most of the people he did charge paid little more than petrol money. He delivered parcels and ran errands and taught the violin to a few pupils, and though he admitted that he himself didn't play terribly well, his pupils always seemed to do well enough. He grew soft fruits and herbs in his garden and sold them to neighbours and blokes he met in the pub. He made false teeth in his garden shed, making them for people who couldn't afford to see a dentist. They were good teeth too and, I gather, lasted for years. He did a little dealing in lower-priced antiques too and was a regular at auctions in the area – usually picking up items that none of the dealers seemed to want but for which he thought he could find a buyer. He was proud that one of his ancestors was a pirate.

He loved practical jokes and silliness and when I had my first book published he had a sign made to fix to the side of my car. The sign read: 'Supplier of essential words and phrases complete with punctuation. No sentences are left in this vehicle overnight.'

I proudly stuck it on the side of the car.

Aunty Bertha had died a year earlier, after a stroke that ended with her spending two years in bed or sitting in a chair beside her bed. Uncle Charlie, I knew, had read to her every day and after she'd died he had visited her grave every afternoon. He'd taken flowers from the garden when they'd been available and he had taken a book which he thought she would enjoy and a camp stool to sit on. He'd sat and read to her from the book he'd chosen. That was true devotion for he didn't really like the sort of books she enjoyed. He used to go to the library every other Wednesday afternoon to change the books.

After he had asked after us all, Uncle Charlie told me that he acquired two tickets for a cricket match at Lord's Cricket Ground in London. He wanted me to meet him in London and go to the match with him.

I desperately wanted to go, mostly because I wanted to see him, but I knew I wouldn't be able to find a locum in time so, with great regret, I had to say 'no'. I told him that we'd fix up something later in the summer. He said he would look forward to that. He sent his love.

And then the phone went as we were having dinner and it was a neighbour of Uncle Charlie's.

He told me that Charlie had died that day. My uncle had apparently been ill for a while but had never said anything to anyone. I had no idea that he was seriously ill. I know too well that most of us die a little sooner than expected or desired, and that we are none of us more than a moment's inattention away from death but from what I subsequently learned, Charlie had known he hadn't got much longer. The day at Lord's was due to be his final hoorah.

When he rang me, Uncle Charlie must have known that he was dying.

Of course, he knew.

I thanked the caller and asked him if he happened to know if Charlie had managed to get to watch the cricket at Lord's.

'Yes he did. He went with a pal from the pub. They went down on the train. The doctor didn't want him to go but Charlie insisted. He was exhausted when they got back but the neighbour said he'd had a good day. It was the last time Charlie left the house. 'I don't follow the game myself but apparently it was a good day's cricket,' said the neighbour. 'You're his nephew, aren't you?'

I said I was.

'He told me that he'd hoped you could go with him.'

I didn't explain why I hadn't gone. I thanked him and put the telephone down gently on the cradle. Patsy and I hugged one another and cried together.

Sometimes, just sometimes, the price of belonging to a country medical practice can seem too high.

A Hard Night, a Long Engagement and Gilly's Rock Cakes

Thumper, Patchy and I were in the bar at the Duck and Puddle. We were sitting with Frank, the proprietor, barman and chief glass washer and fire lighter. I would not presume to place myself in this or any other category but Thumper, Patchy and Frank are all gentlemen in the truest, most fundamental sense of the word.

There is much confusion these days about how a gentleman can best be defined. Some would doubtless argue that the very notion is an anachronism and that gentlemen disappeared for good when men abandoned jousting and stopped carrying swords but I think that's nonsense. Some would suggest that you can't be a gentleman unless you're a member of the upper class, but that too is nonsensical. I would argue that it is more difficult to find a gentleman among the aristocracy or among those dwelling in palaces than it is to find one driving a bus or a tractor or working on an oil rig. Snobs who like to judge people would claim that a gentleman is someone who went to the right school and university, and who has enough money not to have to count it, but I think that's dangerous nonsense. I prefer to define a gentleman as someone who is decent and honourable with a sense of duty and responsibility, a man who in any circumstances always instinctively knows the right thing to do and then instinctively does the right thing without fear or favour. A gentleman never betrays his friends and instinctively treats strangers with respect, until or unless they are proved unworthy. Thumper Robinson, Patchy Fogg and Frank Parsons all meet those criteria most satisfactorily. I would trust each and all of them with my life. What good fortune it is to have such friends.

Thumper and Patchy were both drinking beer. I was sipping a small glass of Laphroaig, my favourite malt whisky in the winter, and reading a postcard which our friend the Professor had sent us from America. The picture side of the card was a photograph of a line-up of Rockettes at Radio City Music Hall. The side with the stamps, the address and the space for a message contained a fulsome account of his first week in the United States, written in handwriting so small that we all needed to borrow Frank's spectacles in order to be able to read it. The Professor was lecturing at Harvard and apparently having quite a wonderful time. Just what the good folk of Harvard thought of their new recruit I couldn't begin to imagine, but American universities coped tolerably well with Dylan Thomas so I am confident that they were finding our erstwhile drinking companion a valuable if slightly eccentric addition to their academic staff.

Thumper Robinson, Bilbury's best known entrepreneur, odd job man and dealer in anything and everything portable or driveable, had his hat on, pulled down over his ears to hide the fact that on one side of his head he had very little hair left. The loss of hair was not due to any naturally produced alopecia, or to male pattern baldness, but was entirely man-made, or, to be more accurate, woman-made.

Thumper's wife, Anne, always cut his hair but on the most recent occasion she had cut his hair with even more enthusiasm than usual and things hadn't gone entirely to plan. (Just about every male in the village had his hair cut by his wife, girlfriend or mother. A visit to the nearest barber, in Barnstaple, would take up half a day at least and no male in Bilbury thought enough of his hair to devote so much time to its care or cultivation.)

'She's edited my head again,' Thumper complained every time he had a haircut, which invariably happened in an evening when he'd fallen asleep in front of the fire. This time the procedure had produced a rather comical look but Thumper wasn't amused. Because his head had been lying to one side as he slept, the hair cut was inevitably rather one sided. From the left he looked fairly normal, that is to say his hair looked as if it had been gnawed by rodents. From the right he looked like an army recruit, fresh from the barber's chair and ready for a touch of square bashing.

Patchy Fogg, an antique dealer who was married to my wife's sister, was looking through an auctioneer's catalogue, hunting to see if there was anything on sale which he could turn into a profit. He was marking possible lots with a stub of pencil which he had been using for as long as I'd known him, and which never seemed to get any smaller or any blunter.

I was struggling to stay awake and make sure I didn't fall off my bar stool. I had been up twice during the previous night.

The first call, at 2.15 a.m., had been to see Mrs Waring. She called me because of a pain in her abdomen which she thought was an inflamed appendix, but which I assured her was more likely to have been a direct result of her celebrating her daughter's engagement by eating a prawn cocktail, two portions of roast chicken, with all the trimmings, two pickled eggs, three large pickled onions, half a jar of pickled beetroot and two large slices of wedding cake, and washing the whole lot down with three pints of stout and several glasses of champagne. While I was there she had vomited and then spent fifteen minutes on the loo. The double barrelled explosions, which would have surely woken the neighbours if there had been anyone living within a mile of their house, had left Mrs Waring with far less pain and a strong case of embarrassment and regret, tinged with inevitable self-recrimination.

'I think I probably did eat too much,' she confessed, just before I left her in her husband's capable hands.

It was when I left the Warings that the rain had started. It wasn't one of those 'is it worth putting on a coat or putting up an umbrella' showers. It was one of those storms, driven from the West with a ferocious wind behind it, which everyone living on or near to Exmoor knows only too well, and knows enough to fear; it was one of those storms which seem to herald the end of the world.

The second call, which had come at 5.00 a.m., just after I'd got back to sleep, had been to examine, diagnose and eventually prescribe an antibiotic for the 18-month-old son of a farm hand who lived five miles away on a scruffy track leading off the road to Lynton. The storm was still raging, the wind blowing dead branches off sleeping trees and strong enough to shake fence posts out of the ground.

I got stuck in thick mud around three hundred yards from the farm house I was heading for, and had to travel the rest of the way on foot. I gave Mrs Smithers enough medicine to last for 24 hours and told her to pick up the remainder of the course of antibiotics from the surgery. The entire consultation had taken no more than ten minutes (including the time I'd spent helping Mr and Mrs Smithers move their five dogs from the living room and into the kitchen, where they had continued to attempt to intimidate by barking incessantly) but the whole visit had taken over two hours, most of which I'd spent having my car pulled out of mud by Mr Smithers' tractor. (It hadn't actually been purely mud though it was brown and sticky and there was a good deal of it. The clue to the nature of the gelatinous morass which had captured all four wheels of my car in an unforgiving grip was that there were around 20 cows in the field, and judging by the state of the car and my legs they had all suffered from diarrhoea. Maybe they had attended Mrs Waring's daughter's engagement party.)

When I finally got back home, tired, stinking, soaked to the skin and desperately in need of a bath, it had been too late to go back to bed. I'd stripped off everything I was wearing and dumped the lot outside the front door before hurrying, naked, upstairs to bathe away the night. My shoes and trousers seemed beyond rescue. I wasn't too bothered about the trousers but I had liked the shoes. They were brogues which I'd bought off the shelf but which fitted my feet perfectly. I'd had a pair of wellington boots in the back of the car but when I got stuck I jumped out to walk to the farmhouse and by the time I realised it was too late to save my shoes it was too late to go back and put on the boots. I suspected that the rest of my clothing was too dirty and foul smelling even to put into the washing machine.

Since, Patsy was awake we'd enjoyed a quiet early breakfast together.

The peace of the morning, before the day really starts, can sometimes be the best part of the day and it is even more relaxing when it marks the end of a hard day's night. I had a huge bowl of porridge, a rack full of Patsy's home-made pumpernickel bread, toasted and liberally covered in homemade, thick cut marmalade, and two cups of excellent, steaming hot coffee to kick-start the day. Patsy's pumpernickel bread is quite superior to anything produced in any commercial bakery and is so rich that I can usually only manage two slices at a time.

Just as I finished the last piece of toast the phone rang. It was Mrs Smithers. She said that her baby was now a lot better and that there was no longer any need for her to pick up more medicine. I told her that it was important that they finished the course of antibiotics and that I'd be expecting to see her or her husband later that day to pick up the rest of the course of medicine that I'd prescribed. After that it was time for the morning surgery, which was one of the quietest I could remember. The tempest was still raging and as a consequence, only seven patients turned up. I had plenty of time to deal with the morning mail and dispense the few repeat prescriptions which had been requested by telephone.

By lunchtime the worst of the storm had passed, heading no doubt for Somerset and then all counties to the East, stopping off at Taunton, Swindon and Reading to send the locals scurrying for cover and excite local weather forecasters (who always do a much better job of reporting on weather that has arrived than they do of warning of weather that is on its way). By the time it reached London the storm would have blown itself out, a ghost of its former menace, reduced to little more than a mischievous breeze, tickling the odd tile off the odd roof and overturning an occasional dustbin, but the news programmes would doubtless give the storm a name and describe it as a gale or possibly a hurricane. If an inch of snow falls in London the city grinds to a halt and dominates the news, with earnest forecasters and doomsters warning everyone to stay at home. The natives pat themselves on the back if they venture out of doors to the corner shop. If a foot of snow falls in Devon we put on our wellington boots and duffle coats and carry on as normal. Everything takes a little longer but life goes on.

After Patsy and I had lunch (homemade vegetable soup and two eggs on plain white toast for me and just the soup for Patsy) I dropped off Patsy at her sister's for the afternoon and drove the 20/25 to the Duck and Puddle for an hour or so. My ever-reliable receptionist, Miss Johnson has the village pub's telephone number next to our telephone pad but she knows it too well to need it written down.

When I arrived at the Duck and Puddle, Frank, the proprietor, a good friend and Bilbury's undisputed champion toper was perched on a stool on the other side of the bar, leaning on his hand with his elbow providing essential structural support. In front of him there was a large whisky which had been much larger just a few minutes earlier. Frank was never drunk but never quite sober for he held, quite passionately, to the view that a publican who does not test his own products regularly, and without unnatural constraint, will be as successful as a doctor who never seems quite well.

'It's all a matter of matching reality, perception and expectation,'

Frank said, in a rare moment of sobriety mixed with philosophy.

No one quite knew what he meant by this but that, of course, is the secret of sounding wise. On the now rare occasions when he imbibed too freely, and faster than his liver could cope, Frank usually managed to remain both upright and seemingly cogent and when asked about this he would tap the side of his nose and explain that it was a trick of the trade. For a while now, under his wife's instructions, Frank had been cutting down his drinking and on days with a 'y' in them he limited himself to just two alcoholic drinks. He was the only person I knew who drank his whisky from pint glasses. He did so because he believed that it looked as though he wasn't drinking quite so much. But this didn't fool anyone and it certainly didn't fool Gilly who had, unbeknownst to Frank, taken to watering down the bottle which he kept under the counter for his personal use.

Frank was popular with everyone, and whenever a new society was formed in Bilbury, he was usually the first person to join. He was a member of the 'Stamp Club' (which had three members), 'The Gilbert and Sullivan Society' (which had five members) and the 'Naturalist Society' which at one point had 15 members (this was put down as being due to a misprint on a poster which had resulted in the society being advertised as the 'Naturist Society') but which now consisted of Frank and Mr and Mrs Porter. A general lack of membership material in a small village meant that Frank was secretary and president of most of these. It went without saying that all local societies in Bilbury held their meetings in the Duck and Puddle.

Frank was still learning how to smoke a pipe which Gilly's sister had given him two Christmases ago, and it was proving to be harder work than he had expected. The pipe, a box of matches, a packet of pipe cleaners, a tobacco pouch and various metal instruments which looked as if they would be more appropriate in a dental surgery, and which had arrived with the pipe, lay on the counter in front of him.

Frank had a tea towel in the hand which wasn't providing support and he was taking a rest from drying glasses. His long-held philosophy, and the essence of an experiment which had been running for some years, was that the glasses which he didn't bother to dry with the tea towel would eventually dry themselves and do so, furthermore, without any smears. They had a dishwasher in the kitchen but, largely through tradition, Frank always washed glasses in the sink behind the bar.

Gilly, Frank's wife, was baking and the smell of bread, cakes, buns and biscuits was wafting into the bar in glorious gusts of almost edible aromas. You'd have to be suffering from a serious case of anosmia, or have a will of iron, not to feel your taste buds twitching when Gilly was having one of her grand baking days. Gilly's rock cakes were famous in three counties and Frank had assured us that they were on the baking list. We could hear her occasionally bursting into song, singing bits from old musicals. Gilly, Frank said, was in a very happy mood because after a lifetime's search her sister (the one who had given Frank the pipe), had sent along a pepper grinder that really worked.

'I had a battle to stop her putting pepper onto my toast and marmalade this morning,' said Frank.

'I hope she isn't too disappointed,' said Thumper Robinson.

We all thought about this for a moment and then looked at him.

'The search is everything,' explained Thumper who, together with Patchy Fogg, had turned up five minutes after my arrival.

'I know what you mean,' I said, after a few moments. 'My life has been a long search for a jacket that has enough decent pockets, and a black medical bag that is light and yet big enough and strong enough to carry a fridge. I'll probably be disappointed if I ever find what I'm looking for.'

'Why would you want to carry a fridge round with you in your black bag?' asked Thumper.

'It was just a figure of speech,' I explained. 'I don't really want to carry a fridge with me. Just a bag that's big and strong.'

'I just hope she isn't so excited with her new pepper grinder that she puts pepper into the scones,' said Patchy, who was obviously still worrying about Frank's toast and marmalade.

'I don't think she will,' said Frank at last. But he didn't sound entirely sure.

There is no television set in the bar at the Duck and Puddle and it is customary for the regulars to find some way to entertain themselves. There is a dart board, a bar billiard table and a miniature skittle table, and there are a box of dominoes and a pack of slightly grubby playing cards on the mantelpiece over the fire which burns through the seasons, but today the four of us had been entertaining ourselves by having a competition to see who could dredge up the most utterly useless fact.

'Did you know that the Bible contains 17 Commandments in the book of Exodus but 21 in Deuteronomy?' said Patchy, who had once claimed that as a boy he had once planned to become a monk. The ambition had been downgraded to priest and then finally had fizzled out completely and for reasons he could not explain, he had acquired a degree in Slavonic languages and half a degree in art history. Just how he had ended up in Bilbury as an antique dealer was something of a mystery.

'If you put in a tennis court it has to be placed north south so that the sun never shines directly into the eyes of the players,' said Thumper.

It was generally agreed that this information could be useful and was, therefore, disqualified.

'If you had a penny that doubled in value every day it would be worth £1million in a month,' said Patchy.

'Where can you get a penny that doubles in value?' asked Frank.

'It's theoretical,' said Patchy.

'It's impossible,' said Frank.

'Psychiatrists are all mad,' I said.

'Is that a fact or an opinion?' asked Patchy.

'Oh, I think it's a pretty well accepted fact. All the ones I've ever known were certifiable. Not that you can blame them for going potty. I heard about one psychiatrist who took a gun out of his desk drawer and shot a patient in the middle of her standard fifty minute consultation. In court he explained that the woman just kept complaining about her problems. 'All my patients are like that,' he said. 'They just go on and on about their problems. They never think that I might have problems too'. I never found out what happened to him.'

'That's quite useful information, so it's disqualified,' said Thumper, who was clearly still slightly irked that his information about tennis courts had been disqualified.

'Until May 1926, the Italians drove on the left in towns and on the right in the countryside,' said Frank.

We all stared at him, agog.

'A slice of toast contains more calories than a slice of bread,' he added. 'Not many people know that. But I saw it in one of those little calorie books that women buy.'

'How can that be?' I asked.

'Maybe the heat does it,' suggested Thumper.

'If that were true then people who sunbathed would all put on weight,' I pointed out. 'And so no one would ever sunbathe.'

'Did you know that Lowry the painter is also a rent collector?' asked Patchy.

'Do you think he would have painted more pictures if he had not spent much of his life traipsing the streets collecting rents?' asked Frank.

'Is he still working?' asked Thumper. 'Having him collect your rent would be like Picasso popping in to fix the plumbing.'

'The real question is would he have painted the same pictures?' said Patchy. 'It was his experiences traipsing the streets collecting rents which made him the artist he was.'

'That's not even a fact,' said Thumper, raising his voice with indignation. 'If my tennis court is disqualified then your Lowry definitely should be disqualified.'

'A shrew weighs 0.1 ounces and can travel at 17 mph,' I said. 'If the shrew were the same size as a horse and ran at the same speed, proportional to its size, it would be able to travel at 500,000 mph.'

'Where on earth did you hear that?' asked Thumper.

'I don't have the faintest notion.'

'Is it true?'

'Of course it is,' I replied, more out of hope than conviction. I honestly couldn't remember where I'd read it.

'Sounds to me as if you made it up,' said Thumper.

'Cynicism among the elderly is merely an outward sign of inner wisdom,' I said. 'But among the young it is unsettling and rather sad.'

Thumper stuck his tongue out. I told him his response was childish. He agreed.

'I read yesterday that researchers at Cambridge University traced the twin brothers of 13 men who were recidivists,' said Frank. 'Of the 13 twin brothers, nine were also recidivists and the remaining four were policemen.'

'I didn't think you knew big words like 'recidivist',' said Thumper.

Frank threw his tea towel at him and missed by a yard.

'That's quite boring,' said Patchy.

I agreed with him.

'But talking of universities, did you know,' said Patchy, 'that until 1948, university graduates had two votes – one in their home constituency and one in their old university?'

We all stared at him. 'Can that possibly be true?' asked Frank.

'Absolutely,' said Patchy. 'My Uncle Jerry told me and I've never forgotten it.'

'The elastic hook thing which connects the two straps of a bra was invented by Mark Twain in 1871,' I said. 'He patented it under his real name Samuel L Clemens. 'His drawing in his patent application shows the little hooks and several rows of suitable eyes so that the straps could be tightened or loosened at will.'

'That's ridiculous,' said Thumper.

'It may be,' I said. 'But it's true.'

'Customers in 18th century London coffee houses who wanted fast service used to drop small coins into a box labelled 'To Insure Promptness', said Patchy. 'Later the label which read 'To Insure Promptness' was shortened to TIP. And thus tips were born.'

'No one ever leaves me a tip,' complained Frank.

I took an old-fashioned sixpence out of my pocket and put it on the counter.

'Thanks,' said Frank, moving faster than I'd seen him move for years, and sliding the coin into his trouser pocket. 'I'll be able to buy Gilly a warm, new winter coat and a pair of decent shoes that don't leak so that we don't let ourselves down when we take our winter holiday in St Moritz.'

'Don't forget to send us a postcard,' I told him. 'That was my lucky sixpence.'

'When I was a boy,' said Frank, 'I found half a crown in the park. I was six or seven years old. I was terribly excited and told my Mum I'd found it and she, being very law abiding, insisted that I take it to the police station. The desk sergeant said I could keep it since it was less than a pound but my Mum insisted we take it to the church and put it in the poor box. I'd never had that much money before in my life and I missed that half a crown very much. I still do. In those days you could buy a comic, a bottle of fizzy pop and a huge bag of sweets every day for a month with half a crown. I used to get four pence a week pocket money. Half a crown was riches beyond a small boy's dreams. Ever since then I've always kept quiet about any stray bits of money that come my way.'

'I learned not to trust people when I was very small,' said Thumper. 'My grandfather put me on the stairs, stood smiling at me and told me to jump into his arms. I jumped and he moved backwards. I fell. He told me it was a lesson not to ever trust anyone again. I think he thought it was a useful lesson for life. In fact it was the only lesson he ever taught me and for a while it taught me paranoia, distrust and a great sense of loneliness. It also gave me a bruised and swollen knee which took weeks to heal. As I grew to hate him so the lesson faded and I forgot about it until a moment ago.'

We all looked at him but no one said anything.

Thumper looked thoughtfully at the fire and decided it needed another log. He jumped up, crossed the room and carefully balanced a huge log on top of the ones that had nearly disappeared.

'That's a yule log,' said Patchy, impressed by a log which looked like half a tree.

'What's a yule log?' Thumper asked. 'I've never really known.'

'It's a big log that lasts all Christmas Day. As one end of the log burns away you just keep pushing the rest of the log into the fire so it saves you going out to the log-shed to get more wood.'

'So it's a 'yule not have to put another log on the fire' log,' said Thumper, who occasionally comes up with excruciating puns which are usually best ignored.

'I suppose you think that's punny,' said Patchy.

'Can we stop this please,' I said.

'Well at least I've got a lucky sixpence,' said Frank, holding up the sixpence I'd given him.

'You can keep it,' I told him. 'I've got a lucky three-penny bit – though that's probably only half as good as a lucky sixpence.'

'And here's a little something to pay for a lift pass for half a day, while you're enjoying your break in St Moritz,' said Patchy, taking a small coin out of his waistcoat pocket and putting it on the bar counter.

'What is it?' asked Frank, examining it. The coin was quite small and clearly very old.

'It's a groat.'

'What the devil's a groat when it's not wandering around the countryside making holes in hedges and eating my wife's washing?'

(This feeble attempt at a joke was a topical reference because a pack of wild goats had been causing mayhem in Bilbury, and had twice eaten some of the prize items from Gilly's washing line at the back of the Duck and Puddle.)

'It's an old English coin – an old-fashioned, silver four-penny piece. This one was from 1841 but I'm afraid it's a fake. I found a dozen of them in a box of stuff I bought at a house auction in South Molton.'

'How do you know it's fake?' asked Frank.

'All the ones in the box had the same date on them – 1849. And all had exactly the same part of Queen Victoria's nose missing. It looks good, though. It's a very good fake.'

'So it's not worth much?'

'Not unless you can convince someone it's real! If you sell them one at a time you'd probably get away with it.'

'So you were ripped off when you bought them?' said Frank, with a grin. None of us had ever known Patchy to be ripped off when buying antiques.

'No,' replied Patchy, with an even bigger grin. 'I bought them in a large, wooden box full of bits and pieces. I paid 50 pence for everything in the box, which also contained three sets of old brass taps, an antique garlic press, a rather nice paperweight, a couple of tin plate cars that were a little rusty, a lorgnette and a pile of costume jewellery that I sold to a small antique shop in Barnstaple for a tenner. I cleaned up the box, found an old key which fitted the lock and sold it, empty, to a furniture dealer in Exeter who gave me £35 for it. There's quite a demand for old wooden boxes.'

We listened in quiet admiration. Local auctioneers organising house sales often put all the small, unclassifiable bits of bric and brac and debris which they haven't listed in their catalogue into a cardboard box and flog the box and contents as one lot at the end of an auction. Most of the bidders have long since gone by then and the professional buyers are usually loading up their Volvo estate cars with their purchases, many of them getting ready for a long drive home. The Volvo estate car, or station wagon as some prefer to call it, has for years been the transport of choice for antique dealers. With a little bit of jiggling, and possibly the help of a piece of washing line, you can fit six dining chairs into the back and the dining table onto the roof rack and save the cost of hiring a van. And yet on days off, the Volvo looks just like an extended version of the family saloon.

Patchy, who drives to auctions in one of his Land Rovers, with a longish trailer attached, only attends auctions he can reach within an hour or so and usually stays right until the end. He always bids on, and usually wins, the 'box with assorted contents' which is the final lot of almost every English auction. He never pays more than £2 and usually wins the lot with a 50 pence bid. I suspect that he always makes a good profit. I was so impressed by this little trick of his that at an auction I attended by myself I tried the same thing. Sadly, the box I bought was full of woodworm and everything it contained was mouldy, or broken quite beyond repair. I spent 50 pence on the lot and lost 50 pence. Patsy made me promise never to buy another 'box and contents'.

'Well, I'm going to put this into the safe,' said Frank, holding up the groat, or rather the fake groat. He turned behind him and pressed a few numbers on the keypad of the tiny safe that a salesman had persuaded him to have installed. None of us could understand why Frank had a safe because even on skittles night the takings were always on the parsimonious side of modest.

'How do you remember the code for the safe?' asked Patchy. We all know that Frank has an appalling memory. 'Aren't you worried you'll forget it?'

'It's easy to remember,' said Frank. 'It's the year of my birth.'

'How many people know the year of your birth?' I asked him, laughing.

'Oh just you lot and Gilly.'

'And your relations, and Peter and your dentist,' said Thumper.

'And the tax people and the bank and the driving licence people,' added Patchy.

'And the insurers and the licensing people and your pension company,' I added.

'But they don't know the safe is there!' protested Frank.

'You can see it from here,' said Thumper. 'You only have to sit by the bar to see that you've got a safe.'

'Well, I'll change the damned password thing,' said Frank, rather crossly.

'What to?' asked Patchy.

Frank thought for a while. 'The last four digits of our phone number,' he said at last, clearly quite proud of himself.

'That'll do it,' said Patchy, and Thumper and I nodded our agreement.

'There's never anything valuable in it anyway,' muttered Frank. 'And I never bothered to fix it to the wall so anyone could just pick it up and walk off with it.'

We all lifted our glasses and toasted Frank's safe.

'Who won our competition?' asked Patchy.

I thought I might have won our competition with my comparison of a shrew and a horse but I had to admit with Thumper that Frank's piece of history about motoring laws in Italy was both extraordinary and, since it was half a century out of date, utterly useless.

Sadly, we hadn't agreed on a prize so he didn't win anything.

'I still don't think I should have been disqualified,' said Thumper.

'Herodotus wrote that when the Persians couldn't agree on anything they discussed it twice,' said Patchy who has a fine classical education. 'They discuss it once when they are sober and once when they are drunk. Only if they agreed on a conclusion when they were both drunk and sober did they agree that a final decision had been made.'

Thumper, Frank and I looked at Patchy.

'The question is,' said Thumper slowly, 'how do you decide precisely when you're drunk and when you're sober? Frank hasn't been properly sober for at least a decade.'

'That's quite true,' nodded Frank, nodding wisely. He started to pack tobacco into his pipe and used one of his metal gadgets to tamp down the tobacco.

Exhausted by this unanswerable puzzle, our flurry of mental activity and the furious nature of the competition, none of us said anything for a while. Thumper put another huge log onto the fire, which did not look as if it were in any danger of going out, and Frank put out two fresh bottles of beer for Thumper and Patchy. They were drinking from the bottle to save dirtying glasses. Since I had a surgery to do later that afternoon I didn't order another whisky but had a black coffee instead, to help me stay awake after my hard night's work.

And so we sat and pondered and enjoyed the smell of Gilly's cooking for a while. Silence between friends is a special and most satisfying silence. Frank popped out to the kitchen, came back and told us that rock cakes would be available in fifteen minutes time. It was universally agreed that this was a good thing.

'That car of yours is fine and dandy for popping to the shop or the pub or for taking your fair lady round to see her sister,' said Thumper, a propos of nothing but presumably referring back to the moment when I'd mentioned my early morning travails in brown, sticky stuff that wasn't entirely mud. 'It's a lovely motor and I wouldn't hear a word said against it. But you need something higher off the ground and fitted with four wheel drive for visiting farms in the winter.'

He was, I knew, quite right. It had been raining, on and off, for over a month and every lane, bridle path and farm track was muddy and almost impassable. Even when the heavy rain stopped there was still a steady, quiet drizzle – the sort of soft rain that convinces you that you don't need a coat and a hat but which has tricked you, with the result that a quarter of an hour later you suddenly realise that you're soaked to the skin and really needed fisherman's oilskins and a sou'wester.

'You need a Land Rover for the lanes,' suggested Patchy, who had recently bought himself a pair of 15-year-old Land Rovers to add to the one he'd already got, and who was so delighted with his purchase that he thought everyone should have at least one.

Frank, I noticed, was still hammering at the tobacco in his pipe. When he'd finished he lit a match and tried to set fire to the tobacco.

'Why have you got two of them?' demanded Thumper, turning in Patchy's direction.

Patchy sighed in immediate defeat and looked down into his pint glass. There was a significant pause before he answered. 'Actually I have three. And I need three because one of them is nearly always broken down,' he muttered, rather reluctantly and half under his breath.

'Exactly!' said Thumper, banging his bottle down on the bar top and startling us. 'Land Rovers are like Gilly's rock cakes. One is never enough. If you have a Land Rover you'll spend half your time on buses and the other half in taxis. And since there aren't any buses round here and not much in the way of a taxi service that leaves walking and cycling. The doc can't go trudging round the village on Shanks's pony! He needs something reliable that'll get him up and down all the farm tracks without breaking down and leaving him stranded in two feet of thick mud.'

'So, what do you reckon?' demanded Patchy, who had apparently immediately given up his advocacy for Land Rovers.

'A tractor,' said Thumper, firmly. 'The doc needs a tractor.' He turned to me. 'You need a tractor.'

Frank, who was still trying to light his pipe, lit another match and burnt two fingers by holding onto the burning match for too long.

'I know two people who died when the tractors they were driving tipped over!'

'They only tip over if you drive them on very steep slopes,' said Thumper. 'They're usually quite safe because they have a low centre of gravity. And I bet you know more people who died in car crashes than died in tractor accidents.'

'But a tractor!' I repeated, rather stupidly, not mentioning that I knew far more people who drove cars than people who drove tractors. I was slightly embarrassed to realise that I'd sounded rather too much like Dame Edith Evans playing Lady Bracknell and saying 'A handbag!' in Oscar Wilde's 'The Importance of Being Earnest. 'I can't see myself driving around on a tractor,' I said with more than a hint of pomposity for which I felt immediate regret.' A tractor isn't very dignified,' I explained. 'Patients don't expect their doctor to turn up on a tractor. And tractors don't have a cab. I'd freeze to death on a January night.'

'People who are ill wouldn't give a damn if you turned up on roller skates or on one of those sit and bounce Space Hoppers!' said Patchy.

I nodded, appreciating the truth of what he said, though still harbouring some reservations.

'They're more dignified than being towed out of mud and cow shit,' Thumper pointed out. 'And I know where I can put my hands on one that has a little cab. Nice and warm too.'

'A warm tractor cab?' cried Patchy, disbelievingly.

'There's a crack in the exhaust and the waste exhaust gases come up through the floor,' admitted Thumper. 'It'll make you cough a bit, but you'll never be cold.'

Patchy nodded as though this made perfect sense.

'And there are three floodlights fitted to the cab roof,' added Thumper. 'I know the bloke who is selling it. He offered it to a second hand car dealer in Barnstaple. They offered him £10 for it for its scrap value. He's now advertising it in the local paper. He's asking for £100 but he knows he's pushing his luck. I can get it for half that. I can probably get it for £35 if I give him cash.'

'How old is it?' I asked.

'Younger than your Rolls Royce!' replied Thumper with a laugh. 'It's still running in. It's a Massey Fergusson. They made good tractors at the end of the 1950s. And I know where we can get a spare engine that'll do nicely. The bloke who has the engine wants a new gearbox for a Ford Consul. I can get a gearbox for £10 and do a straight swap. I can hoist the old engine out and put the new engine in on Sunday. I can get a set of fairly new tyres too. It'll be like a brand new tractor for under £50. I can even weld the leaky exhaust pipe if you don't want the carbon monoxide based heating system.'

Thumper knows people and can always lay his hand on useful things. Much of what he does is simple, old-fashioned trading. Last month he picked up an unwanted new washing machine, still in its box, and swapped it for a pneumatic drill. He then exchanged the pneumatic drill for a freezer and a tumble dryer and then swapped the freezer and the tumble dryer for a two-year-old ride-on mower which I needed because the one we'd had since we bought Bilbury Grange had finally died and gone to lawn mower heaven.

'If you don't have the leak mended you'll choke to death if you spend more than five minutes on it,' said Patchy.

'We can weld the leak and stop the carbon monoxide coming out,' said Thumper. 'Cost nothing and take ten minutes while we're in the garage.'

I trust Thumper totally. Apart from the ancient Rolls Royce 20/25, which I inherited from my predecessor, Dr Brownlow, every vehicle and piece of garden equipment I own or have owned has been found, checked and bought for me by Thumper. I thanked him and said I'd think about it. I needed a few moments to get used to the idea of driving around in a tractor – even if only when making visits in wet weather to patients in farms or cottages, situated at the end of long and difficult tracks. Actually I still wasn't sure whether one drives around in or on a tractor.

But the more I thought about it the more it seemed to be a good idea. My practice is largely confined to the village of Bilbury but there are a few dozen patients in outlying farms and satellite villages, and although most of the cottages and houses I visit can easily be reached in a motor car or even on a bicycle, I would estimate that around five per cent of my patients live in places which can only be reached by travelling along muddy, stony tracks, and opening at least a couple of five barred gates. Those patients are easy enough to reach in the summer but can be something between difficult and impossible to reach during the winter months.

Frank had now given up trying to light his pipe. He put it into his pocket and pushed the tobacco pouch, the matches and the impedimenta (including a smart looking multi-purpose tool, which I confess I rather envied) to one side.

'If you buy it for your practice it'll be tax deductible,' said Patchy, who is considered something of an expert on taxable expenses and who once succeeded in persuading Her Majesty's Inspector of Taxes in Barnstaple that his occasional trips to Paris, Venice, Amsterdam and so on were all completely essential buying trips. He had, moreover, succeeded in convincing the Inspector that his wife's company was also essential.

'If I ever earn enough to pay any tax I'll bear that in mind,' I replied, with a smile. My practice was too small to bring in much more than my expenses, and for one reason and another my income from writing books and articles had shrunk in recent years.

I was still pondering, and my three companions were quietly sipping, and probably pondering too, when the door to the pub burst open and a young man in a dark grey suit burst in, shaking an umbrella as he did so. He had what looked like an expensive haircut, wore string backed driving gloves and his shoes shone in a way rarely seen in Bilbury, where winter mud and summer dust tend to dull any shine so quickly that few people waste much time with polish and brushes.

We were surprised to see him with an umbrella since he couldn't have possibly had to park his car more than twelve feet from the pub door. He had a sharp pointed nose, staring eyes which made him look like an inquisitor and one of those meaningless, all-purpose smiles that minor celebrities, lunatics and sociopaths master; one of those smiles which shows no emotion whatsoever – no happiness, no amusement, no hidden anger, no veiled disappointment – nothing except expensively capped teeth and a pair of shiny pink gums.

'It's blowing a gale out there,' he announced loudly, as though it were our fault and we were unaware of the weather. Actually, the wind and the rain had pretty well stopped and settled down into the sort of weather considered 'normal' for much of the year in North Devon. England is widely supposed to have a temperate climate but Bilbury has weather which has made up its mind to be different, distinctive and determined. Whatever our weather might be there tends to be a good deal of it. If Bilbury had its own meteorological office the daily forecast would remain the same from October to April and would consist simply of the words: 'wet and windy'. The newcomer did not, of course, know this and undoubtedly came from a part of the country where the words 'temperate climate' are still taken seriously.

'There's a really knackered old car dumped outside,' he said. 'Does anyone know what sort is it? It's parked next to an abandoned old Land Rover someone's dumped. It looks like the beginnings of a scrap yard.'

'It's a Rolls Royce 20/25,' I told him. 'It's old but not knackered and it's mine.'

'The Land Rover is mine,' said Patchy.

Most of us in Bilbury try to be warm and welcoming to strangers, aware that many of them are lost and trying desperately to be somewhere else. Those of us not in the hospitality trade try to offer sympathy and calming advice while Frank and Gilly offer hot coffee, cheese sandwiches and, if the pub is empty, a seat by the fire.

'Is it really! Does it go?' He laughed. I was suddenly reminded of that scene in 'A Fistful of Dollars' when the shortly to be shot bad guys laugh at Clint Eastwood's mule. Eastwood's character (sometimes known as 'the stranger', sometimes known as 'the man with no name' and sometimes known as 'Joe') didn't like his mule being disrespected and I felt much the same way about the Rolls.

'Not very good for the environment is it?' the stranger said with a lip curl that Elvis would have been proud of. 'I bet it doesn't do more than ten or twelve miles to the gallon.'

'It's very good for the environment,' I insisted.

His estimate of the petrol consumption was accurate but I didn't bother to tell him that.

'Oil was created by God with the help of a process called photosynthesis – which requires sunshine. And so my Rolls is a truly solar powered form of transport. Moreover, it has a large battery which provides the electrical power for the lights, wipers, indicators and cigar lighter.'

'Well, it looks as if it should be in a museum,' said the stranger, obviously unconvinced. He spoke quickly and glibly, as though his mouth were always at least two steps ahead of his brain. 'Every car I've seen for miles seemed old. Is this a village, by the way? Or just a collection of houses that got lost? Half the houses look as if they're ready to be demolished and the other half look as if the demolition has started.' He laughed again as though we were bound to appreciate his kindness in sharing his brand of big city bonhomie.

'It goes and it's reliable,' I said, defiantly. 'I rather like old cars.'

'Not for me, my friend,' said the visitor. 'Old things are always breaking down and they cost a fortune in maintenance.'

'I doubt if my old Rolls costs more to run that whatever you came in. I doubt if it breaks down any more than anything modern. And if it does break down it's a darned sight easier to repair. The mechanic at the local garage can deal with just about everything with an oily rag and a wrench.'

'I've got a brand new BMW 5 series,' said the visitor proudly. 'Company car, of course. They change it every two years but I always have a BMW. Best cars in the world. German technology, metallic paint, heated seats and a six cylinder engine. Hugely popular Stateside.'

'I prefer old cars,' said Patchy, joining the conversation for the first time and doing so, I suspected, purely out of a sense of mischief. 'They always smell of oil and wood polish and leather – especially the leather. They smell like shoe shops used to smell before they stopped selling proper shoes and started selling plastic sandals and things that used to be called pumps or gym shoes but which are now called running shoes and cost an arm and a leg. Old cars are full of memories but modern cars are all beginning to look the same to me. When I was a kid I could identify just about every car I saw but these days I couldn't tell a BMW from a Ford.'

The stranger looked at Patchy as if he were dangerously mad.

'Oh, I definitely prefer something new and shiny,' he said. 'I like all my mod cons – central locking, lots of lovely plastic, electric windows, a little light that comes on in the glove compartment so that you can see what's in there. In a few years' time cars will all run on electricity.'

'Didn't they try that when they first started building cars back in the 19th century?' asked Thumper.

'Oh, they're coming along leaps and bounds,' said the stranger. 'The petrol engine will just be a footnote in the history books in 50 years' time. By 2020, everyone will have an electric car in their driveway – plug it into a socket at night and drive off the next morning. Cars will have in-built computers which tell you where you are and they'll probably drive themselves. Progress! People will get in, tell the car where to go and whoosh, off they'll go. You can't stand in the way of progress or you'll get run over.' He rubbed his hands together as though excited by the future and unwilling to wait much longer for it to arrive.

We stared at him in disbelief and astonishment. None of us is keen on the future. We rather like what we've got now. Thumper started to laugh and laughed so much that he had a coughing fit that took a couple of minutes to subside. 'Cars that drive themselves,' he muttered to himself and then started laughing again. 'I'd like to see a car driving itself round our lanes,' he said.

The stranger was beginning to annoy me.

'My 20/25 was built 40 years ago,' I told him. 'And it'll still be running in another 50 years when your BMW will have been recycled five times and turned into a pair of ornamental gates and half a dozen toasters.'

The stranger looked at me and his lip curled a little again. 'So,' he said, 'where is the nearest village?'

'You're in a village.' said Frank indignantly. 'It's called Bilbury.'

'Never heard of it!' the stranger said rudely, as though that meant it couldn't possibly exist. 'I'm pretty sure I didn't see it on the map. Are you sure it's a proper village? I'm trying to get from Barnstaple to Taunton,' he said, beginning to get into the rhythm of his monologue. 'No, you know, I have heard the name. Bilbury you say? Hmm. It'll come to me.' He was clearly a man who, as my mother might have said, enjoyed the sound of his own voice. 'You people don't look as if you get about much. I travel all the time. I'm in the hotel trade and travel in soft furnishings. I do 60,000 miles a year and cover pretty much the whole of the West Country. We're the biggest suppliers of soft furnishings to the hospitality trade. Curtains, cushions that sort of thing. If you see a cushion in a pub it's probably one of mine.' He looked around, searching for cushions but there are no cushions in the Duck and Puddle. It's not that sort of pub. 'We're starting a new range of shower fitments – plastic mould-resistant curtains, shower rings and such like. And we do a lovely range of old hunting prints for the walls.' He paused for a moment and looked around, as if he might see an opportunity for an unexpected sale, but quickly changed his mind. 'On the map this looked like a short cut,' he said, as though he felt he needed to explain his unplanned presence.

Generally speaking our truths are different; we all tend to see things from our own perspective. We may see Mr X as cruel, unthinking and selfish. His mother may see him as angelic. And his wife may think of him as a romantic suitor. There are no simple truths where people are concerned. Generally speaking, that is. But there are, of course, exceptions to this rule and I decided that the stranger was an exception. He was so rude and full of himself that I could not see how anyone could not find him loathsome.

'I'm afraid this isn't a short cut to anywhere,' said Patchy. 'If you came to Bilbury without meaning to be here then I'm afraid that you're lost.'

'I doubt if I'm lost,' he said, as though this were not possible. 'I looked at the map before I set off and I'm pretty good at reading maps.'

I was tempted to tell him that the maps which include Bilbury are all misleading. The problem is that the surveyors who were sent to make the maps found themselves completely confused by the web of lanes, bridle paths and tracks which criss cross our part of North Devon. The bottom line is that there is no decent commercially available map of Bilbury for sale though (with help from Patchy and Thumper) I did once put together a map for my own use. In a public spirited mood I printed a few copies and gave them to Peter Marshall to sell in his shop. I priced them at the precise price they had cost me to have made. 'No one ever buys your map, though I explain to them that it is the only accurate map of Bilbury,' explained Peter. 'They all prefer the official map which the Barnstaple Council publishes, which is two shillings more expensive, has a nice cover and is official.'

The visitor snorted, looked around again and didn't seem at all impressed. 'This place could do with a refit,' he said. 'Get some new carpet down, decorate the walls, get rid of all this old wood and replace it with some lovely plastic panelling. Replace your old furniture with some nice pine stuff. We can supply that too. It's Swedish. It comes flat packed and you just put it together yourself. It doesn't take more than a minute to put one of our tables up. Is it always this dark in here?'

Frank nodded.

'Do you have disco evenings? Is that why it's so dark?'

Frank looked at him as if he'd suggested that the Duck and Puddle might install a cremation oven and do funerals as a side-line.

'Night clubs always favour dim lighting so that everyone over 30 looks younger and more attractive,' the stranger explained. He stared at Frank. 'Do you know you're on fire?'

Frank looked down and saw smoke coming from his pocket. He took out his pipe which had, at last, caught fire and lay it down on the bar counter where it continued to smoke. He didn't say anything else to the customer. The fact is that Frank doesn't give a damn how old or young or attractive his customers look. He doesn't much like people spilling beer on the carpet or throwing darts into the wallpaper but he doesn't care what they look like. The Duck and Puddle is dark inside because the windows are small and the only light in the place comes from a 40 watt bulb over the bar. The idea of Frank and Gilly organising a disco evening made me smile.

'You could organise disco evenings,' I said to Frank. 'Buy one of those glitter balls, hire a disc jockey and get him to play some loud music.'

Frank stared at me as though I'd suggested that he organise Sunday lunchtime strip shows or organise an Everest expedition for his customers, most of whom, even when sober, had difficulty negotiating the two steps at the front door.

The visitor rubbed his hands as though suddenly realising that he was in a hurry. 'I've remembered,' he said, clearly pleased with himself. 'My wife was reading a book with Bilbury in the title. Some book about a doctor, I think. Not my cup of tea at all. Was that written about this Bilbury?'

'Probably some other Bilbury,' I said quickly.

'That figures. Can't imagine anyone writing a book about this place!' he laughed and then looked at his watch. 'Is that the time? Tempus fugit, eh? Can't stand here chatting. I've got an appointment in Taunton in an hour but I'm too hungry to wait until I get there. I had a great meal the last time I was there. Met my regional manager and he pushed the boat out because I'd just sold two complete refits to hotels in Minehead. We shared two dozen oysters, pate de foie gras, a capon, half a dozen ortalan buntings and a magnum of Moet et Chandon. Taunton is a great place for cafes. Last time I was there I found one which served mackerel flavoured marmalade sandwiches and teacakes with bits of beetroot and radish baked in. I love something a bit different.'

'Personally, I prefer a cheese and tomato sandwich with a couple of gherkins and a handful of decent sized pickled onions,' said Thumper.

'Could I have a menu?' the visitor asked, ignoring Thumper's remark and walking up to the bar. 'I'm not sure I'll be able to read it but I'd like to see one.' He laughed at his tiny joke but no one else joined in.

'What's an ortolan bunting?' asked Frank.

'Sounds like a string of flags,' said Thumper.

The stranger tutted and closed his eyes and shook his head in apparent quiet dismay. 'I thought everyone knew what an ortolan bunting was,' he told us. 'They're small birds. They're force fed in the dark to soften their bones. When they're ready to eat they're drowned in Armagnac. You eat them whole.'

'Including the bones?' I said, horrified at the thought, from every possible point of view.

'Oh, definitely, including the bones. You have to eat them with a white napkin draped over your head to capture the aroma. Quite an experience I can tell you.'

'If you need to be in Taunton in an hour then you ought to be on your way,' I said.

It is fair to say that I hadn't warmed to Frank's would-be customer and I could tell the others hadn't either.

'It's not an easy road from here. You have to drive through Lynmouth, go up Countisbury Hill and through Porlock. If you get stuck behind a tractor or a caravan you'll be stuck behind it for miles.'

The visitor laughed. 'My BMW does 0-60 in less time than your old crock takes to start. It'll scream past a tractor in no time.'

'The only menu is the one on the blackboard behind me,' said Frank, using his 'I-am-disinterested-in-you-and-don't-give-a-damn-if-you-stay-or-go' voice. 'And I'm afraid I haven't got any white napkins to drape over your head but I can lend you my tea-towel if you want to put that over your head while you drink your soup.' He held up the tea-towel on offer and waved it. Although it hadn't been doing much drying it looked distinctly damp and I suspected that Frank had used it to mop the bar counter.

Frank had recently moved the menu. The blackboard used to be over the fire place but after three people got singed trying to read it, Gilly had insisted that they move the whole thing to a safer location. Frank had protested, arguing that no one had been seriously hurt and that if the menu were moved it wouldn't make any difference because people would still stand in front of the fire to look at themselves in the mirror. The mirror, not in the first flush of youth, had de-silvered and discoloured and anyone wanting to use it had to try to find a part of the mirror which still did what it was supposed to do. The local health and safety officials who had tried to force Frank to replace the log fire with an electric fire had repeatedly complained about the pub having a mirror over the mantelpiece but it remained there. Frank had nodded while two 16-year-old health and safety officials in cheap suits had given him a stern talking to, and had made appropriate noises as though listening carefully, but he had, of course, taken no notice of anything they'd said, and the log fire and the mirror over the mantelpiece remained stalwart fixtures at the Duck and Puddle.

The chalk menu, scribbled on the blackboard, hadn't varied for months and was beginning to fade. When I'd arrived at the pub, Thumper, Patchy and Frank had just finished three large helpings of steak and kidney pudding, roast potatoes, carrots and greens. For pudding they'd shared a Christmas pudding which Gilly had found, forgotten, in their pantry. If the visitor hadn't been so rude he too might have been offered steak and kidney pudding, with all the trimmings. There would have been no pudding, however. That had all gone.

'What else have you got?' asked the visitor. 'Lobster? Crab? We are by the sea aren't we?'

'Everything we've got today is on the menu,' said Frank, without bothering to hide his indifference.

'Down here we never eat shellfish when there's a vowel in the month,' said Thumper helpfully.

'That's it?' said the visitor, pointing to the menu and not

bothering to hide his incredulity or his disappointment. 'A cup of soup and either a cheese sandwich or a ham sandwich?'

Now, Frank can be the most welcoming of hosts; the kindest and gentlest of landlords. I have seen him give double helpings to hard-up campers who were clearly hungry but worried about the cost of sharing the price of a packet of crisps between three. But he had no patience at all with superior and patronising strangers who seem to assume that their big city heritage and pseudo-sophisticated ways entitle them to be patronising and dismissive. 'The soup is home-made,' said Frank coldly. 'And for added excitement we've got crisps,' he added. 'Actually, we've got two types of crisps and one type of pork scratchings. Or, rather, we do usually and if you'd been here last Wednesday we'd have had both, unfortunately, we're out of pork scratchings and to be honest with you we've only got one type of crisp in stock at the moment and they're a month over their sell by date. Some people like them a bit stale and soft and if you toss them in the soup you'll never notice.' As he spoke he moved along the bar slightly, thereby hiding the array of crisp boxes behind him which showed that the bar actually had good stocks of six different types of crisp. 'We serve the soup in a mug but if you have crisps I'll give you a spoon as well. If you're hungry I'd recommend the soup and a ham sandwich. I can't recommend the cheese because we've only got cheddar and I thought it looked a bit mouse-trappish this morning. If you're still hungry after your soup and ham sandwich you could have one of Gilly's rock cakes with your coffee. They'll be ready by then.'

If the fellow had been less full of himself, less brittle and less determinedly offensive, Frank would have made him whatever he fancied, and I definitely knew that there was the remains of an excellent steak and kidney pudding in the kitchen, but when Frank didn't like someone they got their choice of whatever was on the menu behind the bar. Actually the soup was excellent and the sandwiches always far superior to the sandwiches sold in supermarkets and at railway stations.

'I think I'll go somewhere else,' said the visitor, clearly cross. 'I'm hungry and I was hoping for a decent meal. This pub is a disgrace. I shall complain to the management.' And he headed for the door.

'They're big sandwiches,' said Thumper to his back.

'I am the management,' said Frank.

'I'm not sure that's entirely true,' said Patchy. 'What about Gilly?'

'Well, I'm married to the management,' said Frank, correcting himself.

'I was hoping for a proper meal,' said the man with his hand on the door knob. 'Something, perhaps, with gravy or a sauce of some kind; something you eat with a knife and fork. I'll go somewhere else.'

And he left in what my mother used to refer to as high dudgeon but which would today be more likely to be called a huff. His final act of defiance was to leave the door wide open.

'We've got brown sauce and tomato sauce,' said Frank. 'What more does he want?'

'I wouldn't eat gravy with a knife and fork,' said Patchy, climbing down off his stool, walking across to the door and closing it.

'Thank heavens he's gone,' muttered Frank who doesn't much like customers he doesn't know. He took another tiny sip of his whisky as he tried to eke out his day's supply.

Outside we could hear a car struggling to start.

'Where's the nearest place he could get food?' I asked Frank.

'That'll be in Wales, on the other side of the Bristol Channel,' Frank replied, instantly. 'There's a pub in Port Talbot that does snacks. It's only a short ride if you've got a fast boat but it's 170 miles away by road. You have to go to Taunton, get on the M5 and then turn left onto the M4. I hear they've got the usual road works on the M5 so it'll take him about eight or nine hours at least. The pub in Wexford-on-Sea is shut while the landlord's liver is attended to so the nearest practical source of food would be Barnstaple.' He looked at his watch. 'But that's in the wrong direction and by the time he gets there everywhere that is open now will have stopped serving lunch.'

'What happened to that pub on the South Molton road?' asked Patchy. 'I didn't know that was shut.'

'The people managed one season, gave up and went back to Wolverhampton,' explained Frank. The pub's up for sale again.

We sat and thought about this for a while. The closure was sad but not unexpected.

Every year hundreds if not thousands of people who have had a lovely holiday by the seaside decide to move permanently from their home inland. They've spent two weeks sitting on the beach, eating ice cream, having laughs in the amusement arcade and eating fish and chips on the sea front. And they want the fun to continue. They look in the window of an estate agency and see that if they sell their semi-detached house in Walsall they can buy a pub or a boarding house or a café or a shop selling buckets and spades or, if they want to retire, they can just buy a flat or a static caravan or a little bungalow a few hundred yards inland. And they talk about it in their lodgings or in a café where they have lunch or a cup of tea and a toasted teacake and they decide 'what the hell you're only born once' and they take the plunge and do it.

And then, sadly, life isn't what they thought, or hoped, it would be. There are so many pitfalls and hurdles and disappointments to be discovered.

Excited and full of hope they open a boarding house or small hotel or simply make up the spare room so that they can take in paying guests and they put a notice in the window screaming 'Room to Let' and maybe splash out for some adverts in a few magazines but before the first paying guests can ring up and book themselves in, the booking diary fills up with aged parents and aunts and siblings and old neighbours and friends from school or university that they haven't seen for absolutely decades and the vicar and his wife who think they'd quite like 'a break in the country, away from it all, and a chance to catch up with how you're doing because it will be lovely, absolutely wonderful, to see you'. And of course they don't charge the aged parents and aunts and siblings, or the vicar, and not only does their expected income never materialise but they spend all their time and money providing free meals and clean sheets and taking people out and about to show them the local landmarks. And Aunt Edna's daughter is getting married. 'Maybe she and her new husband and the two children could spend their honeymoon with you. Just for the week. It would save them some money to spend on their new home.' 'And we're having a silver wedding celebration and we were going to rent a house somewhere but nowhere could possibly be as lovely as yours.'

Out of season the sea front is always cold and wet and deserted. There aren't any customers wanting pub meals. The fish and chip shops are shuttered. The little shop that was so busy in August is dead because no one wants to buy buckets and spades between October and April. The floral clock is just a memory. And it's colder and wetter and a damned sight windier than it is inland.

And the newcomers don't know anyone. The nearest ironmonger, post office, bank or shoe shop is twenty miles away. And there are no buses. And so the newcomers, still probably not properly unpacked, contact the estate agent, and someone else on their holiday buys the dream.

Only the determined, the hardy and the self-contained survive.

The engine of the car outside eventually started and the driver accelerated away with a squeal of rubber and the sound of an engine complaining bitterly.

'Of course, there is a fish and chip shop near the bus station in Barnstaple,' said Frank. 'But it's only open on Fridays, Saturdays and Sundays and it doesn't open until 6 in the evening.'

'Is it Friday, Saturday or Sunday today?' I asked. I can never remember what day of the week it is unless I am sitting at my desk, where there is a convenient calendar positioned near the telephone. I cross off the days as they pass by so that I can keep track.

'Bad move on his part,' said Thumper. 'Leaving like that.'

'I think it's Thursday today,' said Frank.

'So the chip shop will be shut until tomorrow evening,' I said.

'He's left his umbrella,' said Patchy. 'It must have stopped raining. He wouldn't have risked his hair without an umbrella if it had still been raining.'

'Bet he doesn't come back for it,' said Thumper with a laugh.

'Must be an idiot to try to use an umbrella in North Devon,' said Frank.

'I had an umbrella once,' said Patchy. 'Peter managed to convince me that I needed one and guaranteed that it was gust-proof. I was obviously not operating on all cylinders. I'd only had it for half an hour when it blew inside out, turned into a helicopter and took off. A bloke I knew said he saw it stuck half way up a tree in Porlock. It was apparently there for months.' He paused. 'And the day it took off was a quiet, gentle sunny day. I only put the damned thing up to stop the sun melting my ice cream.'

'I wouldn't ever put an umbrella up to keep off the rain,' said Thumper. 'The rain never comes straight down in North Devon, so what's the point?'

'Talking of Peter, have you noticed that he is getting more and more obsessed with the 1950s?' asked Frank. 'Every time I see him he tells me how much better things were then.'

'I've noticed that,' said Patchy. 'I'm occasionally beginning to find myself agreeing with him. I'm worried that he's got some sort of brain disease and I've caught it.'

'I'll give you something for it,' I told him. 'Something green and foul smelling that tastes really horrid.'

Patchy gave me a dirty look and drank some more beer.

'By the way, our daughter told us that she's in love with your son,' said Thumper giving Patchy a playful thump on the arm. A playful thump from Thumper is like being hit by a steam roller and Patchy nearly fell off his stool. Thumper is, I should perhaps mention, a master at the non-sequitor. Until you know him well it can be difficult to follow a conversation in which he is involved. 'She says he's asked her to marry him and she's said Yes.'

'That's nice. They'll make the perfect couple,' said Patchy, who seemed quite unfazed by this news. He held up his empty beer bottle and Frank gave him a full one. 'When's the wedding?'

'We've persuaded them to wait a while,' said Thumper. 'We told them they should probably wait another 15 years or so.'

'Good idea,' nodded Patchy.

'How old are they now?' asked Frank.

'Lucy will be six next Thursday' said Patchy. 'She's around seven months older than her fiancé. She's having a party on the Saturday and even if you don't come she'll be expecting presents. If you make sure she gets a present she'll make sure you get a piece of cake.'

Thumper screwed up his eyes, did sums in his head and nodded his agreement. 'Around seven months,' he agreed. 'What do you want to do about that tractor?' he asked me. 'I'll need to get over there this afternoon if you want it. The old bugger who's selling it might manage to sell it to some other idiot if we leave it too long. He'll probably have another advert in tomorrow's free paper.'

'Buy it for me,' I told him. 'If it hasn't gone to some other idiot by the time you get there.'

Outside there was an angry roar as a car shot past. 'That'll be the salesman,' said Patchy. 'Lost and going round in circles. He'll still be here next Wednesday.'

'I doubt if it will have gone,' said Thumper. 'I was only teasing. I doubt if anyone wants to buy a clapped out old tractor. Farmers all want one of the latest models with air conditioning, electric windows, radio, tape player and all the other bells and whistles. The banks don't mind lending money if you're using their loot to buy a tractor. I'll get it tomorrow, put the new engine in on Sunday and bring it round to you on Sunday evening. You'll be able to sail through lakes of cow manure without getting your feet wet.'

'If there aren't any shut gates,' pointed out Patchy.

I wasn't terribly comforted by the thought that no one but me seemed to want a clapped out old tractor but I trusted Thumper and I thanked him. 'Do you want some cash?'

Thumper shook his head. 'Settle up with me on Sunday.'

He would not, I knew, charge me anything for his time and labour. No amount of cajoling would ever persuade him to accept a penny for his work.

'Do I need road tax for it?'

'No, not for a tractor. You don't have to pay anything.'

'Insurance?'

'I wouldn't bother. I've never known anyone round here insure a tractor.'

'One other thing,' I said. 'Do you know what colour it is? Patsy is bound to ask.'

'A sort of scruffy, dirty colour,' said Thumper. 'It probably started off red. Henry Ford made black cars but Massey Ferguson always seemed to make red tractors.'

'If you've got a tractor you can pick up a bit of farm work at harvest time,' said Patchy. 'Put one of those sixpenny adverts in the window at Peter Marshall's shop. 'Have tractor will mow.' Stick a bit of straw in your mouth and you'll look just the job.'

'I love those little sixpenny adverts of Peter's,' said Thumper. 'I always make a point of reading them when I'm in his shop.'

I ignored Patchy's business suggestion and looked at my watch. 'Do you think those rock cakes might be ready now?' I asked Frank. I had to be back at Bilbury Grange for the evening surgery in another forty minutes. You can't hurry one of Gilly's rock cakes if you want to avoid indigestion. And, besides, it would be culinary sacrilege to do so.

For once my timing was impeccable, for just then Gilly entered the bar carrying a tray piled high with her scrumptious rock cakes.

I just had time to eat two, and to get Gilly to put half a dozen in a paper bag for me to take home to Bilbury Grange.

Patsy and I decided long ago that if the end of the world is coming and the Government tells us we've got an hour to live, then we will make a feast of all our favourite foods: Patsy's mum's home-made fudge and coconut ice, Patsy's home-made pickle and chunks of Red Devon cheese on thick slices of home-made bread, Patsy's Devil's food cake, and a large bag of Gilly's rock cakes. Gill's rock cakes are six inches in diameter and if I eat more than two at a time I always get indigestion a couple of hours later. But if the world is ending anyway, who cares about the indigestion I'm never going to get. If there is time I'll toast six thick slices of pumpernickel bread on an open fire (you can cut the bread thicker if you toast it with a brass fork in front of an open log fire) smother three of them with her homemade marmalade eat, smother the other three with her homemade plum jam and eat them all, uncaring about the inevitable gastric consequences.

I paid Frank what I owed him and headed for the door.

Outside, there was another roar as the salesman, obviously still lost, drove past again in his BMW, the engine howling and the tyres struggling for traction on the muddy lane. As I left, I looked back and noticed that Frank's pipe was still smoking. The air in the bar was full of the sweet smelling smoke of the tobacco his sister-in-law had bought him.

I drove home and told Patsy that I'd bought a tractor.

'Oh, good,' she said. 'That's nice. What colour is it?'

'I've no idea,' I admitted. 'But Thumper says there's a leak in the exhaust pipe and the carbon monoxide gas that seeps up into the cab will keep me warm on cold nights.'

Patsy looked at me and raised an eyebrow. 'I'm still never quite sure when you're joking,' she said.

The Student

'Do you remember having a student working with you?' asked my friend William (known to one and all as Will), just as I was finishing the morning surgery. I was at medical school with William and he and his family have been down to Bilbury several times. We discuss difficult diagnoses together and on one memorable occasion he and I operated on a patient in a hut in a small forest.

William has been a GP in a fairly large, modern practice for as long as I have been a single handed GP in a fairly remote country practice, and I knew that he had recently taken on some teaching work at the university where we studied and qualified together. In addition to being a GP, Will is now a Professor of General Practice and responsible for ensuring that all students, whether they go into general practice or decide to spend their lives working in hospital, understand a little about the responsibilities of GPs. I wish there had been a similar course running when I was a student. When I first became a GP and walked alone into Dr Brownlow's consulting room to start my first surgery as a GP, it was the first time I had been in a doctor's consulting room since I was a boy, attending the surgery with my mum to have my spots looked at and diagnosed. When I sat down behind the desk I didn't even know how to write a prescription as a GP since the process is quite different in hospitals.

The entire process of choosing and training students has altered dramatically in the relatively few years since I was a student. I knew one doctor who trained at one of the London medical schools where the success of the rugby team is considered more important than academic honours. When my friend attended for his interview to see if he would be accepted as a student, he walked into the interview room and one of six interviewers threw a rugby ball at him – very hard. My friend caught the ball cleanly and threw it back – very hard. That was the end of the interview. He was accepted immediately for admission to the medical school. It was decided that he would clearly make an excellent recruit for the medical school rugby team. Judging students in that way was by no means uncommon.

'I certainly do!' I replied to Will.

'Do you think you could manage another student – just for three days? As you know we want students to get a taste of general practice. We're allocating some to city practices and some to rural practices like yours. Some will go to practices with a dozen doctors and some will go to single-handed practices. What they get is the luck of the draw. When they get back they're expected to write essays and give short talks to the other students. To be honest we're still finding our feet with this project.'

'When do you want this to happen?' I asked.

'Probably tomorrow I'm afraid. I know it's terribly short notice but it's all been a bit chaotic and I meant to ring you sooner.'

'You mean another GP has pulled out of the scheme?'

There was an embarrassed silence. 'I wish it were that simple. Actually, it's worse than that,' confessed William. 'Someone in my office miscounted. We have one student more than the number of GPs ready to take on a student. So unless you can help us out we have a student who'll have to practise thumb twiddling for a couple of days. It's really very embarrassing.'

I couldn't help laughing at William's mild discomfort.

'The University will pay you a modest honorarium,' he went on. 'And if you can put them up at Bilbury Grange, the University will pay you a fee for board and lodging. The modest honorarium really is terribly modest but the board and lodging fee is reasonably generous and if you and Patsy could just give them bread and water for a couple of days you might make a small profit.'

I said I'd speak to Patsy and ring him back a little later.

The morning surgery had been a long and tiring one and I had quite a number of prescriptions to make up, and an order to phone through to the company which supplies me with medicines, so it was a quarter to two by the time I finished. Since none of the day's visits were urgent I decided to have my lunch before I set off round the village.

When I first started in general practice I always tried to finish all the day's visits before I had my lunch but I found that I was sometimes sitting down to lunch at 4.00 o'clock in the afternoon, just minutes before the evening surgery began.

Patsy and I both had a ploughman's lunch (but a rather tastier and more substantial one than the sort of ploughman's lunch usually served up in city pubs – instead of one chunk of cheddar, two solid bread rolls, a pickled onion and a limp lettuce leaf, we had decent sized chunks of cheddar, red Leicester and double Gloucester cheeses, several home-made bread rolls, a good portion of home-made pickle and a decent salad – and after I'd finished my lunch, and drunk a cup of coffee to enliven me for the afternoon, I rang William back.

'I spoke to Patsy,' I told him. 'And we're happy to have a student here and to put them up in the house. Make sure they know there is no television set and that we're vegetarian.'

'Splendid!' said William. 'I'll make sure they know all that. I'll do a little switching around and send you a student who's got their own car because otherwise it's nigh on impossible to get to your place.'

He told me that the student, a girl called Annunciata Beulah Beauregard, had rich parents and drove a fancy, modern sports car. 'She'll be with you sometime tomorrow and she'll stay with you for three days. We get more girls than ever before now. As you probably know the Government decreed that we had to take more female students than male students to try to redress a traditional imbalance between the sexes.'

'You're creating a massive problem for the future,' I pointed out. 'Most of the female doctors you produce will want to work part time so that they can fit in their work with having a family.'

'That did occur to us,' said Will. 'But the politicians only care about how things look so we're doing as we're told. If she gets in the way, or you can't stand her, ring me up or throw her out and send her back.'

I said, of course, that I didn't think either of those drastic options would be necessary. Patsy prepared a bedroom with fresh towels and so on. And she worried, of course, as most people would, about having a complete stranger in the house and about whether she'd be easy to feed. Filled with second thoughts and not a few regrets about saying 'yes' to William (for both Patsy and I prefer to have our home to ourselves), I then went off to do the day's visits and promptly forgot about our forthcoming guest.

I was reminded of my promise the following afternoon when the peace of the house, and indeed the village, was shattered by the throaty roar of a rather expensive, open-topped white MGB sports car skidding to a rather showy halt outside my study window and sending gravel and pebbles flying against the glass.

There wasn't any need to wait for the doorbell to ring so I put down the medical records I was updating, called for Patsy and went out to meet our medical student.

'Is this Bilbury Grange?' demanded a short, confident, rather weary looking girl with wind-tousled long, red hair. You could write what I know about hairdressing on the tip of a needle, leaving room left over to print a copy of the proverbial Lord's Prayer, but it was clear even to me that she hadn't cut her hair herself, and nor had she let a flatmate loose with a pair of scissors and a comb.

She had freckles and wore more make-up than I'd seen for quite a while. She climbed out of the car which, despite its journey through Devon, still shone as though it had just been driven out of the showroom, and deftly switched the flat shoes in which she had been driving for a pair of expensive looking high heeled shoes.

In answer I pointed to the sign she was standing beside. Underneath the words 'Bilbury Grange' it said, simply, 'Surgery'.

'Are you the doctor?' she asked, as though concerned that I might be the gardener or the doctor's handyman.

'You must be Miss Beauregard,' I said, and having admitted that I was the doctor I introduced Patsy.

'How does anyone ever find anything in this village?' she demanded. 'There are no signposts and the lanes are ridiculously narrow and full of tractors. I must have been stuck behind 100 tractors in the last hour.'

She was wearing a mint green suit in what looked like silk and what I assumed was a silk blouse – also coloured mint green. (I'm sure that the fashion house which had produced the suit had a more sophisticated name for it than mint green – just as motor car manufacturers, and the makers of up-market house paints usually manage to think up quite extraordinary names for their products.)

I wondered if all medical students now dressed like that. When I'd been a student I'd almost invariably worn the same scruffy sports coat, a pair of grey flannels and brown brogue shoes that always needed new heels, new soles, new uppers and new laces. Actually, I realised that I was still wearing the same sports coat as I had worn then, though it now had leather patches on the elbows to hide the worn parts. Patsy was wearing a pair of jeans and a blue sweater and I guessed that the clothes Miss Beauregard was wearing probably cost more than everything in Patsy's wardrobe. There were, I couldn't help noticing, a bag of golf clubs and a fishing rod on the back seat of the car.

'Or, perhaps, stuck behind the same tractor 100 times,' suggested Patsy.

The girl frowned, puzzled for a moment. 'Oh yes, I see what you mean!' she laughed. It was a surprisingly deep, throaty laugh. 'Yes, that could well be true.' She turned back to her car and unfastened straps holding two suitcases onto a rack fitted to the boot lid. She then opened the boot itself and started hauling out a variety of squashable bags – the sort that can be fitted into tricky spaces. The luggage, most of it marked with the Louis Vuitton monogram, looked expensive and undoubtedly was. A surprisingly large amount of it had been crammed into the tiny boot. As our visitor bent over to fish out the last piece of luggage, Patsy and I exchanged a glance.

'Three days?' mouthed Patsy. I've never been any good at lip reading but I knew immediately what she meant. I smiled at her. It occurred to me that if Patsy and I put all our clothes into bags we wouldn't fill as many cases and bags as Miss Beauregard had brought with her for a very short stay.

'I can't seem to go anywhere without tons of stuff,' apologised Miss Beauregard, standing up, seemingly suddenly conscious of the number of bags she had brought with her. I noticed now that she was wearing a gold Rolex watch. It was, and still is, the only make of watch I can recognise at a glance. 'I didn't know whether you like to dress for dinner or if we'd be going anywhere requiring a posh frock. I asked a friend who said that country GPs often have quite a few really rich patients with whom they socialised a good deal so I thought it would be wise to pop in a couple of suitable dresses...' The sentence tailed off and I tried to hide the smile I felt. Miss Beauregard then reached into the back of the car and lifted out the golf clubs and the fishing rods. 'Is there a course near here? I suppose there's bound to be.'

'There's a golf course at Ilfracombe – right on the cliff edge.'

'Oh, how terrific! I love links courses.'

'But I'm afraid I doubt if you're going to have time to play much golf.'

'Oh. No, I suppose not!' she said, clearly disappointed. She looked around her, for the first time. 'What an interesting old house,' she said, diplomatically. I looked too and all I could see was brickwork that needed pointing and window frames that needed painting. The two chimney cowls which had been moved by one of last winter's gales were still stuck at dangerous looking angles and the house martins, whose nests were still stuck under the eaves, had left unsightly reminders of their presence down the walls.

We helped her take her luggage into the house and took her to her room. Patsy, after pointing out to her apologetically that she almost certainly had too much stuff to fit into the one wardrobe and the three drawers of the single dressing table the room contained, invited her to settle in (a polite way to say to use the loo and make whatever repairs to her make-up she felt appropriate) and then to come downstairs to join us for a cup of tea and something to eat.

Twenty minutes later, after tea and cake, I showed Miss Beauregard my consulting room. She looked around, with some obvious surprise, at the old, scarred and rather well-worn furniture and the elderly medical instruments laid out on my desk. The bookcase was stuffed with a wide variety of books, most of them rather elderly, and there were piles of old journals stacked on the floor. I found myself looking around with her and feeling a little ashamed of how I realised it must look.

When Patsy and I had first moved into Bilbury Grange I had filled my consulting room with cheap plywood furniture I bought at an auction – the sort that you fix together yourself – but when Dr Brownlow retired he gave me his furniture. I had thrown out my junk and replaced it with his solid furniture – most of the stuff that antique dealers refer to without much affection as 'brown Victorian'. The old telephone on the desk probably looked to Miss Beauregard as if it were a model which Alexander Graham Bell might have felt looked out of date. Dr Brownlow had left me his house and his car too. The house was now Bilbury hospital and the car, the elderly but still reliable Rolls Royce 20/25 which I used every day, was parked at the side of the house and rather in need of a wash.

And I also realised how old I must look to a young medical student. I was really beginning to regret agreeing to William's request.

'Am I right in thinking that you don't have a television?' she said.
'I'm afraid so.'
'Never mind, I brought a small portable one with me,' she said, 'so that I can keep up with my favourite programmes.' I was a little surprised by this too, and I was already beginning to feel my age. No medical student or junior hospital doctor I knew ever owned a TV set and none ever had time to watch television at all – except for glimpses of occasional, major sporting events which might be watched in part but almost never in whole in the doctors' lounge. Miss Beauregard seemed very confident, much more confident than I was at her age. But I suppose that if my parents had been rich enough to buy me an MGB sports car I might have been confident too.

'I'm not sure that your set will work,' I warned her. 'No one in the village has much in the way of reception. Miss Beauregard looked both disappointed and slightly disbelieving.

'What do you want me to call you?' I asked her. 'Miss Beauregard? Ms Beauregard? Annunciata?'

'Oh, Nancy, please. That's what everyone calls me.'

'Fine, Nancy it is then. But when I introduce you to patients you'll be Miss Beauregard. Is that OK?'

'Oh yes.'

'Do you want to do the home visits with me?' I asked her. 'And what about night calls?'

'Oh, I want to be wherever you are,' she replied, with some enthusiasm. 'You're my only chance to see what general practice is really like as a single handed practitioner. Most of the other students in my year are going to large group practices.'

I nodded. 'At night it's probably best to keep some clothes by your bed so that you can dress quickly,' I said. 'I usually aim to get out of the house within five minutes of a telephone call.'

'How many nights are you on call?' she asked.

'All of them; seven nights a week,' I replied. 'That's what single handed means.'

'You don't have an arrangement with another practice?'

'There isn't another practice. At least, there is no practice close enough to share my calls.'

'Oh,' she said, clearly surprised. 'What about weekends?'

'I'm on call at the weekends.'

'What about holidays?' she persisted.

'We haven't actually ever had a holiday,' I confessed, a little embarrassed, though I have no idea why. Maybe I just felt embarrassed at appearing to be such a workaholic. 'But we keep talking about hiring a locum for a week so that we can get away. We've never really got round to it.' I didn't mention that neither Patsy nor I relished the idea of a stranger living in our house and I had become proprietorial about my practice, and didn't really want to go away and come back and find that a strange doctor had put half my patients on a drug of which I didn't approve. I had heard of one doctor who had hired a locum, gone away for a fortnight and come back to find that hundreds of his patients had been prescribed benzodiazepine tranquillisers which they didn't want to stop and which I knew they would find increasingly difficult to give up. I know another single handed GP who went to a great deal of trouble to find a trustworthy locum. He and his wife spent weeks preparing the practice for the locum. The doctor made extensive lists, describing all the patients currently on treatment. The doctor's wife cleaned the house from top to bottom and filled the larder and the freezer with food that she had prepared for the locum and his wife. The doctor and his wife then went to Paris for their first holiday in two decades. While they were away they both worried constantly. The doctor worried about his patients. He telephoned his locum every day to see if everything was going well. The wife worried constantly about the house, the food and the pets they'd left behind. After four days they gave up, paid extra for a flight and went back home.

'How did you get on?' the doctor asked the locum.

'It was very quiet,' said the locum. 'I never saw more than four patients in a surgery and I wasn't called out in the day or at night. Not once. You've got a very quiet life here.'

The GP then paid the locum the full fee for the week and breathed a huge sigh of relief that nothing had gone wrong.

The next morning, his first morning back at work, there were 54 patients filling the waiting room, the hallway, the porch and the driveway outside. 'We're used to you, doctor,' was the commonest remark. 'Better the devil you know,' was the cruellest. The telephone rang incessantly with requests for visits. By the time he went to bed that night, the GP was utterly exhausted and in desperate need of a good holiday. There were four requests for home visits during the night.

Nancy didn't say anything but I was beginning to get the feeling that any affection she might have felt for the idea of single handed medical practice was beginning to ebb away.

'Surely, there should be a better way to do things,' she said at last. 'I think we have to manage our commitment and our expectations more critically.'

'I can't think of a better way to do things,' I replied. 'I'm the only doctor for about an hour in any direction. In the dark of winter, when it snows, we can be cut off for days. If someone injures themselves I'm the ambulance service too. It's a big responsibility but living in a small village like this means that we are all interdependent on one another. We rely on the one garage, the one village shop and the one pub. There are problems and disagreements but on the whole the people who live here recognise that we need one another. In towns and cities, the lack of any real sense of responsibility, and the fact that most people live rather lonely lives, means that workers go on strike without any thought for their neighbours or the consequences for their community. Here, if the village shop closes we are all in trouble. Peter Marshall, the shop keeper, was ill with a bad back last Spring. Half a dozen villagers helped out, looking after the shop for him. When he went back to work he found that everything had run smoothly and efficiently and the money in the till matched precisely what he thought it should be. The volunteers all refused payment – they were just happy to help out. When the garage owner was ill, one of his former mechanics came out of retirement and managed things for a fortnight for him.'

'And what about if you're ill?' asked Nancy.

'Ah,' I said, flummoxed. 'I'll worry about that if it happens. But the point is that if you get rid of single handed country GPs, as I know a lot of people in the profession would like to do, then there will, inevitably, be no medical care at all for country folk. In the end, everyone living in the country would have to move into the towns and cities.'

'But what about your work/life balance?'

I looked at her, puzzled. It was the first time I'd heard the phrase.

'It's a new concept one of our lecturers talked about; the need to balance the demands of your working life against the right to have a private life.'

'Why can't your work and your life be one and the same thing?' I asked. 'If you love your job, and I do, then the distinction between the two is artificial. Lots of people have jobs which consume their lives and they don't see anything strange about it. Work is a vital part of our existence – that's why so many people struggle with a sense of worthlessness when they retire. Trying to separate work and life, as you put it, is quite artificial.'

'I can't see many doctors being prepared to work the hours you work,' she said. 'There are quite a few students who feel that single handed practice is too demanding, particularly for women. We don't think it's fair that doctors, particularly female ones, should be expected to visit patients in their own homes, particularly at night.'

'You think single handed doctors are dinosaurs? And that I'm past my sell-by date?'

'I'm not actually sure that there is any role at all for GPs,' she said, to my astonishment. 'People who are ill should go to hospital and be seen by a specialist.'

'But experts are often wrong,' I pointed out. 'They're accustomed to looking through the telescope so they don't see the big picture. If a patient goes to see a surgeon then the surgeon is going to think about operating. If the patient sees a heart specialist then the doctor is going to look for heart problems and might miss other health issues. Do you really think everyone would be better off without any GPs?'

She was saved from answering my question by the sound of the telephone. She sat down and picked up a copy of *The Lancet* while I answered the call.

Less than three minutes later, I put down the telephone, picked up my black bag and headed towards the door. 'I've got a visit I need to make,' I said. 'Do you want to come with me or would you rather have another cup of tea and relax a little? I know you've had a long, tiring drive.'

'Oh, I'll come with you,' replied Nancy. 'Can you just give me two minutes?'

She ran out of my consulting room and I heard her running up the stairs.

'I'm sorry, love,' I said to Patsy. 'I've got to go out. Nancy is coming with me.'

Nancy then came running back down the stairs. She was wearing a freshly starched white coat and had a stethoscope hanging around her neck and an ophthalmoscope and a patella hammer sitting neatly in a pocket. She was carrying a notebook and a pen. She looked very professional, as if she was ready to walk onto the set of a TV programme about doctors and hospitals.

'You look very smart,' I told her. 'But I'm afraid that white coat will scare my patients to death.' I opened the door to the cupboard under the stairs and picked up a shopping basket. 'Put your stuff in here for now.'

Nancy, looking rather surprised, obediently put her notebook and pen and the contents of her pockets into the bag and took off the white coat. Patsy took it from her and hung it up on the hall coat rack. It looked rather incongruous, hanging next to a row of raincoats and waxed jackets.

'I hope you don't mind but this isn't the sort of village where the doctor wears a white coat,' I explained, as we walked to the car.

'I brought three clean white coats with me!' said Nancy, hurrying to keep up with me. 'My GP always wears a white coat so I thought...' She suddenly stopped as we approached my car. I opened the car's offside back door and tossed my black bag onto the back seat and then started to climb into the driving seat.

'Is this your car? I'm sorry that was a stupid thing to say. Is this the car we're going in? Is the door on this side open?'

'Yes, yes and yes,' I replied. I started the car as Nancy climbed in. She looked around rather anxiously.

'Where's the seat belt? I can't find it.'

'There aren't any seat belts, I'm afraid. Would you feel safer in the back? I can put on a peaked cap if you like and you can wave at the sheep.'

'No, it's OK. It's just that I've never been in a car without seat belts before. It feels rather illegal. Is it legal? What is this car? Is it a Rolls Royce? Do you use it for all your visits? Don't you have anything smaller?'

'Classic cars don't need seat belts. It's my only car so yes I use it for all my visits. It's a 1934 Rolls Royce 20/25. A company called Thrupp & Maberly built the body and put it on a Rolls Royce chassis.'

I waved as I overtook a tractor being driven at 5 mph in our lane.

The driver of the tractor, Paul Bolton, had pulled over into the hedge to give me room to get past.

'I've never seen that before,' said Nancy, half turning in her seat to look behind her. 'Did that tractor driver really pull into the hedge to let us go past?'

'He recognised the car,' I explained.

'I suppose he would,' said Nancy softly. 'I don't suppose there are many elderly Rolls Royce motor cars around here.'

'As far as I know this is the only one.'

'How fast does it go?'

'It's a 3.7 litre engine but it's nowhere near as fast as your car. Forty years ago it would reach 75 mph; today it'll reach 65 on the straightest bits of the A39 between Lynton and Barnstaple.' I noticed that she had one hand hanging from the strap above the door while the other was gripping the dashboard. Are you OK?'

'Yes, it just feels strange to be in a car without seat belts. Where are we going?'

'We're going to see a lovely lady who has fallen in her living room. She's worried she might have broken something. It's not far.'

I knew that Mrs Dorian was approaching her 80th birthday but when we got to her cottage I discovered that the big day had arrived and 'Happy Birthday' cards were proudly displayed on the table in her narrow hallway. Several of the cards were French and wished her 'Bon Anniversaire'. The front door was open (I'd never known it to be locked) so I let myself in and called her name.

'I'm on the floor in the kitchen,' she said. 'I need a hand up, please.'

Followed by Nancy, I led the way into the tiny kitchen which smelt of a delicious mixture of peppermint and hot chocolate. The kitchen contained an old, scrubbed pine table with two matching wooden chairs, a refrigerator which should have been in a museum and a small AGA which, as far as I knew, hadn't been allowed to go out since I had first arrived in Bilbury. In the winter the kitchen was the only room that had any heat in it. The AGA provided hot water for washing and two ovens and a hot plate for cooking. Mrs Dorian was lying on the floor, with one leg underneath her. She had managed to pull the telephone down from a shelf with the aid of a kitchen broom. I introduced Nancy and we both wished her happy birthday.

'Do you mind Miss Beauregard staying with us?' I asked.

From her uncomfortable vantage point, Mrs Dorian studied her for a few moments. 'I don't mind at all. She's a medical student isn't she? Just working with you for a few days? She looks strong and healthy. She can help you lift me up into a chair.'

So, together we gently unravelled Mrs Dorian and put her into a chair. We both examined her and could find nothing broken.

'My 80th is probably the last significant birthday in my life,' said Mrs Dorian. 'The only thing left is the funeral and I've left strict instructions in my will that there is to be no service whatsoever. The cremation people can do with me what they will. I don't think anyone over 50 should attend funerals and, other than you doctor, everyone I know is much older than that.'

'Why shouldn't people over 50 go to funerals?'

'Funerals are too much of a reminder of the future which lies ahead of them,' replied Mrs Dorian instantly.

'What happened?' I asked, after I'd listened to her heart and taken her blood pressure. Nancy checked both too. We agreed that both were entirely normal.'

'Did I have a fit? One minute I was about to make a cup of tea and the next moment I was flat out on the floor. Do you think I've broken anything? As far as I can see, everything seems to be working. I haven't had a stroke have I?' She looked worried and I was reminded that, as Dr Brownlow had once pointed out to me, old people are more conscious of death, and therefore more conscious of life, and often keener to hang on to what is left than many people believe. Twenty year olds don't think of death, often regarding themselves as immortal, and to them death is a theoretical concept, whereas the elderly, who see their friends disappearing at an exhausting rate, are only conscious of death's quiet inevitability.

The only souvenir of Mrs Dorian's small misadventure was a graze on her left elbow which was bleeding slightly. I cleaned the area and put on a sterile dressing. Mrs Dorian didn't flinch.

'What do you think happened, doctor?' she asked.

'I think you probably had a mini stroke,' I replied. 'It happens sometimes.'

'What's a mini stroke?'

'It's actually called a transient ischaemic attack or a TIA. It's like a stroke but a very small one. And yours appears to have been a very, very small one.

'I don't suppose, by any chance, it's something that happens more frequently with older folk?'

'Indeed it is.'

'So what do I have to do?'

I turned to Nancy. 'What would you like to know before deciding on treatment?'

'Do you smoke?'

'No.'

'You're obviously not overweight but do you have a balanced diet?'

'I think I do, yes.'

'How much alcohol do you drink?'

'A small sherry in the evening. Nothing much else except at Christmas.'

'Do you take any exercise?'

'I look after myself, the house and the garden.'

'So, what treatment do you recommend for Mrs Dorian?' I asked Nancy.

'You could prescribe a blood thinner,' she suggested. 'Warfarin?'

'What are the side effects with warfarin?'

'Well, the biggest danger is bleeding.'

'Exactly. Do you think the potential upside is worth the potential downside?'

Nancy thought for a while. 'I don't know.'

'But you want to prescribe something don't you? You feel you need to do something?'

'Well, yes.'

'I'm not going to prescribe anything,' I said. 'Warfarin is quite dangerous. I think it's too dangerous for a single mini stroke.'

'No pills?' said Mrs Dorian.

'No pills. But you ring me if anything like this happens again. The minute you get any symptoms, you ring me.'

'OK, doctor,' she said.

'You need to change that dressing regularly for a few days. Just a big sticking plaster will do.'

'Oh dear, I'm afraid I haven't got any big sticking plasters. I've only got the little ones and the long thin ones for poorly fingers.'

'I'll get you some from Peter's shop,' I assured her. 'You make yourself that cup of tea and we'll be back before you've finished drinking it. Your garden is looking wonderful, by the way. What are those big pink flowers called?'

'They're dahlias, you big tease. You know darned well what they are. It's hard work to create a traditional, wild-looking kitchen garden so I'm glad you like it. Do you know that Monet used to have six gardeners to make his garden look wild, with one gardener employed solely to dust and wash his lilies for his paintings? Can you imagine?' She suddenly burst into laughter; it was the bright, tinkling laughter of a young girl.

'How did she know who I was?' asked Nancy, when we got back into the car.

'This is a very small village. Everyone in the village probably knows who you are, why you're in Bilbury, what make of car you drive and, quite probably, what size shoes you wear.'

'Really?' asked Nancy as I drove off.

'No,' I confessed, laughing. 'She just guessed. She wanted me to know that her mind is working fine.'

'That's why you asked about the flowers you pretended you didn't know were dahlias?'

I nodded, and swerved slightly to avoid a pheasant which was trying to commit suicide.

'You're really not going to start her on any treatment?'

'I'll keep an eye on her. She has intermittent atrial fibrillation and ten years ago, before I came here, she had a heart attack. Her pulse is steady now and she has no signs or symptoms of having had another heart attack. I'm not going to treat her because she doesn't need treatment. One of the things I've learned in general practice is that knowing when not to treat someone is as important as knowing when and how to treat them. I could send Mrs Dorian to the hospital for a whole series of tests but constantly visiting the hospital and sitting in waiting rooms will make her life a misery for months on end and once they've got their teeth into her they'll never let go. Whatever test results we get won't change my mind on not treating her so why do the tests? If she sees a consultant they'll probably put her on some new wonder drug that will produce fearful side effects and ruin her life. It's what they do. Specialists are paid to do something and they find it difficult to do nothing. Mrs Dorian will ring me if it happens again. And I'll pop in to see how she is in a day or two.'

'It must be difficult to be so old,' said Nancy. 'I think I'd be waiting for problems to appear: a heart attack, a stroke, an unexpected, unexplained lump and all the rest of it. You'd be watching yourself deteriorate – it would be like owning an old banger of a car and being forever on the look-out for holes in the bodywork or problems with the ignition or the exhaust and so on.' She suddenly stopped. 'Is that a terrible thing to say?'

'No, course not, though I don't think of Mrs Dorian as old and she certainly doesn't. Most people don't think of themselves as old. But in my experience they see life a little differently. People in their twenties are thinking forward, planning their careers, establishing a position in life where they feel comfortable, looking for a partner and so on. But although people who are fifty years older are still often looking forward – most often than you might imagine – they are also able to look backwards and see things in perspective. And their priorities are different too. As you say, an 80-year-old woman will probably be more aware of health problems developing – a skin problem, an irregular pulse, lumps and bumps that weren't there before. It's not surprising that sometimes older people become obsessed with their health. But then teenagers, and 20-year-olds, can become obsessed and can start imagining all sorts of problems that aren't really there.'

'That's true. I think every student in my year has had at least one fatal illness in the last twelve months. They teach us about a disease and the next day someone decides they have all the symptoms.'

'It's always been like that,' I agreed. 'The trick, I suspect, is to try to differentiate between the things that matter and the symptoms and signs which can be ignored. As we age we all lose some of our flexibility, strength and skills. Nothing works quite as well as it did when we were 20-years-old. It is, of course, possible to get something done about most of the things that are faulty, or not working as efficiently as they did previously, but that can mean making quite a sacrifice in terms of time, pain and money. And there are risks in having surgery or taking pills. There are inevitably going to be consequences as the machinery becomes worn.'

'People deal with ageing in very different ways. And their expectations are important. Many people find it difficult to accept that things aren't going to work as well when they age. An American whom I saw when he and his wife were passing through told me (with considerable pride) that he and his wife between them had four new knees and three new shoulders fitted. The joints God gave us can last 70 or 80 years without too much difficulty. But the expensively produced artificial joints do well to last five years.'

'That's a lot of surgery!'

'It is. And he admitted that neither he nor his wife was in great pain before their surgery and they could both get around quite well, though he sometimes used a walking stick. I find it strange that anyone would rather go through the pain, risk and expense of so much major surgery to avoid the relatively mild inconvenience of using a walking stick. But it's a matter of choice. Many people's lives are occupied by a constant search for surgery and new treatments as they fight the daily battle against decaying teeth, increasing deafness, constant indigestion, breathlessness, pain in every joint, backache, palpitations, forgetfulness, poor circulation, leg ulcers, hair loss, high blood pressure, skin discolorations and more. Millions go to an optician every six months to have their eyes tested, and to a dentist every six months to have their teeth and gums assessed. They have regular bowel, breast and heart checks. The slightest abnormality must be investigated at length and then treated (also at length) with the side effects of the treatment then requiring more tests and more treatments. Patients in their 60s and older are often taking a dozen or more different types of drug every day. They need charts and special pill dispensers to help them keep a check on what they have taken and what they need to take. I knew a woman well into her 70s who insisted on having surgery performed on her hardly visible varicose veins. Dodgy knees, elbows, shoulders and hips need regular testing. There are endless procedures to be undertaken and regular screenings to be endured. There are injections to have and vaccinations galore to protect against the flu, shingles and a range of disorders. These constant visits to doctors and other health professionals create a sense of victimhood and passivity which the health professionals encourage. Regular praise is offered to those who remember their name and age correctly.'

'It is no big surprise that no one over the age of 18 wants to be older and many over the age of 50 have started working out how many days of life they might have left. In the country of the old there is no normal. It's perhaps no surprise that suicide is highest among those over the age of 75. I read a book the other day in which the author, still only in her 70s, confessed that she spent 80% of her time visiting doctors and clinics of one sort or another. Moreover, her friends thought that this was fairly normal. Gore Vidal called his final years 'the hospital years'. But if you live another ten years and spend eight of them in hospitals or doctors' waiting rooms, you are arguably worse off than someone who lived another three years without bothering with doctors. And, of course, this ignores the pain, discomfort, cost and inconvenience of all the treatments that will be offered and doubtless accepted. There is no drug or surgical treatment that does not come without side effects. I'm afraid that doctors and drug companies have a distinct tendency to oversell themselves and their products. I've visited care homes and nursing homes where all the emphasis on illness and treatment means that most old people spend their days moaning about their ailments, talking about their friend's ailments, attending funerals, remembering those who have gone, and abandoning all their hopes and plans because it becomes impossible to fit hobbies and interests in between all the hospital and doctor appointments. It seems to me that the elderly are entitled to have a little more fun. As the responsibilities and obligations have lessened a little (maybe) then the time has come to be more daring and adventurous; to stop worrying about what other people think and to take on new challenges. There isn't much point to being older if all you do is try to repair, to restore and to delay the inevitable aging process. Keeping occupied with projects that are a challenge, and fun to do, seems to me to be the only way to meander through old age with any sense of self-respect and purpose. I am always astonished by people who want to retire at the age of 50 or 55 (or even earlier) and who genuinely seem to think that they will be satisfied if they spend their remaining years sitting on the beach, sipping cocktails and playing an occasional round of golf. I wonder how many of those who embark on a long, long retirement doing nothing eventually find themselves fading away from boredom and a lack of a challenge. Retirement is an entirely artificial concept and it's important to remember that when pensions were invented in Germany, the age of 65 was chosen as the official retirement age because that was, at the time, the average age of death in Germany. In my experience, loafing is only enjoyable if you have a great deal to do. And only if you don't entirely fill your days with doctors' appointments, visits to the dentist and the optician, sessions with a physiotherapist and so on, can there possibly be time to take on the sort of projects that are worth the time. Sadly, the problems of being older are exacerbated by the fact that the elderly are often discarded or rejected merely because of their age.'

'How many of your patients are elderly?'

'More than usual. Younger people move to towns and cities because that's where the fun is and where the work is. Older people come to the countryside to wind down and enjoy life. And the ones who have most fun are the ones who are able to accept that they are old and that some things won't work as well as they did. Look at this car, my old Rolls Royce 20/25. The petrol gauge doesn't work, the clock doesn't work, the temperature gauge suggests that the car is over-heating even before I get out of the driveway. The passenger side door doesn't lock properly. And so on and so on. But if I leave the car at the garage to be repaired I'll never be able to use it. So I compromise. I ignore the small niggly problems. You can apply the same philosophy to everything in life. If I had a pain which kept me awake at night and which wrecked my days, I would try to have something done about it. But if I could find a way around it then I would.' I looked at Nancy. 'Anyway, that's my philosophy of life and general practice. You'll need to find your own philosophy of life and you'll need to decide what sort of doctor you want to be and how you want to help people.'

'You've given me a lot to think about,' said Nancy, quietly. 'We don't get encouraged to think much at medical school.'

'Good. Peter Marshall's shop is just round the next bend. Peter is what is sometimes called a character. He can be amazingly rude and he does crazy things but he's a real friend. If I need him at 3 o'clock in the morning I just have to ring him and he'll come.'

'Have you ever had to do that?'

'What?'

'Have you ever had to ring him at 3 o'clock in the morning?'

'Yes.'

'And he came?'

'Yes. Immediately and without asking questions.'

'Wow. I wish I had friends like that.'

'And Mr Marshall runs the local shop?' asked Nancy.

'Peter owns and runs and is the entire staff of the village shop –

it's the only shop for miles around but you can buy just about everything there. If you want a needle for a wind up gramophone Peter will have one. If you're searching for new leather bindings for your wooden skis then Peter Marshall is the man to turn to. I have known people to come from as far away as Taunton or Exeter in search of size 14 high heeled shoes or the original cast recording of Gilbert and Sullivan's Mikado. People who travel say that Peter Marshall's shop has more delights and surprises than Harrods, Bloomingdale's or Galleries Lafayette.' I laughed. 'Once you've seen it you will never look upon any retail establishment with anything other than mild disdain.'

A couple of minutes later we drew up outside Peter's shop and I strode in through the front door with Nancy scurrying after me.

'Aren't you going to lock the car?' she asked, from behind me. 'Your drug bag is inside. And someone might steal the car.'

'The passenger side door doesn't lock properly,' I replied. 'I'm worried that if I do manage to lock it I won't be able to open it.'

'Oh yes, you said,' said Nancy. She remained standing beside the car, clearly concerned and unwilling to move away. 'Would you like me to stay with it?'

'Don't worry,' I reassured her. 'I never lock the car. But just make sure the door is shut. I've discovered that dogs like climbing into cars if the doors are open. I once got back home and discovered I got two stowaways fast asleep on the back seat.' I had to turn round and drive straight back with them. They didn't wake up until I lifted them out of the car.'

'But aren't you worried the car will be stolen?' She seemed astounded. 'It is a vintage Rolls Royce!' My father has a Jaguar and he's paranoid about it being stolen.' Suddenly I heard myself asking my Uncle Charlie the same question.

'I looked around. There wasn't another building or vehicle visible. I could faintly hear a tractor working in a field in the far distance.

'No,' I said. 'No one is going to want to steal a 40-year-old Rolls Royce. The market for cars built in the 1930s is surprisingly small, the cars are really only saleable when they have some history – servicing and repairs paperwork and so on – and I keep all the paperwork at the house. Besides, although it's a Rolls Royce, the 20/25 isn't a very valuable model. And old cars aren't the easiest of cars to drive, either. There's no automatic gear box and no power steering, the brakes aren't anywhere near as sharp as the brakes on modern cars, there are no heated seats, no heated steering wheel and the windows only go up and down when I wind a little handle.'

'Look at this!' cried Peter, the minute he saw me. He pointed to a huge mountain of shoe boxes that were filling up most of the shop. Quite a number of the boxes looked singed, as if they might have been in a fire.

'They look like shoe boxes!' I said.

'They are shoe boxes! You can't go wrong with shoes,' said Peter. 'Everyone needs shoes. No one ever goes broke selling shoes. So I heard about these and bought them. The people selling them promised me that they would be all different styles and different sizes.'

'You've bought enough of them!' I said. I introduced Nancy.

Peter shook her hand. He was, however, clearly distracted by all the boxes.

'Where did you get them?' I asked him.

'A man rang up and we did the deal on the phone. He brought them round in a big van. You can't trust people these days. I hate to think where it's all heading.'

The Bilbury Stores shop keeper (famous for his slogan 'Pay for Three, Get Two' which had, a few years ago, taken him to national prominence when a holidaying journalist had seen, photographed and shared the sign with their readers) has for some time had a deep conviction that the world was going to the dogs. We all tend to look at life through the retrospectoscope – a clever instrument which enables us to look back and remember only the good things that happened – but no one does this with as much enthusiasm as Peter Marshall. He regularly insists, to anyone who will listen, and indeed, anyone who doesn't want to, that nothing now is as good as it was and that nothing in the future will ever recapture the delights of yesterday.

'How long will it be before everyone has a car and a telephone in their house?' he demanded. 'I know several people who've been to London and two who have been abroad? What's the world coming to when people go abroad for their holidays?'

I sometimes started to argue with Peter but I could never quite summon up the enthusiasm these days. The problem was that deep down I rather suspected that he was right. The past always seems better and less stressful than the present because it's gone and you know you got through it alive, or at least nearly alive. It is, I suspect, for this reason that the elderly prefer to reside in the past and to eschew the present.

A well-built, middle aged woman in a bright blue, low cut sun top, bright pink shorts and bright yellow flip flop sandals came into the shop. She was almost wearing clothes which, apart from the bright yellow flip flops, would have looked skimpy on someone a third her size. She was as broad as she was tall and she shook like a 200 pound jelly when she moved. A few moments later I discovered that when she laughed she shook even more noticeably. When she stopped laughing, it took her bits and pieces several minutes to settle into something approaching a state of repose. She was wearing sunglasses and carrying a beach bag. I thought it reasonable to assume that she was a holidaymaker on her way to or from the beach. Since none of the visible skin looked sunburnt it seemed reasonable to guess that she was on her way to the beach.

'Can't you stop the cheque if they lied to you?' I asked Peter.

'Do you have any of those square cheese slices to put in sandwiches?' the woman demanded, ignoring me.

'I paid cash,' said Peter, who, I remembered, wasn't fond of cheques. He probably hadn't seen a cheque since the 1950s. 'They unloaded them so fast I didn't have time to check the boxes. You can't trust people these days. There are so many crooks around. It wasn't like this back in the 1950s.'

Peter was very fond of the 1950s and from what I could remember his sense of nostalgia was probably justified. He turned to the woman. 'I sell groceries Madam and those square cheese slices don't count as a grocery item. If you want to sole your shoes I can sell you rubber soles and a tube of glue. But I cannot sell you cheese slices.'

'Oh,' said the woman, pouting. For no reason she laughed and jiggled all over.

'I have square bread,' said Peter, helpfully. 'And cheese which you could cut to fit the shape of the bread. Or, if you're feeling ambitious I have round bread which would allow you to be more imaginative when cutting up your cheese.'

I smiled. If Peter ever wrote a book it would be called 'How to make enemies and annoy complete strangers in thirty seconds'.

'Oh,' said the woman, clearly disappointed. 'We stopped on the way down here and bought bread and milk, and most of the things we would need for our stay. We found a nice supermarket somewhere, I can't remember where. But I forgot to get the cheese slices. It's the only sort of cheese my family like. My children call the slices 'real cheese'. Oh, are those walnuts up there?' She pointed to a box of walnuts propped up on a wooden shelf.

'It's terrible when you can't even trust crooks anymore,' I said drily. 'Do you have any large sticking plasters, please, and a birthday card for someone celebrating their 80th birthday?'

'They're walnuts,' replied Peter, answering the woman.

The woman reached up and knocked a dozen or so walnuts out of the box. Most went on the floor but one fell into her cleavage and disappeared.

'I'll sue you!' she shouted, and laughed again. There was more general jiggling. I think the comment was meant light-heartedly but it is always difficult to tell these days. Holiday makers and tourists are becoming increasingly litigious. A tourist from Germany had recently threatened to sue me because I had politely declined to operate, without delay, on varicose veins which he had clearly possessed for several years. 'One of your walnuts has dived into my cleavage,' she added in explanation.

'I'll sue you back unless you buy it,' said Peter drily. 'I can't possibly sell that one now, considering where it's been.'

'What's wrong with where it's been?'

'It's been in that canyon you call a cleavage. I can't sell it now.'

'Did you hear that terrible man?' the woman screamed, presumably shouting to a husband or boyfriend waiting outside. But there was no answer and the woman, offended and still bereft of cheese slices, left.

Peter watched her go with quiet satisfaction. He is a shopkeeper but, like many of his calling, he doesn't much like customers and he especially doesn't like demanding customers who come from outside and behave aggressively. Anyone who hasn't lived in Bilbury for at least two generations is a foreigner as far as Peter is concerned. This means, of course, that I am very much still a foreigner, though Patsy, whose family has lived and farmed in Bilbury since the beginning of time, is very much a local, and I derive a certain amount of kudos from this. I sometimes think the word xenophobia was invented specifically for Peter Marshall.

'You want what?' he asked. 'A toothbrush and a box of toffee? In all the excitement I've forgotten what you wanted. Did you say toffee or coffee?'

I raised my voice. 'Large sticking plasters and a birthday card for someone who is 80.'

Peter nodded his understanding, disappeared behind the pile of shoe boxes and re-emerged a couple of minutes later holding a packet of large sticking plasters, a large, colourful card with a big 80 on the front and an iced birthday cake in box. He handed them all to me. 'I bought 1,000 pairs of men's shoes and 1,000 pairs of women's shoes,' he said. 'The man who called said they were from a very reputable wholesaler. They're supposed to be overstocks.'

'It might take a while but I'm sure you'll sell them in the end.'

I heard a car start up outside and then, turning my head, saw the car drive away. The passenger in the front seat, the woman in the uncoordinated outfit, waved two fingers. Peter, the would-be recipient of this example of sign language, was showing shoes to Nancy and did not see the finger display, which was a pity for it was well-executed.

'They're all the same colour, the same style and the size!' said Peter. 'The men's are all size eight and the women's are all size 6. The men's are all too small to sell round here and the women's are all too big.' He picked a box off the top of the nearest pile and opened it to show me the contents. The shoes inside were very utilitarian to say the least. They looked to me as if they were made of plastic. Worse still, they were made of green plastic.

'Cut the front off the men's shoes and sell them as sandals,' I suggested. 'And stuff cotton wool in the toes of the women's shoes.'

Peter thought about this for a moment. 'Do what?'

I repeated my suggestion.

'Ah. Yes, I could. I suppose I could.' He disappeared for a moment and then returned with a saw. To Nancy's obvious astonishment he proceeded to cut the toes off one of the shoes.

'Are you going deaf?' I asked him.

'Am I what?' He held up the amputated shoe and examined it. 'What you do you think?'

'It looks like a shoe with the toe cut off.'

'I've cut the toe off. It looks awful. That was a terrible idea.'

'Are you going deaf?' I shouted.

'Sorry, you'll have to shout. I think I'm going a bit deaf.'

I didn't say anything but went out to the car, opened my bag and took out my auriscope. I then went back into the shop.

'Stand still,' I told Peter as I looked into his ears. Nancy, who was clearly not accustomed to seeing a doctor examining a patient in the middle of a shop, stared in astonishment.

'Is there something wrong?' asked Peter.

'I can cure your deafness,' I told him. 'You've got about a pound of wax in each ear. Come to the surgery tonight and I'll syringe your ears for you.'

'You want a pound of wax? What on earth do you want wax for? Are you making candles? I've got some good ready-made candles.'

'Your ears are blocked with wax,' I shouted. 'Come to the surgery. I'll syringe them for you this evening.' I removed the plastic end from the auriscope and dropped it into a nearby waste bin that now also contained the sawn off shoe.

'Can't you do them here and now?'

'No. Come to the surgery tonight. How much do I owe you for the plasters, the card and the cake?'

'Tell Mrs Dorian that the cake is a present from me,' he said, having correctly guessed why I was buying the card. 'The sell-by-date was up yesterday but it'll be fine.'

He told me how much I owed and I took out some cash and paid him. I then wished him good luck with the shoes, went back to the car, put the auriscope away in my black bag and climbed into the Rolls. I took out a pen, wrote a cheery birthday message for Mrs Dorian and signed my name underneath. Nancy climbed into the passenger seat. I was about to drive off when Peter came rushing out of his shop holding a large, brown paper bag. 'Are you going past Mrs Askew's's cottage? It's on your way back to Bilbury Grange.'

I said I could easily go that way.

'Would you drop these off for me?' he handed me the bag. 'Mrs Askew has these once a fortnight and she's due for a delivery today.'

I looked inside the bag. It was full of walnuts. 'What's she going to do with all these walnuts? It's going to be a very big cake.'

'She feeds them to the squirrels,' he said. 'Do you really think there's a pound of wax in my ears?'

'I was exaggerating,' I told him, as we left.

'I expect so,' said Peter, looking up at the sky. 'But it'll only be a short shower.'

'Back to Mrs Dorian?' asked Nancy, who was carrying two shoe boxes and a large, brown paper bag.

'Back to Mrs Dorian. Sign this.' I handed her the card and my pen.

Nancy signed the card and we drove back to Mrs Dorian's cottage. Nancy seemed quiet and a little embarrassed. 'I bought some sweets,' she admitted quietly. 'I haven't seen some of these sweets since I was a kid. I wonder where he gets them from.' She opened the bag and showed me what she'd purchased. There were two packets of sweet cigarettes, a huge gob stopper, a Barratt's Sherbert Fountain in a yellow packet that looked like a Roman candle (with an edible liquorice straw for sucking up the sherbert), a paper packet of humbugs, a packet of Refreshers, half a dozen blackjacks, a packet of jelly babies, some Palma Violets, a tube of love hearts, a packet of fruit salad sweets, a quarter of a pound of dolly mixtures, a box of butterscotch and a large quantity of midget gems.

'Your dentist will be thrilled!'

'I know,' murmured Nancy.

'You missed the little hats by a fortnight,' I said. 'I think they've all gone now.'

Nancy looked at me.

'What do they call those tiny hats that women wear when they go out somewhere posh but don't want something huge that will blow away in a breeze?'

'Fascinators.'

'That's the word. Peter bought a load of them. The women of Bilbury thought they were too small and looked silly so Peter persuaded them to wear two at a time – one at the back of their heads and one at the front. It became quite a craze for a while and he got rid of the hats twice as fast as he'd expected.'

Nancy stared. I'm not sure that she believed me but it was true, of course. What might be surprising elsewhere always seems quite normal in Bilbury. I remember we once had a villager who invented a pencil with a sharpener fixed at the end where a rubber is usually fixed. Several of us tried to explain to him that a sharpener at the wrong end of a pencil would be of no value but he wouldn't listen, pointing out that someone had made a fortune out of fixing little rubbers to the end of pencils. He had 1,000 of these made and gave them to Peter Marshall to sell. Peter sold them all, though it took him two years to do so. He sold them as curiosities to holiday-makers who wrongly thought they were intended as some sort of a joke and bought them to give to friends, relatives and workmates when they got home.

'If you come back when our local Women's Institute has a jumble sale you'll probably be able to pick up any number of fascinators,' I told Nancy. 'The fad will almost certainly be over by then. Mind you, Peter will have something else on offer. He once bought 100 old-fashioned tin baths, the sort that people used to use when they wanted to bathe in front of the fire. Unfortunately, most people have a bathroom in their homes these days and the baths proved more difficult to sell than Peter had expected. Still, he managed it in the end. He also sold 100 pairs of ski boots and, most notably, he managed to sell 50 trouser presses. That was impressive before no one in Bilbury had ever been seen in public in pressed trousers and even after the trouser presses had sold this was still the case. The trouser presses had, however, proved surprisingly popular as Christmas presents and Patchy Fogg, and his wife Adrienne, each bought one for the other. I seem to remember that Adrienne didn't speak to Patchy for a fortnight.'

Nancy was quiet for a while. I don't think she'd ever known anywhere quite like Bilbury.

'Mrs Dorian is very sweet,' said Nancy at last. 'I expect reaching 80 is the highlight of her life. One of the lecturers at medical school said that although most people, especially women, are reluctant to divulge their age this changes once people get over 70. He said they become very proud of their age then because it's a major achievement.'

I looked at her and for a moment didn't speak. I wanted to drive up to my old medical school and throttle that ignorant lecturer.

'Not quite,' I said, trying to stay calmer than I felt. 'Mrs Dorian is half French. During the Second World War she was parachuted into France as a liaison with the British. She married a Frenchman who was killed by the Germans in a gunfight in St Germain. They'd only been married four months. She never married again. The Germans captured her after two years and tortured her for a month. She didn't tell them anything. Both the British and the French gave her some medals after the war, though she never talks about them. In the 1950s she worked in the City of London as a stockbroker but she found broking stocks boring so in her spare time she was a racing driver. She was the best woman driver for years and won quite a lot of races. She has a pile of cups and trophies which she keeps tucked away in the cupboard under the stairs. She knows Stirling Moss very well and he's been to Bilbury once or twice to see her.'

Nancy didn't say anything for a while. Not a word.

And then, very softly. 'Is that all true?'

'It's all true.'

'I feel very small,' she said after a long silence.

'It's easy to think of old people as just old,' I said as we drew up outside Mrs Dorian's cottage. 'We often forget that they used to do all sorts of things. I've never yet met an old person who didn't have a fascinating story to tell.'

I picked up the plasters and got out of the car. 'Don't forget to bring the card with you. And give me back my pen, please!'

She gave me back my pen which I slipped into my pocket.

'Have you bought some of Peter's shoes?' I asked, nodding towards the two shoe boxes on the back seat of the car.

'I seem to have done,' she admitted. 'I don't really understand what happened and I have no idea what I'm going to do with them.'

'Wait a few years and green, plastic shoes will probably be very fashionable,' I told her. 'Collectable even.'

'He gave me a 10% discount for buying two pairs,' she said weakly.

I grinned at her and, picked up all the stuff from the shop and got out of the car.

'We've brought you a card and Peter has sent you a fancy birthday cake in a box,' I told Mrs Dorian a few moments later. She was sitting at her kitchen table. There was a pot of tea in front of her and three cups and saucers beside it. I looked at the cake for the first time and noticed that it had the words 'Happy Christmas' on the top. There was a small Father Christmas and a tree stuck into the icing.

'Peter sent you this and said to tell you that it's only a couple of days out of date,' I told her. 'But he might have meant months. Or even years. With Peter who can tell? I think he regards sell-by-dates as of interest only to historians. This cake may well be collectable.'

'That's very kind of you both and very kind of Peter. That's a lovely card. Bless the old reprobate. You must both stop and have a piece of cake with me.' She put the card on the mantelpiece, went to a cupboard and took out three plates and then took a large knife out of her cutlery drawer. She put pieces of cake on each plate. 'How was Peter?'

'He's just taken delivery of a huge quantity of shoes which seemed to have fallen off the back of a lorry. Sadly, they're all one size and they look awfully nasty and cheap. Nancy succumbed to his extraordinary charm and skill and bought two pairs so he'll be very happy. Oh, and he has gone quite deaf but I think I can probably cure him.'

Mrs Dorian laughed. 'I shouldn't laugh,' she said, with a slightly guilty look.

'Oh, yes you should,' I told her. 'Peter wouldn't mind. He'll somehow get rid of all the shoes and laugh about it himself in a week's time. A coachload of Japanese tourists will stop in the village and each of them will buy six pairs of Peter's shoes because he'll convince them that they're the coming thing in English fashion.'

Nancy and I sang a couple of choruses of Happy Birthday and ate pieces of Mrs Dorian's birthday cake. It wasn't in the slightest bit stale, or at least it didn't taste stale to me but Patsy always tells me that I have useless taste buds and can never tell if something is stale or not.

'I don't suppose I should eat this,' said Mrs Dorian, looking at the cake on her plate. 'It's bound to give me indigestion.' She laughed lightly. 'I sometimes stop and think, with sadness, disappointment and regret, and not a little frustration, of the things I can't enjoy anymore. Most of the foods I like best upset my tummy. Whisky gives me a headache and stops me sleeping. Long walks exhaust me. Still, when I get maudlin I try to remember that I could be dead and that would, on balance, be distinctly worse.' She laughed and we toasted her in tea and wished her Happy Birthday again. I wished I'd bought her a bottle of champagne at Peter's shop and then I remembered that the champagne Peter sold didn't come from France but from Poland or Bulgaria or somewhere else a long way from the champagne country – and it was terribly acidic and not the thing for anyone with a sensitive tummy.

'You have a lovely cottage and a wonderful garden,' said Nancy. The garden was visible through the kitchen windows.

'Thank you, dear. Are going to become a GP like my lovely doctor?'

'I don't know. I don't think so. I'm rather planning on becoming an orthopaedic surgeon.'

'Good heavens! Isn't that a little brutal for a young girl? Chopping up bones and joints and so on. Why on earth do you want to be an orthopaedic surgeon?'

'I want to be a surgeon,' said Nancy. 'I've been told that the quickest way to become a consultant is to specialise in orthopaedics.'

'Oh, no, dear, that's not the way to decide on a career,' said Mrs Dorian. 'You should follow your heart. Pick a career that will mean something to you. Since it is my birthday I feel entitled to offer you three pieces of advice. First, if you have a choice always take the challenge. If you walk away from it you will always wonder what would have happened. The unknown is intimidating but invigorating and few things are more irritating than regrets. Second, if you wait for the right time and the right place to do something then whatever you are planning or hoping for will never happen because the right time and place will never coincide. And finally, never assume that the people in authority know what they are doing. The people in authority may know what you are doing and they almost certainly know what I am doing but they don't have the faintest idea what they themselves are doing. When I look back, the only regrets I have are the time I wasted doing things that didn't really matter to me or anyone else. Do you really want to spend your days and your talents replacing hips and knees? Think about how you can make a difference and what you can do that will give you satisfaction and pleasure. I look after my garden as best I can but I don't spend much time weeding these days. I haven't got much time left and I don't intend to waste a minute pulling up weeds. I'd rather write an article to try to make people think, or even a letter to make someone happy, though I hardly have any friends left now, or read a good book, than pull up a few more dandelions. Besides, dandelions are very pretty and the birds love the seeds. Have you ever watched a bullfinch feeding on dandelion clocks?'

Nancy shook her head.

'I ramble a little sometimes,' apologised Mrs Dorian. 'It's a privilege of age.' She paused and thought for a moment. 'When I was your age I didn't realise that older is different. The accumulated stresses of a lifetime build up and tend to make you feel quite full of experiences. All those failures and frustrations mean that you begin to expect disappointments and so when you see the next generation making the same mistakes it is impossible to keep quiet. I don't expect you to take any notice because no one ever learns from the past. Finish your cake, it's not too stale is it?'

Nancy smiled and shook her head.

'Apart from my garden, I love reading books,' said Mrs Dorian. 'And I keep hoping that the doctor here will put me into one of his books about Bilbury.' She looked at me and raised an eyebrow. 'He keeps promising.'

'You'll be in the next one,' I promised her.

Nancy looked surprised and turned towards me. 'You write books about Bilbury? About your practice here?'

'He certainly does,' said Mrs Dorian. 'There are dozens of them.'

'Not quite dozens,' I murmured, feeling embarrassed.

'They're wonderful books,' said Mrs Dorian to Nancy. 'You should read one or two if you want to find out what general practice in the country is really all about. She took another bite of her birthday cake. 'I'm going to regret this later,' she said, brushing crumbs from around her mouth. 'Still, I don't care. It's my birthday. I've decided to stop worrying too much. A few weeks ago I found myself constantly waiting for something to go wrong – a pain in my chest, a slight paralysis somewhere that might be a sign of a stroke, that sort of thing. And then I realised that was a stupid way to live.' She paused and looked straight at Nancy. 'Have you thought about being a GP?'

'No, not really,' said Nancy. 'I think it's a good idea that we have to spend a couple of days finding out what general practice is like, and being a GP is always something to fall back on but at the moment I'd rather aim a little higher than general practice.'

Mrs Dorian raised an eyebrow and looked at me.

'Oh, I am sorry,' said Nancy, blushing. 'That was very rude wasn't it? I didn't mean to be so rude.'

I smiled and muttered something soothing about not being

offended. I stood up. 'We'd better get back to the house,' I told Mrs Dorian. 'Thank you for sharing your cake.'

'Give me a birthday kiss,' she said.

I bent and kissed her forehead. Mrs Dorian closed her eyes and smiled.

'What was that little red ribbon in her cardigan?' asked Nancy, when we were back in the car.

'The Legion d'Honneur. She also has a George Medal which I've never seen her wear, but she always wears the Legion d'Honneur ribbon. Most people don't notice it.'

I pulled the Rolls a few inches closer to the hedge as a small van approached. The driver also pulled over and waved. I waved back.

'Did you see that?' asked Nancy. 'I've never seen that before?'

'A van pulling over?'

'No, the name on the van: 'Horton and Father'! I've seen lots of vans with 'Smith and Son', 'Jones and Sons' and so on but I've never seen one with 'Father' after the name.'

'Joe Horton came here a few years ago and started a chimney sweeping business. The previous sweep had retired years ago and people had to bring in a guy from Barnstaple which wasn't very practical. He wasn't too keen about coming this far.'

'And he kept getting lost?'

'Yes, he did get lost a good deal. Another fellow tried chimney sweeping but his brush got stuck in a tricky chimney and he gave it up. I think he was worried that he'd do some damage or get a brush permanently stuck. So Joe Horton started work as a chimney sweep. He'd never done it before but he bought some brushes and it apparently isn't that hard to learn how to sweep chimneys. Modern sweeps use vacuum cleaners but Joe still uses brushes. Then when he started to be successful he needed some help. He was about to advertise when his Dad asked if he could have the job. His Dad had been a machinist in a car factory and he'd retired to Devon when Joe and his wife moved here. He decided he was too young to just go fishing and grow onions so he joined Joe's business which therefore became Horton and Father.'

'Do you know everyone round here?'

'I think I probably know everyone in Bilbury, yes.'

'And all their secrets?'

'Probably that too!'

'Mrs Dorian mentioned writing articles. Who does she write for?'

'She writes a column on English gardening for a French gardening magazine and writes fortnightly articles on European politics for Le Figaro, the French newspaper. The French pretend to hate the English but they envy us some things – and our gardens are probably top of the list.'

'She writes in French? Oh yes, of course she does. I feel ashamed of thinking that being 80 would be the highlight of her life.'

'Remember what I said: I've never yet met an elderly person who doesn't have a fascinating story to tell!'

'I think I tend to just think of old people as old, not remembering that they've not always been old.'

It occurred to me that if that was the only thought Nancy took away from Bilbury, then her visit would have been well worthwhile.

'I've just got to drop off these walnuts for Mrs Askew at 'No Turning' and then we can go home.' I looked at the clock in the car, remembered it didn't work and looked at my watch. 'It's a bit late for afternoon tea but just in time for the evening surgery.'

'Is this a normal sort of afternoon for you?'

'Fairly normal,' I agreed. 'Though I haven't had to buy an 80th birthday card for a while.'

A few minutes later I stopped the car and delivered the bag of walnuts.

'Is that house really called No Turning?'

'It is. At least that's what everyone calls it. And that's the name on the gate. There's a house on the other side of the village which is really called Mon Repose but the only visible sign is one that screams 'NO PARKING.' I gather that the owners put the sign up outside their house in the summer of 1957, after a holidaymaker parked in their driveway to have a picnic. I don't think they've had any more trouble but the sign is still there. Maybe it has worked. Anyway, the people who live there decided they didn't like the name 'Mon Repose' so they took it down and all that is left is the NO PARKING sign. There's another house in Bilbury which has a sign on its gate which says: 'Before parking here please notify your next of kin.'

'But why on earth would anyone call their house 'No Turning'?'

'You may have noticed that the roads around here are rather narrow and there aren't many signposts. The ones which were here were taken down at the start of World War II so that German parachutists would wander around, get lost, have to ask their way and be reported to the village bobby who would duly arrest them for being German, for vagrancy or, quite possibly, for simply being lost.'

'Were there many German parachutists dropped on Bilbury in World War II?'

'Oddly enough, I don't think there were. In fact I don't think there were any. You'll be surprised to hear that Bilbury wasn't a major target for the German High Command and I don't think the Luftwaffe came this way a good deal. But, logical or not, that's why they took down the signposts.'

'So, why haven't they put up new ones?'

'Well, there's a rumour that the council did send a van full of signs...'

'...but it got lost?'

'It did.'

'Because there weren't any signposts?'

'That's the story we tell visitors, though the truth is that I suspect that the council just forgot. We're a bit cut off and that suits us fine. They did put up a bus shelter once, which was nice of them.'

'Do buses come to Bilbury?'

'Not really. There's a bus between Barnstaple to Lynton twice a week but it doesn't come to Bilbury anymore, and hardly anyone uses it because the bus that goes from Barnstaple to Lynton sets off just a few minutes after the bus from Lynton to Barnstaple arrives and so there isn't a lot of point to it.'

'So, why is there a house called 'No Turning'?'

'Sorry, I forgot the other half of the explanation. Motorists and delivery drivers who don't know Bilbury are always getting lost and when they get lost they sometimes panic and turn round and try to go back the way they came. Mrs Porter's house has a long driveway and apart from a couple of permanently muddy farm gates a hundred yards up the road, it's the only place to turn. Mrs Porter is the kindest person you could meet but she got fed up with people reversing into her stone pillars and knocking bits off, so she put up the No Turning sign. When the driver of a huge lorry got lost trying to deliver a fridge to someone in Barbrook he managed to knock down her very nicely painted house sign. So all that was left was the

'No Turning' sign. And so that's what why the house is now known to everyone as 'No Turning'. The postman told me that Mrs Porter has her mail addressed to 'No Turning, Bilbury, Devon.'

I braked and parked the Rolls behind a rather battered tractor that was parked on the verge, and which had probably been blue when it had been in the showroom a hundred years ago. 'You can stay in the car if you like. I'm just going to give Rupert a helping hand.'

'What's happened?'

I pointed to a man struggling to manoeuvre a piece of rusty corrugated iron into the position where he wanted it. I got out of the car, fetched a pair of thick gloves out of the boot, and went through a nearby five barred gate into the field. ('Now that you live in the country,' Dr Brownlow had said to me within a week of my arrival in Bilbury, 'you must keep a pair of thick gloves or gauntlets in your car boot. You will find yourself using them more times than you can imagine.' He'd been perfectly right.)

'Damned sheep keep getting out,' said Rupert, when he saw me arrive. He is what most people would call a character. He looks as if he had been manufactured from other people's leftovers. He has uncommonly short legs, unusually long arms and a head that would be in proportion if he were seven feet tall. He was wearing a pair of worn and stained jeans, a blue woolly jumper full of holes, an old Barbour coat and a battered brown trilby. I had known him since I've arrived in the village and I had never seen him wearing anything else. 'They've made a hole in the hedge,' he said glumly. He managed to seem surprised though sheep are always making holes in hedges. It's one of the things they do best.

I picked up one end of the sheet of corrugated iron and together we pushed and wriggled it into a position where it blocked the gap. Despite the gloves I found myself being badly stung by nettles. There always seems to be a gap between the cuff of my coat and the beginning of my gloves. Not even gauntlets prevent this problem.

I was suddenly aware of someone standing behind me. I looked round.

'Can I help?' asked Nancy.

'I think we're about done,' I said. 'But thank you.'

Rupert gave the corrugated iron a final push to make sure it was firmly fixed and then looked at Nancy. I introduced her and explained that she was working with me for a few days.

'Oh, you're the student,' Rupert said to her.

'I am.'

Rupert nodded, thanked me and wandered off to untangle a sheep which had got itself caught up in a bramble bush.

'Will that repair be temporary?' Nancy asked me when we were back into the car and once again headed for Bilbury Grange. I rubbed at the nettle stings with a large dock leaf which I'd picked from the verge.

'That depends on how you define temporary. He'll layer the hedge and it'll grow back quite quickly.'

'And then he'll remove the corrugated iron?'

'By then it'll be impossible to remove the corrugated iron,' I said.

'It won't look very pretty.'

'No, but it'll keep his sheep in place. What else is he to do? He hasn't got the money it would cost to put up a sheep proof fence.'

'I've ruined my skirt and my shoes,' she said softly. 'And I didn't do anything.' I glanced down. Her shoes did look a mess and her skirt had been snagged in several places by a bramble bush.'

We drove back to Bilbury Grange just in time to wash and brush up a little before the evening surgery was due to begin. Nancy remembered to put the roof up on her sports car and moved it to the side of the house, leaving more room for patients to park. Patsy, who is infinitely more adept with mechanical devices than I am, offered to help with the hood but Nancy said it would take her only a minute. It actually took five but I was impressed, I'd always thought car hoods took ages to erect. One of Patchy's Land Rovers has a roof that comes off in sunny weather and can be put back into position when the weather changes, but it usually takes him so long to put the roof back on that the weather has usually changed back again long before he's finished.

It was a good job that Nancy had put up her car roof because twenty minutes later the skies went dark and five minutes after that the rain started. It was one of those all-too-common storms which come in from the Atlantic Ocean and drive with unabated fury along the North Devon coast. Storms like this tend to last for hours. Even inside the house the sound of the storm was almost frightening and I found myself hoping that I didn't have to do any calls during the night ahead.

Evening Surgery

The evening surgery took a little longer than usual because I had to explain to every patient just who Nancy was and what she was doing there. I then asked every patient if they were happy to have a student sit with me during the consultation. When I had to listen to a chest, or palpate a lump, an abdomen or a breast, I asked the patient if they objected to Nancy listening or palpating when I'd finished. When Peter Marshall came in to the surgery to have his ears syringed I did the right side, showed her exactly what to do and let her do the left side.

The surgery was really quite routine, though there were one or two patients with unusual problems.

Mrs Rogers, a holidaymaker staying at a local caravan site, came in convinced that she was losing her sight. She was also getting regular headaches.

'Do you think it's a brain tumour?' she asked me, clearly very distressed. 'I read in a book that my symptoms could be a cancer in the brain.'

I asked her when she got the headaches.

'If I've been reading for a while,' she said.

'Only then?'

'Yes, only after reading.'

'And how is your sight?'

'Well, I recently got new spectacles and to be honest my sight has been worse since I got them,' she complained.

'Where did you get the spectacles from?'

'I bought them at a jumble sale. They're nice looking spectacles with expensive frames,' she said, pulling what I assumed were the spectacles in question out of her handbag.

'Did you have your eyes tested?'

'No, I didn't bother. I thought that if I just bought some spectacles I wouldn't need an eye test. The spectacles were only 50 pence.'

A brief examination showed that there were no signs of any tumour in her brain and so I told her to stop wearing the spectacles that were clearly quite inappropriate, to go to see an optician to get her eyes properly tested and, if she needed them, to wear suitable glasses.

A man called Herbert Acton came in to have some stitches removed from his abdomen. He had fallen down the stairs at home while holding a glass of beer right in front of his body. Luckily he didn't break any bones but the beer glass broke as he fell forward and a decent sized sliver of glass sliced into his abdomen, cutting open a piece of skin. Again he was lucky that the sliver of glass didn't pierce his abdomen or cut into his intestines or any vital organs. I'd put the stitches in myself.

'You were very fortunate!' I told him as I removed the stitches. The wound had healed nicely and he wouldn't have much of a scar. I was quite proud of it. 'If you walk up or down stairs carrying a glass always hold it well away from you!' He thanked me and seemed to look at his new scar with some pride. He was not a man who spoke a great deal because he had spent his working life deep in the London sewers where it is wise to keep your mouth shut as much as possible. When he did speak, Herbert tended to open his mouth no wider than a good ventriloquist would.

Another holidaymaker, an overweight woman in a skimpy beach outfit, came in asking for advice for healthy eating. It didn't take long for her to hint that she wanted me to prescribe some slimming pills.

I gave her a copy of a diet sheet which I had had printed and asked her about her eating habits.

'Oh, I eat plenty of vegetables and fruit,' she said.

'What vegetables and fruit have you eaten today?'

'I had a Cornish pasty together with onion and garlic crisps,' she began, rather proudly. 'There was potato in the pasty and potato, onion and garlic in the crisps. And I had a strawberry ice cream. Strawberries are good for you, aren't they?'

I quietly pointed out that strawberry ice cream doesn't count as a fruit and that crisps don't count as vegetables. I suggested that she go to see her own doctor when she got home. She left the surgery looking rather cross and disappointed.

'What did she want you to do?' asked Nancy.

'Wave a magic wand or, more likely, prescribe some powerful slimming pills.'

The next few patients were fairly straightforward. We saw an 18-year-old making a good recovery from glandular fever, a 46-year-old woman struggling with a frozen shoulder (but showing some signs of improvement), an elderly man with a Dupuytren's contracture affecting his right hand and a young woman with carpal tunnel syndrome. After asking their permission, I allowed Nancy to interview, examine and diagnose all four patients. We were both delighted when she made four correct diagnoses. I didn't tell her but it wasn't entirely by accident that we had four such interesting cases to examine. The gentleman with Dupuytren's and the woman with carpal tunnel syndrome had both come into the surgery at my request – purely as a test for Nancy. (Patsy had rung them up while Nancy and I were out. When they left the surgery, Patsy gave each of them a £5 note as a thank you. Since neither of them was working, both were very happy with the arrangement.)

And then there was Mr Rossington who came into the consulting room just before Peter Marshall. He was not one of the patients I'd invited in as a test for Nancy. He is a small, neat man, who always moves firmly, decisively and a little more speedily than seems entirely necessary, as though he is proud of the fact that he still remembers how to do it or, perhaps, because he is worried that if he delays too much he might forget and have to ask someone what you do with your feet. Or maybe he is always just in a hurry. You can over think things.

'I keep hearing a ringing noise in my abdomen,' he complained when he'd sat down and made himself comfortable. I introduced Nancy, examined him and put the end of my stethoscope against the upper part of his abdomen. At first I couldn't hear anything but when he moved I could hear a definite ringing sound.

'See what you can hear,' I told Nancy.

It took her slightly longer but she too agreed that she had heard a tinkling sound.

For a moment I was puzzled and I then remembered about a story I'd read in the local newspaper.

'Didn't I read that you'd eaten a bicycle for charity?'

'Yes!' he said, very proudly.

'Did you get any indigestion?'

'No, nothing at all. Six months ago I ate a piano.'

'But you ate the bicycle two weeks ago?'

'Yes, that's right,' he said, rather proudly. 'I had to saw up the frame and the wheels, but quite a lot of it I ate whole. I swallowed the chain in one piece. We raised nearly £150 for charity.'

'And the bell?'

'The bell?'

'The bicycle bell? I assume that there was a bell on the bicycle. Did you eat that?'

'Yes.' He seemed proud but after a moment he started to go a little red.

'You swallowed the bell whole?'

He nodded. I couldn't help noticing that Nancy was now grinning in a rather unprofessional way.

'The bell rings when you move. Did you have difficulty in swallowing it? How big was it?'

'It wasn't easy but I swallowed it in the end. It was quite a small bell.'

'If it doesn't pass through the various sphincters it will meet on its way through your intestinal tract you'll need to have an operation to have it removed,' I told him. I sighed. 'These daft charity stunts nearly always end up costing more than they raise. Come back and see me in a couple of days and let me know how things are going. I'll have a listen and see if I can work out where it's got to.'

'He's going to have a devil of a job passing that if it gets to the end of its route,' said Nancy, when he'd gone.

We agreed that we didn't envy him the price he would have to pay for his daft stunt.

'People do some very silly things,' said Nancy.

'Everyone does silly things. The secret is to try not to do silly things that can kill you. I knew a doctor who was having chest pains. He wondered if he was having angina. Instead of having some tests done he decided to see what happened when he ran up several flights of stairs in the hospital where he worked. He got as far as the fourth floor before he had the heart attack that killed him.'

'Is that really true?'

'Yes. That really happened.'

Over dinner that evening, Nancy gave Patsy a summary of all the patients we had seen that evening, and everything she had learned about general practice.

'The amazing thing is that when the next patient comes in, you don't have the foggiest idea what you're going to see!' said Nancy in amazement. 'I'm used to the teaching hospital where you know exactly what is wrong with every patient before you see them. I hadn't realised that general practice is a constant stream of surprises.'

We were then treated to a blow by blow account of every wheeze, every rash and every lump. By the time we were ready for coffee I felt as though I'd done the same surgery twice.

'Do you always syringe ears yourself?' asked Nancy.

'Always. There's no one else to do it.'

'We were taught that GPs should have their practice nurse do the syringing, to save their time. Do you take blood samples yourself too?'

'Always. I don't have a practice nurse. But even if there was someone else to do the syringing and blood taking and removing of stitches I'd prefer to do those things myself.'

'Why?'

'First, the patient has already waited to see me. It seems rude to tell them they've got to wait again to see a nurse just to save two minutes of the doctor's time. Some practices make patients make another appointment for a few days' time, or even a few weeks' time ahead. That seems unfair. Patients are often worried when they visit a doctor. It's much better for them if everything is done at once. Patients often have to make two long difficult and expensive journeys to get to and from the doctors' surgery. If a mum has to take a child to the hospital in Barnstaple to have stitches removed it'll take her a whole day. And probably cost her two taxi fares. Many of the people living in Bilbury are poor, and have lots of things they have to do. Removing stitches takes me two minutes. Second, when GPs tell patients to make an appointment to see a nurse or technician to have a blood sample taken there is usually a delay – which may be a week or two or even more. And this creates a much bigger problem. Either, the patient must wait for their treatment to start until the blood samples have been taken – meaning that the patient must wait additional weeks for essential medication to begin. Or, the patient will be started on treatment before the blood sample is taken in which case the blood sample and the blood tests will be useless because the blood will be contaminated by whatever treatment has been initiated. So, for example, if a patient is given steroids then their ESR will be reduced and their white blood count altered too. Blood tests should be taken the moment the doctor decides they are necessary. And third, I believe that doing these little tasks help build the relationship between doctor and patient. When ears are blocked with wax I can cure deafness in a couple of minutes. When I remove stitches from a child I stick the stitches on a visiting card so that they can show their pals at school.'

'Do you ever wish you worked in a large, modern practice?' asked Nancy. 'You know, one with several doctors, nurses and so on. Most GPs work in groups of three or more. I heard about a practice in the South East which had twelve partners and heaven knows how many assistants. They have a computer, a sophisticated appointments system and a huge staff of receptionists. Patients who ring up to see a doctor just get slotted in to see the next doctor who has an appointment available.'

'That wouldn't suit me.'

'But don't you think patients are better off seeing different doctors? If the first doctor misses a diagnosis, or makes the wrong diagnosis, a second doctor may make the right diagnosis.'

'I doubt if it works like that,' I said. 'Once a patient has been diagnosed and labelled then that diagnosis and label will probably stay with them. Besides, there's good evidence that if patients always see the same doctor, they're more likely to be honest about their symptoms, more likely to take whatever medicine is prescribed, more likely to follow advice and likely to live longer, healthier lives. A doctor who sees the same patient several times over a few years will get to build up a professional relationship – there will be trust and understanding on both sides. And the doctor will know a good deal about the patient's health and susceptibilities. Moreover, I think you'll find that patients far prefer to see the same doctor every time they need advice or treatment. Patients get to trust a doctor over time and find it easier to talk about personal problems. Most people get embarrassed when talking about their bowels to a complete stranger. Besides, a village like Bilbury wouldn't merit a big practice with lots of doctors.'

'Do you worry that in the end they'll close you down again? The administrators prefer big practices, don't they?'

'They did close down my practice once. But Bilbury is too far from any other town or medical practice. I do worry that the bureaucrats would like to have us all living in towns and cities. Villages and hamlets are inconvenient, messy and inefficient. I do worry that when the 21st century rolls round the bureaucrats will decide it's time to move everyone into little urban communities. The people will all live in blocks of flats and there will be one school, one medical practice, one supermarket and one little park. People will work in offices within their community and there won't be any need for cars or trains or commuting or pubs. Everyone will use a computer for shopping and learning, and spend their evenings watching television and eating television meals on trays. It'll all be like Fritz Lang's 'Metropolis', George Orwell's '1984' and Aldous Huxley's 'Brave New World.'

'I suppose the administrators would argue that it would be a more efficient way to organise society,' said Nancy.

'It would be a bit soulless though, don't you think? Don't you think it's the mystery and the unexpected that give life its flavour? When I wake up in the morning I've no idea what problems I'm going to face or where I'll need to go. My boundaries are circumscribed, of course, largely within a roughly seven mile radius I suppose, but every day is a new adventure.'

I was, I confess, beginning to feel something of a dinosaur; leftover from a way of life that would soon be discarded, forgotten and lost forever.

'My lecturers say that it's very wasteful for doctors to drive around the countryside to see patients,' said Nancy. 'Don't you think it would be much more efficient if they all came to your surgery?'

'I suppose it would,' I agreed. 'But a lot of them haven't got cars, there's no bus service and most couldn't afford a taxi even if it were easy to find one. Besides, if you're feeling poorly the last thing you want to do is trek five miles to the doctor's surgery and then trek five miles back home afterwards. Quite a few of my patients are in their seventies, eighties and nineties. It wouldn't be right to expect them to walk all this way – especially in the rain or the snow.' I finished the rest of my coffee. 'If I get called in the night do you want to come with me?' I asked Nancy.

'Oh yes,' she said immediately.

'I usually try to be out of the house within five minutes of a phone call,' I told her.

She looked a little startled, but said quite firmly that she wouldn't keep me waiting. She then went upstairs to finish writing up her notes for the day, leaving Patsy and I alone.

It was, however, a quiet night – quiet that is until I was woken the next morning, not by the telephone but by a scream.

'Did you hear that?' whispered Patsy.

'What the devil was it?' I asked. I had, for the moment, forgotten that we had a student staying in the house.

'I think it was Nancy. It sounded like a woman's voice.'

We both leapt out of bed, pulled on our dressing gowns and headed downstairs. We found Nancy in the kitchen, fully dressed, leaning against the huge old table in the centre of the room.

'I'm so sorry,' she said, looking as apologetic as she sounded.

'Are you OK?' asked Patsy.

'I'm fine. I'm so sorry. I woke early and it seemed such a wonderful, sunny day that I thought I'd just take a walk in the garden.' She paused and apologised again for screaming. 'I opened the back door and suddenly I was in the middle of one of those Disneyland cartoons where there are animals everywhere.'

I knew immediately what had happened, and so did Patsy.

'There were half a dozen squirrels, heaven knows how many rabbits and two pheasant standing there just waiting and looking up at me,' she said. 'The squirrels all ran towards me and I was worried they'd jump up onto me or try to rush past me into the house. Two rabbits hopped towards me. And there was a pig running towards me. I didn't realise pigs could run that fast. I just managed to shut the door and I'm afraid I screamed. I'm not used to seeing so many wild animals so close to me. Actually, they didn't seem particularly wild. They all seemed so friendly – almost tame.'

'They just wanted their breakfast,' explained Patsy. 'We throw out nuts for the squirrels, carrots for the fluffle of rabbits who live with us, and sunflower hearts for the pheasant. We have a pile of hazelnut trees, a dozen beech trees and one walnut tree in the garden and we collect the nuts and dole them out during the year to the squirrels. Summer is actually a bad time for them.'

'But don't squirrels just bury nuts in the autumn so that they've got food all year round?'

'Oh they do, but most of the time they forget where they've

buried them. That's why our garden is full of young hazel bushes. So we store up some nuts for them and dole them out like pocket money at times of the year when they'd otherwise be hungry.'

'But there was a pig too!'

'Oh that was Cedric,' I explained. 'He is supposed to live in a very comfortable sty but he's learned how to open the latch and so occasionally he wanders out, sniffling out the nuts the squirrels have buried.'

'He seemed to want to come into the house!'

'That was my fault,' admitted Patsy. 'He had a cold and was bit poorly a few months back so we brought him into the kitchen and let him lie down in front of the AGA. He rather liked it…'

'Oh!' said Nancy, who seemed rather surprised by this.

'Did you sleep well?' asked Patsy, keen to gloss over this incident. Cedric had been almost impossible to remove from the kitchen.

'Like the proverbial log. I finished writing up my notes about the patients I'd seen with your husband. I thought I'd try to watch my little television but as you said it didn't work. All I got was a fuzzy white screen. And it didn't matter at all because the minute I lay down I must have fallen asleep straight away. I had a novel with me in bed and in the morning I found it on the floor. I hadn't opened it. By the way, do you think I could make a telephone call? I promised to ring my parents to let them know I'd arrived OK, and the day was so busy I completely forgot.'

'Use the phone in the consulting room,' Patsy told her.

We then all had our breakfast, a little early.

And afterwards I introduced Nancy to more of the joys and quirks of a rural general practice.

A Miracle in a Stable

I didn't have to wait long to use my new tractor.

When the telephone rang at 3 a.m. I woke instantly, as I always do when the telephone rings at night. I can sleep through all sorts of other noises, even the alarm clock, but the telephone's familiar ring acts like Pavlov's bell, but except for my mouth watering at the prospect of food I simply wake up ready for whatever the emergency might be. As I sat up and reached for the telephone, I could hear a storm still raging outside. The weather had gone from sunny to stormy in just a few hours.

The weather on and around the cliffs of North Devon is not the sort of weather that the Devon tourist board likes to promote. When we get wind we get WIND, spelt out in capital letters; it is the sort of wind that demolishes sheds, takes down trees and strips slates off roofs faster than any human hands could do it. The only reason the wind doesn't actually do those things more often is that most of the sheds in Bilbury have already been demolished and most of the surface rooted trees have gone. You won't see many beech trees in North Devon; their roots are far too shallow to provide a solid resistance to the wind. On Exmoor anything over ten feet tall is rare for a tree, those trees which survive look like bushes and are shaped in such a way that you can easily read the direction of the prevailing wind. Devon doesn't get the sort of breezes that tickles the undergrowth and ruffles the skirts of Burberry coats in West End London (breezes which are often dignified with names because they dare to enter the capital); Devon, particularly our part of North Devon, gets storms and gales on a regular basis. The wind roars in over the Atlantic, throwing huge breakers over the rocks and smashing into even the most sheltered of harbours. Lynmouth harbour has such a tight entrance that it's notoriously tricky for sailors, and Boscastle, down the coast in Cornwall, long ago learned that even nature's own protection isn't always enough when the wind brings storms and rain. You won't find many smart pleasure yachts moored in North Devon harbours. Weekend sailors much prefer the harbours of the southern coast: Axmouth, Torquay and Lyme Regis in Dorset.

Rain was hammering against the bedroom windows and I couldn't help hoping that all the animals we care for, know well and regard as friends, were tucked up safely in their nests, drays, lairs, burrows and dens. (Our pets would be fine, of course, tucked up and cosy and Cedric invariably seems to sleep through storms.) One of the saddest sights on the morning after a heavy wind is the sight of a shattered dray on the ground, the newly homeless squirrels who have been unceremoniously thrown out of their homes in the night, frantically trying to salvage what twigs and moss they can as they hurry to build a new home. At least the animals who live underground are usually tucked up and safe – as long as their homes don't flood and the entrance isn't blocked by a fallen tree. However careful you might be, nature can all too often find a way to cause disruption.

'I'm sorry to ring you on a night like this,' said a woman's voice which I didn't recognise at first, though that was probably because she was so distraught. 'Can you come please? The ambulance will take too long – even if it can get to us. Gerald is unconscious. He's been injured. I think he might be dying.'

'What's happened?' I asked, climbing out of bed and pulling my trousers on top of my pyjama trousers.

I now knew who it was, of course. It was Brenda Rathbone. It was typical of her that in an emergency the first thing she would do would be to apologise for disturbing me.

Brenda and Gerald Rathbone live on a farm which many (particularly the authorities and those corporate farmers who regard 1,000 acres as a 'small' farm) would dismiss as nothing more than a smallholding. They grow cabbages and potatoes to feed themselves, grow oats and turnips as fodder and use seaweed as manure. Brenda knits jumpers which Peter Marshall sells to tourists. But whether you call it a farm or a smallholding it was their life, their world and their livelihood. They kept a couple of dozen sheep, a few cows, a few hens and a gaggle of geese. Brenda looked after the hens and the geese and grew strawberries, blackberries and raspberries in torn and repeatedly mended cages. They sold the eggs and the soft fruit at a stall by the side of the road because, as Brenda had once explained to me, if they sold their produce through a shop they would earn too little to make it worthwhile. I remember that one year they paid for a market stall but the cost of the stall, and the diesel to take themselves and their produce to the market, far exceeded their income. Now they sold what they could to passing tourists though since the lane past the gate to their farm was way off the beaten track they got very little custom. Occasionally, Patsy would drive out that way and buy produce from them, though to be honest we didn't need it because we had our own hens and a huge soft fruit cage which kept us well supplied. Patsy and Brenda were much the same size and Patsy would also take Brenda clothes which she didn't much wear. The first time she did this she worried that Brenda might be offended, but Brenda was delighted. Their farm house, which is tiny, has just two rooms downstairs (a kitchen and a living room) and two rooms upstairs (a bedroom and a small bathroom). Their heating is provided by a coal fire in the kitchen and when they want hot water they hang a pan on an iron hook over the fire. There is no washing machine and no fridge. In the darkest and coldest days of winter they pretty well live in their kitchen because the other rooms are just too cold for habitation. The telephone, which they had installed two years ago, is the only real evidence that they're living in the second half of the twentieth century. Before they had the telephone installed, they used a call box three miles away. If you wanted to telephone them you had to write and ask them to be at the call box at a particular time. It was not a system which worked particularly well.

'Gerald is injured,' said Brenda. She was so distraught that she was struggling to speak. 'He's badly injured, doctor. I think he's going to die.'

'Tell me what happened so that I know what to expect and what I need to bring,' As I spoke, with the telephone tucked between my head and shoulder, I put on my socks and somehow managed to pull a thick, polo neck sweater over my pyjama jacket. I keep the thick sweater next to the bed on cold nights and hardly ever wear it except when I go out on a call at night.

'Go and bang on Nancy's door,' I whispered to Patsy, 'and tell her I've got to go out and if she wants to come with me she needs to be ready in a couple of minutes.'

'The storm blew part of the roof off our stable,' explained Brenda, her voice full of fear and tears yet to be shed. 'When we heard it crash, Gerald went out to see that the animals were OK. He brought them in when the storm started because there's no real shelter in the fields.' She paused, obviously and understandably distraught. She was having difficulty talking.

'Go on.'

'When he didn't come back after ten minutes I went out to see if he was OK. We'd been sleeping in the kitchen for warmth and because the roof over our bedroom leaks when it rains. He had taken our only big torch so I lit an old hurricane lamp we have and took that with me. The rest of the roof had fallen down and trapped Gerald underneath it. I don't know where I got the strength from but I managed to pull some of the debris off him. He's barely conscious, doctor, and he looks really bad. The animals were all gathered around him and I was frightened they'd tread on him so I opened the doors and let them out into the field.'

'So he's in the stable next to the house?'

'Yes. We used to keep horses in it but we haven't been able to afford horses for a while. Now we use it for the cattle and the sheep when the weather is really bad.'

'Did you see any bleeding?'

'No. I couldn't see anything. The lamp wasn't very good.'

'What's the track like to your house?'

'It was flooded yesterday morning. It'll be worse now.' She thought for a moment. 'I don't think you'll get up it in your old car,' she said. She suddenly started to cry.

'I've got a tractor,' I told her. 'I'll come in that and I'll bring a couple of good lamps. If I can get close enough to the stable I'll use the tractor lights. I'll be with you as soon as I can. Put something over him to keep him warm and to keep the rain off him.'

'Shall I ring for an ambulance?'

'If the track is flooded, they'll never get an ambulance to your place,' I told her. 'I keep asking them to invest in a four wheel drive Land Rover but they won't. I'll be there as soon as I can. I'm leaving now. I'll probably have a student with me. Is that OK? Another pair of hands might be useful.'

'That's fine, doctor,' said Brenda. 'I'll go back to him and wait for you. You know where the stable is, don't you?'

I told her that I did, put the phone down and picked up my black bag which I keep in the bedroom at night. I then picked up another emergency bag which contains two huge battery powered lanterns which I always keep charged and I hurried out onto the landing. As I got there Nancy came out of her bedroom. She was wearing jeans and a thick sweater, with an anorak on top of the sweater. I was pleased to see that she hadn't wasted time putting on make-up.

'You'll need a waterproof hat and some decent boots,' Patsy said to Nancy. 'Follow me and I'll lend you mine.'

The three of us hurried down the stairs, I picked a huge, waxed Barbour coat off the coat rack, shrugged into that and added a woolly hat that was big enough to come down over my ears. I had a sou'wester somewhere but the ties had broken and I hadn't got round to mending them. Besides, no hat except a woolly hat will stay on a head in a real North Devon wind. The winds we get in North Devon would all be given names and classified as hurricanes if they blew through South East England in general or Greater London in particular. In London, when the wind blows, the news broadcasts are full of nothing else but the news programmes never bother to mention storms which affect North Devon or any other remote parts of the countryside. Friends of ours who live in the Peak District in Derbyshire were snowed in for three months one winter and the media hadn't once mentioned their plight.

A minute or two later Nancy and I were out in the storm, glad of our waterproof clothing. I carried my black bag and gave the student the bag containing the lanterns to carry. Patsy had turned on all our outside lights so at least we could see where we were going as we made our way to where the tractor was parked. Leaves and twigs went by and occasionally hit our backs. This was clearly a bad storm

'I'll stay by the phone in case you need anything else,' cried Patsy as we left. I could only just pick out her voice as the wind whistled past the house and through the trees.

'I'm glad we're going in your car,' shouted Nancy. 'Mine would be stopped by the first puddle. Will your car be OK if the roads are flooded?'

'We're going in a tractor,' I shouted back, 'though I suppose it's probably more accurate to say we're going on a tractor since the only protection from the elements consists of a flimsy little home-made cab that has no heating.' I didn't mention that if there was any heating it would be carbon monoxide leaking from a cracked exhaust pipe. I couldn't remember whether Thumper had managed to mend it.

'I love tractors,' shouted Nancy.

'Really? That's good. I'm afraid I've never driven one in anger before – I gave this a five minute run around one of our fields but that's all.'

I could sense, rather than see Nancy looking at me.

'I bought it the other day,' I explained.

We arrived at the tractor, which was parked inside one of our empty barns. I climbed up into the tiny cab and put my black bag into the small space behind the driver's seat. Fortunately, the single bench seat was big enough for the two of us. Nancy had to keep the bag containing the lamps on her lap because there wasn't room to put it anywhere else. 'Cross your fingers!' I told her. I pressed the starter button, with my heart in my mouth and breathed a sigh of relief when the engine started first time. It occurred to me that if the tractor hadn't started I would have had no way at all to reach the Rathbone's farm except on foot.

'My uncle has one just like this,' said Nancy. 'It's his oldest and quite his pride and joy. It's a John Deere two-cylinder diesel, isn't it? My uncle says that when they were introduced they were considered to be the bees knees in power and reliability.'

'Your uncle has tractors?' I said, surprised. I put the tractor into gear, managing to find something appropriate, and edged forwards slowly.

'He's got seven tractors, and three combine harvesters.'

'This one is what the French would describe as 'nouveau' rather than 'neuf',' I explained. 'It's new to me but not new to the world. It was built in the 1940s. Why does your uncle have seven tractors?'

'My uncle collects them. He used to have a farm but he sold that. He's still got some land, though, and he collects tractors and farm machinery. It's just a hobby. He takes his tractors to shows and exhibitions. How far are we going?'

'As luck would have it we're going to the edge of the Bilbury boundaries. The Rathbones are about as far away from Bilbury Grange as any of my patients. By one of those strange quirks of fate which seem to rule general practice, patients who live just round the corner from the doctor's home rarely seem to have emergencies when the weather is really bad.'

'Does your tractor have lights?' asked Nancy, tactfully.

I thanked her for reminding me, and turned on all the tractor's lights. It was my first night-time call on a tractor. As we drove towards the farm I explained to Nancy what had happened to Mr Rathbone.

The tractor's replacement engine, newly installed by Thumper, was surprisingly quiet but I had to shout to make myself heard above the howling of the wind; it was screeching and screaming as though it were a living thing, angry or in great pain. It was no surprise that there were no other vehicles on the road and we had the lane to ourselves.

'These tractors are supposed to be incredibly reliable,' said Nancy. 'They just go on and on for ever.'

'That's good to know!'

'How many nights a week do you have to get up and go out?'

'Not usually more than two or three, sometimes one call in a night, sometimes more. It's busiest in the summer when there are tourists around – some living in caravans and tents and staying in boarding houses.'

'Don't you get tired of always being on call?'

'I don't really think about it because it's what I do. And it wouldn't work any other way. There isn't enough money coming in to pay for another partner. I came here as an assistant because Dr Brownlow, my predecessor, was getting old and needed to slow down.'

'For me,' said Nancy, 'the really frightening thing is not knowing what you're going to see when the door opens, or when you go into someone's home. As I said before, it's different in hospital because the patients are all lined up in neat rows. They all wear pyjamas or night dresses and they all have diagnoses written on the charts at the end of their beds. A friend of mine said she was dreading her three days' work experience in general practice. She said she thought it would be dead boring – just sitting in an office writing out prescriptions for antibiotics and handing out sick notes.'

'Is that what you thought it would be like?'

'I suppose I did. I didn't realise it would be like this.'

The headlights picked up a branch which had fallen across the road. I started to slow down, thinking I would have to get out and move the branch and then I realised that the tractor would just ride over the branch with ease – which it did.

'There's a philosophy that is taught at the moment which says that we should all manage our expectations,' said Nancy, 'that we shouldn't hope for too much and that we should keep our feet on the ground.'

'That's a pretty dreary philosophy,' I said. 'Rather defeatist.'

'I think so too. But it's popular at medical school.'

'I wouldn't think it's the sort of thing Will would teach,' I said.

Nancy laughed. 'No, it isn't. Not at all. Have you known him long?'

'We were at medical school together.'

'Oh yes, he said that you had been.'

We trundled on, getting wetter and wetter. The canvas cabin kept out some of the bad weather but there were gaps at the corners that seemed to grow wider as we travelled. The wind whistled through the gaps, bringing gallons of water with it. The windscreen wipers, which were clearly a later addition, and had presumably been fixed in position by someone who lived more in hope than expectation, made all the traditional side to side movements but didn't move much of the water off the windscreen.

'I think this canvas stuff is more trouble than it's worth,' I said. 'And the windscreen is useless too. I'll rip it off tomorrow and just buy a pair of goggles.' Just as I spoke the wind decided to agree with me. It lifted the make-shift canvas cabin off the tractor and hurled it into the sky. The windscreen, which was fixed to the home-made cabin, went with the canvas, leaving the windscreen wipers to float pointlessly from side to side, with nothing to wipe clean. I caught hold of the one on my side and tore it free of its flimsy moorings and dropped it onto the floor. Nancy did the same with the one on her side of the tractor.

(At the time I had no idea where the canvas and the windscreen had gone but four days later a farm labourer found them three quarters of a mile away and brought them to Bilbury Grange with a slight grin. No one else in Bilbury would have driven a tractor with such a strange contraption attached to it. I put the unwanted wreckage into a barn where it lies still and will doubtless one day be discovered by an antiquarian dealer specialising in farm equipment. He will ponder long and hard over its provenance and purpose.'

Despite the lack of a windscreen, and the absence of goggles, I found that as I grew more confident I could increase the speed at which we were travelling. When the cab went, we also lost the two spotlights but the tractor's own lights were adequate for the speed we were travelling. I don't know how fast we were going because the speedometer didn't work (indeed, most of the instruments didn't seem to work) but I'd have guessed that we must have been doing 25 miles an hour, or even a little faster. The only snag was that at that speed Nancy and I were constantly soaked with spray which consisted of an unpleasant mixture of water, mud and worse. I decided there and then that my first task the following day would be to visit Peter Marshall's store and buy some suitable goggles and a ski mask of some kind. Meanwhile, thinking of my patient who used to work in the sewers, I decided to say as little as possible so that I didn't have to open my mouth more than was absolutely essential.

When I recognised the turn off into the track to the Rathbone's farm, I pulled the tractor to a shuddering halt.

'Shall I open the gate?'

'Yes, please!'

Nancy jumped down with far more agility than I would have been able to summon, opened the gate, waited while I drove through the gap, and then closed it again. I waited and she then jumped back onto the tractor. The track, which was very rough and nigh on impassable in a car even in good weather, was now covered in thick mud and several inches of water. I knew without a doubt that I wouldn't have been able to travel more than ten yards in the Rolls Royce.

Seven or eight minutes later, and after going through another gate, I drove up the final stretch of the track to the farmhouse. The tractor's headlights lit up Brenda Rathbone, soaked to the skin, who was standing waiting for us. She was wearing an old, grey dressing gown over a nightie and had wellington boots on her feet. Her hair was plastered to her head and her clothing looked as if it had all just been pulled out of a washing machine. Two sheep dogs, both of which also looked as if they'd had a bucket of water thrown over them, stood beside her, barking furiously. A couple of geese wandered around a couple of yards away. The dogs ignored the geese and the geese ignored the dogs and I, well aware that farm animals can be unpredictable and protective of their territory, tried to ignore them all.

'He's over here!' said Mrs Rathbone, pointing to what was left of the stable which had been attached to their cottage. The stable now looked more like the untidy dump found at the back of a yard occupied by a builders' merchant. Not for the first time it occurred to me that country homes, especially those on cliff tops or in exposed positions, should be round, rather than square. A building with no corners is far less susceptible to the wind.

A few unhappy looking cows and sheep, which had previously regarded the barn as their home, mooched around among the wreckage looking puzzled and disgruntled. Mrs Rathbone was holding an old hurricane lantern which flickered, constantly threatening to go out and providing very little light. Suddenly, the darkness was temporarily forgotten as the sky was lit up with a flash of lightning and the whole earth seemed to shake with the accompanying thunder. The lightning showed just how much damage had been done by the storm, and for an instant I could see that part of the cottage roof had been torn away when the stable had collapsed. If the cottage had been a car, the insurance company would have written it off as beyond repair. The rain, which had already appeared to be coming down at the maximum allotted rate, managed to move up another gear. It occurred to me that this was a terrible way for anyone to live, if you could call it living. The Rathbones, like so many of my patients, worked hard but barely scratched a living out of their land. At the same time, drenched, freezing cold and with no idea what to expect, it also occurred to me that I had discovered a crazy way to earn a living. I felt ashamed of myself for that. It was what I'd chosen to do. You can't pick out the good bits to keep and discard the uncomfortable bits.

I took the two huge torches from the bag which Nancy had been nursing, gave one to Nancy and kept the other for myself. I climbed down from the tractor, leaving my black bag where it was for the moment, and asked Brenda Rathbone to take us to her husband. I left the tractor where it was parked. The twin headlights, suddenly appearing brighter than before, lit up the yard and the front of the cottage.

The last time I'd seen the Rathbone's cottage the weather had been glorious and the picture had been very different. The cottage had looked welcoming and idyllic, with a border of geraniums brightening up the front wall, and the two dogs looking peaceful and bucolic, had been asleep beside a few bales of straw. If would-be holidaymakers with a penchant for country living had seen a photograph of the scene in a travel brochure they'd have booked their two weeks 'away from it all' in an instant.

It had looked like paradise on earth.

It now looked like hell; something conjured up by Dante in a nightmare.

Brenda Rathbone led us through a small gap in the rubble and as we walked, I tried to use my torch to light the way for her. The dogs stayed with her, occasionally turning round to scowl and snarl. It is my honest opinion that no animal on earth can look quite as menacing as a farmyard dog. But then, of course, I've never come face to face with a lioness protecting her cubs.

It took several difficult minutes for the three of us to make our way through the rubble to the spot where Gerald Rathbone was trapped. Every few moments we could hear the broken beams shifting slightly and a little more rubble would fall. I turned round to Nancy, who was following behind me.

'Go back to the tractor, please. Wait for me there.'

'No, thank you.' Her voice shook slightly but she sounded quietly determined.

'This is dangerous. There's no need for you to be here.'

'There's every need for me to be here. I want to see what general practice is all about.'

I looked at her. She was clearly determined. I nodded. There didn't seem any point in telling her to be careful.

'Here he is, doctor,' said Mrs Rathbone eventually. She pointed to her husband who was lying underneath a pile of loose rubble and a beam from the roof of the stable. Only his head, his left hand and forearm and his left foot were visible. Everything else was hidden. When I first saw him I honestly thought he was dead. The word pale doesn't begin to describe his colour. He was ashen; quite grey. His eyes were shut and his face had that waxy look of the new corpse. Both dogs started to whimper. One moved forward and licked his hand.

'It's the doctor,' said Mrs Rathbone softly. She stooped so that she could touch her husband's arm. Gerald Rathbone opened his eyes and tried to smile. 'The roof fell in on me,' he said softly. In the light of my torch I could see that his lips were blue. He did not look well. He wasn't dead but he looked as if he might soon be. I put my torch down on a piece of masonry so that the beam shone on him. He closed his eyes as the light hit him. I reached forward and felt for his pulse. It was so fast I couldn't count it, and it was feeble. His heart was clearly struggling to keep him alive. His body was clearly not getting enough oxygen.

'Bit difficult to breathe, doctor,' said Gerald Rathbone. The words came out individually, in gasps. Each word required an effort. He spoke slowly, from one side of his mouth, and his speech seemed slightly slurred, almost as though he had been drinking. He attempted a smile but it was curiously one sided and unbalanced. A cow tried to wander into the part of the stable where he was lying, seeking shelter or human comfort or both, though there wasn't any shelter to be had in the collapsed stable now that there was no longer a roof. Mrs Rathbone shooed out the cow as easily as one might shoo an annoying hen or pheasant out of the way. The cow backed out into the rain, mooing quietly in disappointment.

'Just lie still while we try to sort you out,' I told Mr Rathbone. 'We need to get some of this rubble off you so that we can see what's what.'

At this point, I had no idea what we would find. Broken bones? Crushed ribs? A punctured lung? I had no idea how much blood he had lost.

'It's the beam,' he said. 'It feels like it's crushing my chest.' Again, each word was produced with great difficulty and again the words were slurred as though he'd been drinking. I bent forwards to smell his breath. There was no trace of alcohol.

Nancy balanced her torch on another piece of fallen masonry and the three of us worked together, pulling the debris from his body. We worked as gently and as quickly as we could. The bricks and chunks of plaster were easy enough to move but the half of the beam that lay across his chest was difficult to budge. I was terrified that we would be able to lift it a few inches but would then drop it and cause yet more, possibly fatal, damage.

And all this time the storm continued, the rain fell as though God had found himself overstocked with the stuff and was having a special sale. The light from our torches was supplemented now at irregular intervals by flashes of lightning. The whole scene was definitely biblical.

'Somehow we have to move this damned beam,' I said, a

comment which would have won a prize for banality since it was the obvious thing we needed to do. I wondered if it would be possible to get help. But where on earth could we find the people we needed? I could call the police or the fire brigade in Barnstaple but they would take the best part of an hour to arrive – even if their vehicles could fight their way up the farm track. I tried to think of a neighbour I could call but the Rathbone's farm really was isolated. I knew that Thumper Robinson or Patchy Fogg or Peter Marshall would come and help but once again it would take at least half an hour for either of them, or anyone else, to reach us. We had to move quickly and we were on our own.

I thought for a moment about using the tractor to pull the beam clear. But I didn't think I could move the tractor through the rubble, and pulling the beam off Mr Rathbone was simply too dangerous. The only answer was for the three of us to lift the beam, move it off Mr Rathbone and then drop it down somewhere where there was no risk of it landing on him again. I told Mrs Rathbone and Nancy what we had to do. We moved more of the rubble out of the way and then each one of us positioned ourselves beside the beam.

'Once we move it we have to keep hold of it and lift it away from him,' I said. Even as I spoke I realised it was another statement of the obvious. The trouble was that I didn't have time to filter what I thought before I actually said it. My mind was racing faster than I could think as I tried to sort through all the possible complications that might be waiting for us. What were the chances of a broken rib puncturing a lung? Would moving the beam make things worse? What about his spine? Could that be broken? I tried to think of all the things that might have happened but I couldn't think fast enough. Emergency medicine had recently become a medical speciality and surgeons were trained to deal with situations like this. Based in the Accident and Emergency Departments of big hospitals they would be well prepared for all such emergencies. They would have lifting machinery, portable X-ray equipment, a generator with bright lights, and, of course, a great deal more experience and knowledge than I possessed. I felt as inadequate as I could remember feeling ever before. My mind flashed back to the time when I'd had to deal with a man whose leg was trapped between two rocks. The tide had been coming in fast and I'd had no choice but to amputate his leg. I still had occasional nightmares about that day. Miraculously, the man had survived. He still wrote to us regularly and had visited Patsy and me several times since that awful day. He had learned to manage well with his artificial leg. Thinking of all this took up no more than a nano-second and in a strange way I suppose it gave me the strength, the courage and the confidence I needed.

Each of us put our hands underneath the beam and then together we strained and pulled and lifted and eventually the damned thing began to move. As I slid my hands beneath the beam I realised, with great relief, that the heavy rafter had not crushed Mr Rathbone. It had trapped him but it was resting at each end on piles of smashed masonry. The chances of a miracle suddenly increased massively. Ever since we'd first seen Mr Rathbone I had been quietly convinced that we would be lucky to save him. Now, for the first time, I began to feel a little hope.

The three of us struggled to get hold of the slippery wood and we strained, with every bit of strength we could find, to lift the beam. In the torch light I noticed that there were what looked like spiders' webs around the beam and I suddenly realised that they weren't webs but strands of dry rot. It was no wonder that the stable had collapsed so easily and so completely. How badly was the cottage affected by dry rot? How weak was the roof? What else was going to collapse? I had no idea. I could feel my muscles groaning and complaining and I knew the other two must feel the same. I tried to keep my back straight so that I could use my leg muscles to help me lift, instead of destroying my spine. Probably unnecessarily, I reminded the others to do the same. I was scared that if we let the beam fall it would truly crush his chest and that Mr Rathbone would be in an even worse position than he had been when we'd found him.

And at last we moved the beam high enough up for us to be able to move it to one side. And then, when we were clear of Mr Rathbone, we began to lower the beam. As soon as it was safe to do so we let it crash safely to the rubble on one side. Mr Rathbone gasped with relief as the beam was taken from his chest. Nancy and I sat back, partly out of exhaustion and partly out of relief, on various pieces of the rubble. Brenda Rathbone moved, naturally, to hold her husband. Suddenly I realised she was trying to put her arms around him to hug him.

'Don't!' I screamed, desperate to make myself heard above the noise of the storm.

Mrs Rathbone stopped and looked at me, startled.

'Don't hug him!' I told her. 'If he has broken ribs or a damaged spine you could make things worse.'

I really didn't want him to be paralysed because we weren't being careful. And I didn't want a broken rib piercing his chest cavity. I suddenly realised how exhausted I was, both physically and mentally. I looked across at Nancy. She was bent forwards, almost in a foetal position. She looked utterly drained and I wondered if I looked as bad.

But there was no time to rest. We had to assess the damage and see what bones were broken. It seemed inconceivable that there would not be serious damage to deal with. And still the rain kept coming. The thunder and lightning had abated but the storm had not. Now that Mr Rathbone was no longer underneath the stable beam, I was suddenly aware that we were all in an immensely vulnerable position. I looked up, picked up my torch and shone it on the side of the cottage. The roof of the stable was there no more because we were sitting or standing on it. But the top part of the end wall of the cottage, the part of the cottage to which the stable had been attached, was leaning outwards at a dangerous angle and the cottage roof looked as if it were about to collapse at any moment. The stable had been built later than the cottage and yet the two had clearly been dependent upon each other. On the roof, a huge brick chimney had moved slightly and was doing its own impersonation of the Leaning Tower of Pisa. It looked as if it was about to come crashing down upon us, and if it did the four of us would all be in danger. We needed to move Gerald Rathbone out of the stable as soon as possible. But before we could do that I needed to assess his condition and find out what damage had been done. You can cause a great deal of permanent damage if you move an accident victim without first checking to make sure that you know what sort of condition the patient is in.

Suddenly, I heard a noise behind me.

Worried that something else was about to fall down, I turned my head and saw that a sheep was trying to get to us and had dislodged some of the rubble. Bricks and pieces of plaster moved. One of the sheep dogs lowered its head and growled at it and the sheep backed away obediently.

I turned back from the sheep and saw, to my horror, that Mr

Rathbone had levered himself into a half sitting position. Mrs Rathbone had her arm around him and Nancy was trying to tell him that he shouldn't move.

'Try to keep still while we take a look at you,' I told Mr Rathbone. 'Do you have any pains?'

He said something unclear which I assumed was a 'No'. I asked the question again. The answer was definitely a 'No'.

I moved the remaining bits of rubble from Mr Rathbone and pulled aside an old mackintosh gown and a pyjama jacket. He had clearly not had time to dress before he'd gone outside to check on his animals.

'You check that side, I'll check this side,' I said to Nancy, who was now on the other side of Mr Rathbone. I was really worried about the risk she was taking. Mrs Rathbone was there because it was her husband we were trying to rescue. I was there because it was my job to be there. But Nancy didn't have to be there.

I checked Mr Rathbone's ribs and then the bones of his right arm and then the bones of his right leg. I could find no sign of any broken bones and nor could I find any blood. I did a quick and rather superficial neurological examination to see if there were any signs of spinal damage.

'I can't find anything abnormal,' said Nancy.

'There's some weakness on this side,' I said. I checked his pupils, checked his neck and skull and looked for but didn't find any signs of a head injury. I found a safety pin in my jacket pocket and used it to check his right arm and leg. I then did the same tests on his left arm and leg. There was no doubt there was some sensory loss on the right side of his body.

'How is your vision?' I asked him.

He squinted at me and shook his head.

I repeated the question.

He answered but I couldn't make out what he had said. The sound of the rain made it difficult to hear anything.

I repeated the question.

He repeated his answer, whatever it was.

'He says everything is blurred,' said Mrs Rathbone.

'What do you think has happened?' asked Nancy.

'I think you've had a stroke,' I said to Mr Rathbone. 'Do you think you can stand?'

He said something incomprehensible, struggled to his feet and promptly fell over. We helped him to his feet, and with Mrs Rathbone on one side and me on the other he made his way out of the destroyed stable and into the cottage. Nancy and I removed our waterproofs and our boots and we all went into the sitting room, on the side of the house which was not attached to the stable and which was, therefore, marginally less likely to collapse.

When we had examined Gerald Rathbone again, out of the rain and the storm, it became clear that although he had, miraculously, escaped injury when the stable had collapsed on top of him, he had suffered a mild stroke. He told us, with some help from his wife, that while standing among the debris of the stable, and seeing and hearing his animals in distress, he had suddenly had a terrible pain in his head and had then collapsed. Moments after he had fallen to the floor, the rest of the roof had collapsed and the beam had trapped him on top of the rubble. It made sense that the stress of everything happening around him had caused his blood pressure to rise dramatically and had triggered a bleed within his skull. That, at least, was my best guess.

There are two types of stroke. In the commonest, affecting around nine out of ten stroke victims, the symptoms are caused by a clot. Less commonly, the symptoms are caused by a bleed.

'Are you going to give him an anti-coagulant?' asked Nancy.

Giving an anticoagulant, such as aspirin or warfarin, is a common treatment for a stroke caused by a clot.

'I don't think so,' I said. I explained that it made sense to assume that the stroke was caused by a bleed rather than a clot and that an anticoagulant could make Mr Rathbone's symptoms far worse.

I sat there in the Rathbone's living room for an hour, waiting to see how Gerald Rathbone's condition would develop. Mrs Rathbone made mugs of hot, sweet tea (which normally I hate but which on this occasion I actually welcomed) and fed us huge cheese sandwiches.

'I'll arrange for an ambulance to pick you up and take you into the hospital,' I told Mr Rathbone. 'But not until it's light, and the rainstorm has abated a little. It'll be a lot easier for the ambulance in daylight. The ambulance can park on the road and I'll come and take you from the cottage to the ambulance on my tractor.'

I then asked if I could use their telephone to ring Patsy, first to explain what was happening, and why we had been away so long, but also to check whether any more calls had come in.

'I'm afraid there's one more call to do before you can come home,' said Patsy. She gave me the patient's name and their address. It wasn't a patient of mine but a holidaymaker staying in a self-catering cottage.

Inevitably, as luck would have it, the cottage was on the far side of the village.

The cottage, called 'Sunny Days', is owned by someone who lives in London and is let out constantly to holidaymakers, walkers, fishermen and so on.

There was a small, neat car of an indeterminate make parked on a small area of ground in front of the cottage. I parked the tractor on the lane. There was nowhere else to put it.

'I'm so sorry it's taken so long to get to you,' I apologised to the woman who opened the door. She was fully dressed in jeans and a sweater and had freshly done make-up. Not many of the patients who call me out at night are fully dressed and fewer still have bothered to put on their make-up. There were several suitcases standing in the hallway behind the woman.

'It's been three quarters of an hour!' complained the woman, pointing to her watch as though she were speaking to a foreigner who might not understand her.

'I do apologise,' I repeated. 'I got here as quickly as I could. I've been dealing with an emergency on a farm.' The rain had slowed to a drizzle but I was still soaking wet and a puddle was forming around my feet.

Nancy, standing beside me, started to say something.

'Well, it's not good enough,' snapped the woman before she could speak. 'And I've half a mind to make a complaint about you.' She looked at Nancy. 'And who is this?'

'Miss Beauregard is a medical student,' I explained. 'She's working with me. If you object to her presence I can ask her to sit on the tractor.' I looked at her and couldn't help thinking that Nancy was as wet as if she'd been swimming fully clothed. It occurred to me that I must look just as bad.

'Tractor?' exclaimed the woman. 'You are supposed to be the doctor, aren't you? I didn't call for anyone on a tractor. I don't want a field ploughed.'

'It's been raining and I had to go to a farm. The farm track was flooded.'

The woman looked beyond us and saw the tractor parked in the lane. It was covered in mud and looked as sorry for itself as Nancy and I doubtless did. The woman snorted. She didn't invite us into the house.

'We were just leaving,' she said. 'We want to set off early to beat the traffic.'

I looked at my watch. It was just past seven o'clock. If I was lucky there would be just time for a shower, a change of clothing and some breakfast before the morning surgery started. 'What's the problem?' I asked.

'The problem is that it took you so long to get here,' said a man suddenly appearing in the hallway behind the woman. He was holding something but I couldn't see what it was. There were two small children with him. In the background I could hear a dog barking. It was more of a yap than a bark.

'I'm not going to invite you in,' said the woman defiantly. 'I've hoovered and if you come in there'll be mud everywhere. If the place isn't left clean we'll lose our deposit.'

'That's fine,' I said. I was beginning to feel a trifle weary. 'But what did you telephone me for?'

'Show him, Reggie,' said the woman, standing to one side so that Reggie, who I assumed was her husband, could move forward a little.

Reggie held out a piece of toilet paper for me to examine. I peered at it and then moved aside so that Nancy could look at it too. I didn't take the paper from him.

'Worms?' Nancy suggested.

'Worms,' I agreed.

'So, what are you going to do about it?' asked the man.

'Someone has got worms.'

'We know that,' said the man. 'We're not stupid.'

'Who has the worms?'

'Duncan.'

'Your son?'

'Yes.'

'How old is he?'

'Four.'

'What's his surname?'

'The same as ours – Smith.'

'Is he taking any medicines, Mrs Smith? Does he have any allergies?'

'No. Apart from having worms he's fine.'

'If you come to my surgery at midday there will be some medicine waiting for you,' I told them.

'Can't you just give us a prescription?' demanded the man. 'We want to get on the road.'

'So that you'll miss the traffic?'

'Exactly.'

I reached into my jacket pocket and pulled out a soggy ball of paper. 'I always carry a prescription pad with me,' I said. 'But this one has got a little damp.' I squeezed water out of the useless ball of paper. 'May I ask why you decided to ring me so early in the morning instead of going to see your own doctor when you get back to London? Worms doesn't really count as an emergency.'

'Oh, it's nigh on impossible to see our doctor,' said the woman. 'Unless you're dying it takes three weeks to get an appointment.'

'And he wouldn't like it if we asked for a home visit for a case of worms,' added her husband.

'I'll put out a bottle of medicine for you,' I said wearily, far too tired to protest. Every muscle I had was screaming in protest. Moving the beam had drained me physically. And I have never really got used to missing a night's sleep. 'It'll be ready after midday when I've finished my morning surgery.'

'That's no good at all!' said Reggie. 'We'll be nearly home by then.'

I turned and squelched back to the tractor, trying hard not to feel too angry. Without that call I could have snatched an hour in bed before the morning surgery.

'I shall make a complaint about your attitude and your appearance,' said the mother of the boy with worms.

'That was unbelievable!' said Nancy, as we drove back to Bilbury Grange. 'Does that sort of thing happen often?'

'Occasionally. Two women who were on a walking holiday called me out once to look at their dog who had scratched himself on some barbed wire. It was a nasty looking dog that didn't stop growling. It terrified me to be honest.'

'What happened?'

'I asked them why they hadn't rung a vet or gone to visit one. I pointed out that there was a vet no more than a quarter of a mile from the caravan site where they were staying.'

'What did they say?'

'One said they'd have to pay if they visited a vet. And the other added that you had to pay extra if the vet did a home visit.'

'What happened?'

'I told them that I wasn't legally allowed to treat dogs and that the vet and I had an arrangement – he didn't treat my patients and I didn't treat his. And then I went home.'

Ten minutes later we were back at Bilbury Grange. I parked the tractor and we trudged into the house, leaving our boots and soaking wet outer clothing hanging in the porch. I hugged Patsy and explained what had happened. Nancy had a shower, I had a bath and then we both had a huge breakfast. Afterwards I arranged for an ambulance to take Mr Rathbone to hospital and I went back in the tractor to carry Mr Rathbone down the still muddy track.

I was late starting the morning surgery but there were very few patients, thank heavens, and Patsy explained where I was. I managed to get through the morning without any obvious blunders, and without falling asleep on my blotter.

The first two patients, Mr and Mrs Pilling, came in together, as they always do. They have their blood pressures taken every three months and they are always the first to enter the waiting room and, therefore, the first to enter the surgery. I don't think I've ever seen them apart from each other.

'Mr and Mrs Pilling will have been married 80 years in another month,' I said to Nancy, when I had introduced them to her and her to them. I turned to Mrs Pilling. 'I know diamond is the 60th wedding anniversary but what's the name for an 80th wedding anniversary? Is there a special name?'

'Our son says it's an oak anniversary. He lives in Exeter and he looked it up in a book at the library.'

'So you have to buy each other oak trees?' I said, jokingly.

'That's exactly what we're doing,' said Mrs Pilling with a big smile. 'We've got all the oak furniture we can fit into our cottage so we've bought ourselves two young oak trees and our son is going to plant them at the bottom of the garden. The best time to plant an oak tree is fifty years ago and we know we won't have the pleasure of seeing them grow but it's nice to think we're leaving a real legacy. Our son is having a small plaque made which we'll fix into the ground near the two trees, explaining their history.'

'You must have been very young when you got married,' said Nancy.

'Oh we were. I was 16 and Kenneth, my husband, was 17. We were very proper in those days you know. We kissed just once before we got married and afterwards I worried for a month that I'd get pregnant.' She laughed. I checked their blood pressures. They were both fine. When they'd gone I scribbled a note to myself to ask Peter if he had any special 'Congratulations on your 80th Wedding Anniversary' cards.

'I'm utterly drained,' admitted Nancy, after the last patient had left, an hour and a half later. For the first time in weeks there were no calls to be done. 'Do you mind if I have a nap?' she asked. 'I have to be back at the university in the morning so I'm afraid I'll have to leave after lunch.'

I'd forgotten that she was leaving. 'Will you be safe to drive?'

'I'll be fine, thank you. Your wife kindly said she'd make me a flask of coffee so that if I feel drowsy I can stop and have a blast of caffeine.'

I made up the prescriptions (including the medicine for Duncan's worms – which was never collected, of course) and we had lunch together. Two hours later, after she'd had a nap, Nancy came downstairs with her bags packed and ready to leave.

'I know I should have a bunch of flowers or a bottle of wine to give you as a thank you,' said Nancy, when she'd managed to stow all her luggage into her car. 'But I haven't had time to go to Mr Marshall's shop. You've been incredibly kind to me. I came here as a complete stranger and I feel that both of you are now friends. And I've learnt so much about general practice.'

'Do you know the film 'The Blue Dahlia' starring Alan Ladd and Veronica Lake?' Patsy asked her.

'I don't think so,' said Nancy.

'It's an old film noir,' said Patsy. 'The script was by Raymond Chandler and it's all wonderful but there's one really terrific line it. Veronica Lake, talking to the Alan Ladd character, says: 'Practically all the people I know were strangers when I first met them.''

Nancy smiled. 'I like that.'

'Let us know how you get on,' I told her. 'If you're coming down this way take a detour and come and see us.'

'I'd love to do that!'

She hugged Patsy, shook hands with me and climbed into her sports car. A minute later all that was left of her was the throaty sound of her car disappearing up the lane.

'I think she'll make a good doctor,' said Patsy.

'She'd make a darned good GP,' I said. 'It's a pity she's set her heart on becoming a hospital specialist. You can't blame her, I suppose. There's more money and more kudos for hospital consultants than there is for general practitioners. But it's a pity.'

'You never know,' said Patsy. 'People do change their minds.'

'Hmm,' I said thoughtfully. I didn't think she would change her mind.

'Would you like another cup of coffee?'

'That's a splendid idea.'

I made a lemon meringue pie this morning. I put a couple of slices in a box for Nancy, to go with her flask of coffee. Would you...?'

'...it would be a pity not to have a slice,' I said, not waiting for her to finish. 'Lemon meringue pie always goes off very quickly if you don't eat it straight away.'

'Where on earth did you hear that?'

'Oh, I think I read something about it in the 'British Medical Journal'.'

Patsy laughed.

It was very good lemon meringue pie. I had two slices and felt I'd earned them.

We'd both enjoyed having Nancy as a guest but we agreed that it was good to have Bilbury Grange to ourselves again.

Chase Anderson

The final patient, who came in right at the end of the evening surgery, was an American. I didn't even need to hear him speak to know he was American. He was huge, around six foot five or six foot six inches tall, and he looked like a professional wrestler or, more probably, a professional American football player. Stick padding on him, as American football players are fitted out, and he would have been as big as a small house. As he entered he removed a most extraordinary hat which, even after some thought, I find difficult to describe. It looked a little like a round Fedora with the brim turned up all around. He removed the hat with a theatrical flourish and I was slightly disappointed when he did not skim the hat across the room and have it land, with precision, on some suitable surface. When he smiled, which was most of the time, he displayed two rows of perfectly white, natural teeth which reminded me of the film star James Coburn. His blond hair was cut in a crew cut and his face was sunburned, not in the curiously artificial way people get sunburned when they've spent two weeks lying on a beach in Spain, but in the natural way people get sunburned when they spend a good deal of their time out of doors in a warm climate. He looked like the sort of man who wore faded jeans a good deal and who spent more time chopping wood or breaking horses than he spent sitting by the pool sipping Martinis. He wore a green and tan checked sports coat which fit him so well that it had obviously been made for him, a green open necked shirt, tan coloured trousers and cowboy boots. On his wrist I could see the shine of a gold Rolex which no mugger would have dared to try to take from. He was the sort of fellow that even would-be muggers would be polite to. 'After you, sir,' they'd say, holding the door open for him. If he'd come in and put his passport down on my desk it wouldn't have been easier to guess where he came from.

I said hello and pointed to the chair on the other side of my desk, hoping that it wouldn't give up the ghost when he sat on it. Before he sat he held out a huge hand. Nervously, I took it and shook it. His grip was firm but I was grateful that he was gentle with my hand. He told me his name was Chase Anderson.

'Hi, doc,' he said. 'Thanks for seeing me.' He looked around. 'This is amazing. I just arrived here ten minutes ago and here I am sitting down opposite a doctor. In the States I'd be grateful if I could see my doctor the same week, let alone the same day. When I spoke to my agent in London an hour ago she told me I'd probably have to wait a few days or even a week or two to see anyone.' He looked around again. 'Please don't be offended but this looks like one of those 19th century doctor's surgeries they had in Victorian times.'

'The furniture is mostly Victorian,' I admitted. 'And I'm not offended. What can I do for you?'

'I've developed this pain in my foot,' he said. 'I know it probably sounds crazy but it feels as though I'm standing on a sharp piece of glass. I've looked at my foot and I'm darned if I can see anything wrong with it.'

'One foot or both feet?'

'Just the one foot. The Left one.'

'Have you ever had anything like it before?'

'No. Never had a day's illness except the measles and the chicken pox when I was a kid. I've been blessed with good health.'

'You don't take any medicines?'

'Nothing. Not a thing.'

'Whereabouts on the foot is the pain?'

'Right near the heel bone.'

'Does anything seem to make it better or worse?'

'Well, the funny thing is that it's worse when I'm lying down in bed. You'd think it would be better then but it isn't. It wakes me up sometimes. And then when I get out of bed in the morning and put my foot on the floor the pain is excruciating. Seriously, the first time it happened I felt sure I'd trodden on a nail in the floor, or a piece of glass.'

'When you walk about does the pain get worse or better?'

'That's the other funny thing about it – if I walk about a bit the pain goes away. Just disappears.'

I examined his foot and there was nothing to see except that there was a little tenderness where the plantar fascia met his heel bone. 'Let me look at the other foot.'

He removed his right boot and sock and I examined that foot. Again there was no sign of anything wrong.

'But the pain comes back?'

'It comes back sometimes when I walk or run. Not always, but sometimes.'

'And it's bad at night.'

'Exactly. Do you know what it is, doc?'

'The pain is mainly around the heel?'

'Yes it is.'

'Does it go towards the toes?'

'Funny you should ask that, yes it does!'

'You've got something called plantar fasciosis,' I told him. 'It's sometimes called plantar fasciitis but that would suggest an inflammation and there isn't usually any inflammation. You can put your boots and socks back on.'

'So, two questions, doc. What caused it and can you do anything about it? Do I need any tests?' He paused, as he put his socks back on. 'Please don't tell me I need an operation. I hate hospitals. I think I may have a phobia about them.'

'I think I can help you get rid of it,' I told him. I didn't mention that there were three questions, not two.

'That's great news!' said the American, now struggling a little with his boots. They were dark brown leather, extensively tooled and had very high heels. 'Thanks, doc! So what do we have to do? No drugs I hope.'

'No, no drugs. If it doesn't go away and you're still around here we could try corticosteroid injections but I'd rather not. Do you ever walk barefoot?'

'Yeah, in hotels or round my ranch, I do. I like feeling the ground under my feet.' He had now finished struggling into his boots.

'Well, don't. Not for the time being.'

'OK, doc.' To my astonishment he then reached into his right hand jacket pocket and took out a leather pouch. From the pouch, which was full of tobacco, he took a packet of cigarette papers and removed a single paper. He put the packet back into the pouch and then began to roll a cigarette. I watched, fascinated and appalled as he produced an almost perfect looking cigarette in very little more time than it would have taken the average smoker to shake a machine made cigarette out of its packet. He looked up and saw me watching.

'Oh, don't worry, doc!' he said, grinning. 'I'm not going to smoke it here. I just find it relaxing.' He examined the finished cigarette and slipped it into the breast pocket of his jacket. He then put the leather pouch back into his pocket.

'Do you jog?' I asked

'Yes, I do.'

'Well, don't do that either. Not for a while. Walking is fine. But walk with shorter strides. Stretch your calf muscles and your feet a couple of times a day.'

He wiggled his feet and pulled his toes up towards his knees. 'Like this?'

'Just like that!'

'And put those boots away for now and get some really well fitting shoes that provide good support for your feet.'

'Is there a shoe shop round here?'

'There are a couple in Barnstaple. There's a shop in Bilbury and it sells shoes but although the guy who runs it is a friend of mine I don't recommend you go there. He'll sell you cheap plastic shoes that won't do your feet any favours.'

'Thanks for that. And what's caused the damned pain in the first place?'

'Underneath your foot there is a band of fascia which runs from your toes to your heel bone. The pain is caused by constant stress on the fascia. Wearing high heels and walking barefoot make it worse. As does jogging – particularly on hard ground.'

'I understand!' he said, with a huge cheery smile. 'This all sounds like good news. No need for X-rays and so on?'

'We could get some X-rays done, or even an MRI scan, but I don't think they'll help much with the diagnosis or the treatment. How long are you going to be in Bilbury?'

'I'm really down here looking for somewhere quiet to rest up while I finish a book,' he said. 'I've been in London seeing my UK publisher and they and my British agent were nagging me about the book I was due to deliver two months ago. My agent, who is bossier than my first wife who was as bossy as I thought a human being could be, told me to get away and find a cottage somewhere, preferably in the very middle of nowhere, where I could hide away, be done with life, avoid the inevitable distractions to which I am a constant victim, and get down to finishing the book. They're a bit peeved because they've sold the book, the paperback rights and the film rights. My agent assures me that Al Pacino and Gene Hackman are pretty well signed up to play the leads though there isn't a script or a title yet and agents lie more than estate agents. And there's vague talk of getting Brando to play a super heavy – just a week's work for a couple of million dollars sort of thing. Apparently, the producer sees him sitting in a poorly lit corner while glaring and growling menacingly. Brando doesn't like having too many words to remember so glaring and growling will suit everyone. If I don't produce the book pretty quickly we'll lose them all. If I go back to the States I'll mess around for six months so I thought if I could find a little cottage somewhere I could just lock myself away and finish the darned thing. But I'll need someone to come and cook my breakfast and luncheon, do the shopping and the laundry, clean and tidy and make the bed. I can finish the book in another six or eight weeks if I find the right place. If I stay in a hotel I'll be distracted – I'll find someone interesting to talk to, or a pretty girl to flirt with and the book will never get done.' He grinned at me. 'Have you ever noticed that life has no neat plots? I get distracted very easily. I'm a sucker for a good story or a pretty face and a few curves in the right places,' he confessed. He leant forwards, as though he suddenly thought of something that was important. 'I don't suppose you know anyone who has a cottage I could rent? Somewhere in the middle of nowhere would suit me down to the ground – but not so far from civilisation that I couldn't pop to a pub in the evening. By the way is there a pub round here? One of your old-fashioned English pubs with a skittle alley and a genial landlord but preferably none of your lubricious young English barmaids? I believe a fellow is entitled to a drink after work and I prefer to drink in company. A couple of cocktails help ease the blood around the brain. Do you know that productivity was never as high in America as when the executives were all drunk after lunch? The economy grew by 9% a year when the happy hour was at lunchtime.' He thought for a moment and smiled. 'And I've done a good few interviews with Fleet Street journalists and believe me they can put it away by the bucket load. Most of the ones I've met really do keep a bottle of gin in the bottom drawer of their filing cabinet.'

'You're not married?'

'Not at the moment, as far as I'm aware. I keep trying but it never seems to take! Maybe I've got some sort of allergy. I've got a couple of kids at college. One is studying flag design and the other is studying the evolution of the lanyard in Western society. Or something like that. They both change courses at least once a term. Life for me has always been a long train journey. Some of the time I just sit there comfortably, enjoying the ride. Looking at the scenery and enjoying the peace and quiet. And then we go into a tunnel and everything goes black and noisy and you don't know how long it's going to last. And then someone walks by and spills coffee all over you. And then you go to the bar and meet someone interesting. And all the time you have this feeling that the train is going to crash and end it all. Which, of course, it will because in the end we all die.'

I looked at him and waited for the rest of the monologue. It was, I thought, a good job that he was the last patient of the day.

'I have an odd way of looking at life,' he said with a smile and a shrug. 'But it's probably having an odd way of looking at life that enables me to earn a lot of money so I'm not complaining.'

'There's a pub in Bilbury called The Duck and Puddle,' I told him. 'You go past Jarvis's Field, turn left at Holborrow's corner, follow the road past Tolland's Two Fields' and then go left when the road sort of peters out and there's a narrow lane on your right.' I couldn't help laughing at the look on his face.

'Don't the roads around here have names?'

'Not officially,' I said. 'Fields usually have names and landmarks have names. But the council never got round to naming the lanes and we like it that way. But finding the pub is easy. If you just drive round the village you'll pass it eventually. It's almost impossible not to.'

'Almost?'

'Almost.'

'What's Holborrow's corner? Is there a building or some natural landmark there?'

'There's absolutely nothing to see. But it's where a farmer called Jimmy Holborrow fell asleep at the wheel and drove his tractor into a ditch in 1935.'

'That's it? That's all? And he gets a corner named after him?'

'Well it did happen approximately once a week for seven months. Then he filled in the ditch so that it couldn't happen again.'

'What's the pub like? Hunting prints on the wall? Juke box in one corner and a Space Wars machine in the other? Brassy barmaid? Collection of horse brasses nailed up above the fireplace? Framed mottoes hanging on the wall behind the bar? Favoured customers' mugs hanging on nails?'

'None of those. Absolutely none of those.'

'Good. That's excellent. And this is the best pub in the neighbourhood?'

'It's the very best in the village. Actually it's the best in Devon. The best in England.'

'Is there another in the village?'

'No.' I laughed again. 'Actually, I'm serious, it's the best pub you'll ever find anywhere. They have a skittle alley, a very genial landlord and a landlady who makes the very best pub food you could ever hope to find. Skittles is nothing much like ten pin bowling – you do know that, don't you?'

'I gather skittles is the father of ten pin bowling.'

'More like the grandfather. The skittles – or pins – are usually fairly roughly-made, and carved from heavy pieces of solid wood, and the bowling balls are solid wood too, with no finger holes. The spectators tend to stand each side of the skittle alley and the ball and the skittles are quite likely to go flying – making it a very dangerous game for the spectators rather than the players. Ten pin billing, the modern version, is pretty sanitised in comparison. I can't remember the last time the Duck and Puddle had a skittles competition without someone being injured. I'm the official Medical Officer for all skittles competitions.'

'For a substantial fee I hope!'

'Free whisky and as many free attempts to win the pig as I can manage.'

'Is bowling for the pig the same as your skittles?'

'Yes, it is. I've never won a pig but the last Americans who came to Bilbury won a pig in a Duck and Puddle competition. Sadly, although he was quite small at the time, they didn't think they could smuggle a pig onto their aeroplane, and their pig, called Cedric, is now a permanent resident of a pigsty in our garden. If you need a bed for a night or two, the Duck and Puddle has rooms to rent, and Frank and Gilly who run the pub will look after you so well that you'll probably never want to leave and probably never write a word of your book. Just as you finish breakfast it'll be time for your eleven o'clock scones, rock cakes and coffee. Then there's lunch. And when you've got past lunch you'll segue straight into afternoon tea.'

'And then into dinner and supper.'

'Precisely.'

'Apart from excellent food does this pub have any of those wonderful little historical artefacts that make your English pubs so irresistible?'

'Well, there is Lord Turnberry's Crack in the wall along the side of the car park. I think that counts as a historical artefact.'

'What in the name of everything blazing is Lord Turnberry's Crack?'

'Back in the 16th century, Lord Turnberry, who owned several thousand acres of Exmoor, lived in a mansion of which the wall is now the only bit still standing. In a drunken rage, he killed three of his servants, an osler, an under gardener and a footman. Afterwards, he was so full of remorse that he killed himself. He jammed the hilt of his sword into a crack in the wall, so that the blade was pointing straight out. He then walked away, turned, faced the sword and ran straight onto it at full speed. It was his own personal version of hari kari. He apparently lived for three weeks in absolute agony, before dying during the night. Apparently the screams could be heard as far east as Lynton and as far West as Barnstaple.'

'Is that true?'

'So they say. They also say that the wall is haunted. Every year Frank fills the crack in the wall with cement and every year the cement falls out within a week.'

'I must make a point to see Lord Turnberry's Crack!' laughed the American.

'I can probably help you with a cottage too. A couple of my patients have just bought a huge house a few miles from here and they have a house to rent. I haven't seen it but it might be suitable. You won't have difficulty finding someone to be a housekeeper for you while you're here. If you have any problems with that let me know and I'll ask around.'

'I guess you know a lot of the people in this village?'

'All of them, and most of them intimately.'

'I guess you would at that. Do they mix drinks and make cocktails in your Duck and Puddle?'

'What sort of cocktail did you have in mind?'

'Oh, a 'Singapore sling' or a 'sidecar' and for the morning after a 'horse's neck', 'sufferin' bastard', 'third rail', 'corpse reviver' – that sort of thing. Great pick me ups, hangover cures, hair of the dog I think you call them.'

'I'm not sure Frank makes a lot of cocktails.'

'Frank is the barman?'

'He's the landlord. He runs the pub with his wife Gilly. You'll like them both. Frank looks after the bar and Gilly prepares the food.'

'Well if they're running a pub they must be able to mix drinks!'

'Well, I'm sure they can make you a shandy, I suppose you could call that a sort of English cocktail.'

'I've not heard of that one. What's a shandy?'

'It's half beer and half lemonade. If you have a pint of shandy it contains half a pint of beer and half a pint of lemonade.'

Mr Anderson looked at me as if I were having fun with him. 'Is that for real? The English mix beer with lemonade and call it a cocktail?' He laughed, rather nervously I thought.

'Well, they don't actually call it a cocktail. But it's a mixture of two drinks. It's popular with women and men who are driving and don't want to lose their driving licence if they get stopped by the police on the way home.'

'Do you have many policemen in the village?'

'No. Our last one died and never really got replaced. Once in a blue moon one wanders by. You have a car?'

'Oh yes, I have a car. I bought a Jaguar in London. One of those E type fancy sports cars that are still all the rage – they call it the Jaguar XK-E back home in the States. But I think I should have perhaps bought something a little tougher, higher off the ground and more suitable for your tiny lanes. One of those Land Rovers or a Jeep might be better, don't you think?'

'Probably,' I agreed. 'You can probably rent an old Land Rover at the Bilbury garage. Or you can drive into Barnstaple and rent something from one of the big hire companies.'

'Oh, I think I'd rather get one locally. '

I gave him the address of the Bartons at the Bilbury garage. I was beginning to feel like an information office.

'Sounds perfect. I could park the Jaguar at the garage and rent their Land Rover.'

He stood up, towering above me, though I now realised that at least an inch and a half of the height was down to the boots.

'Thanks, doc,' he said. 'Thanks very much.'

'What sort of books do you write?'

'Oh, when I was an associate professor at Yale I used to write serious literary stuff – books on English literature that sold 100 copies and that no one ever read, and novels that got marvellous reviews but sold in minute numbers. I discovered that I am not by inclination a teacher. Do you remember that stupid adage your school days are the best days of your life?'

I laughed and nodded.

'Well most people I know would agree that, on the whole, their school days were pretty miserable. Most of the university staff I worked with wanted to do something else for a living but had settled into the comfortable life. Like dentists! Have you noticed that dentists all want to do something else? They want to do something else but can't give up their job because the money is too good.'

I couldn't help smiling. I knew one dentist who still dreamt of becoming a professional golfer and another whose heart was still set on becoming a painter. Both had big mortgages and posh cars and knew, in their hearts, that they would never realise their dreams.

'I always wanted to be a writer and so when I started out I wrote the sort of books that I thought I was supposed to write. However, I discovered that the literary novel is pretty well dead now. Modern critics sneer at anything written before 1960 and not many of the great authors of the 19th and 20th centuries will survive. Only the genre novel is still alive and kicking – romance, crime and thrillers are big money earners. But go into a bookshop in London and look for books by H.G.Wells, D.H.Lawrence, Arnold Bennett, Thomas Hardy, Evelyn Waugh, Somerset Maugham, Aldous Huxley, John Galsworthy or George Bernard Shaw and you'll struggle to find more than one or two of their best known books. 'Brideshead Revisited' and 'Scoop' are pretty well all that are left of Waugh. Shaw is remembered for 'My Fair Lady' which is only pretty loosely based on 'Pygmalion' and Orwell just for the books they filmed – '1984' and 'Animal Farm'. Even the best thriller writers are forgotten. Eric Ambler, the best of them all, is already damned near forgotten, bless him, and John Buchan, Sapper and Dornford Yates are all regarded as politically incorrect. Charles Dickens is still around, by the skin of his teeth, but the politically correct want him banned and they will doubtless succeed. Jane Austen and the Brontes survive because of the films but how many people actually read their books? Incidentally, I feel so sorry for Branwell, the wretched brother of the Bronte sisters. Is it any wonder that he drank? We'd all drink if we had to live with those three. Wilkie Collins is gone and William Makepeace Thackeray is now just remembered for 'Vanity Fair' and then only for the Myrna Loy film.' He sighed and there was, I thought, some sadness in it. 'American authors are treated just the same. Hemingway and Scott Fitzgerald are legends because of the films and the biographies. And J.D.Salinger is J.D.Salinger but how many people now read Herman Melville, Henry James, William Faulkner, Toni Morrison or John Steinbeck for pleasure? Students read the condensed exam versions but how many people walk onto a plane with a book by Mark Twain in their pocket? When did anyone last read 'Gone with the Wind'? How many copies of Emily Dickinson's books do they sell in the stores? When did anyone last pick up anything by Kafka, Tolstoy or Dostoyevsky at an airport? How many people read Goethe or Mann? Everyone knows about Victor Hugo, Balzac and Alexander Dumas, pere et fils, but they know the films that have been made of the books – not the books. Poets live on only in books of quotations, unless they have a talent for turning their rhymes into songs or making fools of themselves when drunk or have a small talent for appearing on television as your John Betjeman has. I wish it weren't so but it is. Maybe one day, in the 1980s, 1990s or 21st century, someone will find a way for people to read books on computers and then they'll be fashionable again. Who knows? I'm afraid I don't have the patience to wait and I don't have any yearning to be a personality on television a la Mailer and so I've gone over to the dark side. I was speaking at a book convention in Ohio one winter and at the end of the convention, I went to the hotel desk to ask the receptionist to phone for a cab to take me to the airport. 'When is your flight?' she asked. I told her. But then the author standing behind me, a guy who writes very successful thrillers, asked her to fix him a cab. She asked him the same question. 'Whenever I arrive at the airport,' he replied, completely dead pan. There and then I decided I wanted to be successful, and to have my own jet which took off when I got to the airport, and so I decided to write the sort of books that people want to read. I quite quickly found, to my surprise and delight, that they were the sort of books I enjoyed writing. So now I just write thrillers and comedy westerns which are most definitely what the public want. I tried writing a bodice ripper but the result was embarrassing so I didn't do any more. Fortunately, I had published it under a pen name and it was soon forgotten. I resigned from Yale after I sold my first film rights. Since then it's been all downhill to the bank. 'Death Wears Red Velvet Slippers', 'His Gun Talked Softly but Spoke of Death', 'He Carried Death in his Holster' – that sort of stuff. They mostly have a smoking gun and a pneumatic blonde on the cover.'

'Not the sort of books they hand out as Sunday School prizes?'

He laughed. 'Possibly not.'

'But obviously very successful! I've heard of all those.'

'Oh, there's quite a market for my sort of books. Heaven knows, I'm living proof that money can't buy you love but a fat wallet can buy you a suite in a fine hotel, a splendid meal, a bottle of champagne, a decent brandy, an excellent cigar and enviable companionship. People think it's only old men who read westerns but I've got as many women readers as men. The marketing people tell me the average reader of westerns is 46-years-old and works in an office. The same is true of the readers of thrillers. People from 12 to 102 read them. I don't get any reviews in the smart papers or the monthly magazines and if I do any interviews they usually manage to write something snide about me. Some guy over here got really peeved when he told me that I sold more books than anyone else in England. I don't know why he blamed me for it but he certainly did. He said I was the only author in the world who wrote downmarket of Mickey Spillane. They don't much like Mickey either. A guy complained to Mickey that he had written seven of the world's top ten bestselling books – ever. Mickey told him it would have been more but at the time he'd only written seven books.' He grinned. 'But I don't lose too much sleep over any of those people. The book I haven't yet finished has already been sold to publishers in 32 languages. They'll print a quarter of a million.'

'What's your new book about?'

'I wish I could tell you.'

'You haven't started it?'

'Not exactly in the sense of having words on paper,' he said. 'But this one is a thriller and I've got some ideas. I write thrillers and westerns alternately. I have a regular hero who appears in all my thrillers. Readers like some continuity. In this book he's going to help some unfortunate dame out of a corner, trade wisecracks with a pal in the police force and beat up an assortment of bad guys.' He laughed. 'You may recognise the storyline. Real life is unbelievable because there is no plot and the characters are entirely unpredictable and unreliable. Readers who buy my books, bless them, want a plot and some predictable, reliable characters. I'm selling entertainment and escapism not education. I know a guy who writes romantic fiction, you know the beating heart, heaving bosom sort of stuff. He starts with the last line and works his way backwards. I don't think I could work like that. I like to start at the beginning, meander about a bit, bury some bad guys, give the hero some good times and end up happily ever after.'

'I do seem to remember having come across that plot.'

'Exactly. It's what the readers want. If they want round wheels, give them round wheels say I. Let someone else try to persuade them to like square wheels.'

'Do you write on a computer?'

'Not on your life. If they ever make genuinely portable computers I might try one. Most of the ones I've seen weigh a ton and a half and need two men to move them and connect them up. I type on a battered old Olivetti portable and then make a copy of the pages every night and put the copy in a safe place somewhere. Do you know where I can rent a photocopier?'

'Ask Peter Marshall at the village shop,' I suggested. 'I've no doubt he'll be able to fix you up.' I felt confident in saying this. Peter would find a giraffe if a customer wanted one, especially if they were cash buyers.

He picked up his hat as he prepared to leave.

'I do like your hat,' I told him. 'What's it called?'

He looked at it, held it by the brim, and moved it around as if he'd never seen it before. 'In America we call it a Gambler's hat, in England it's a Chesterton, after G.K.Chesterton the author who always wore one like it, and in Ireland it's called a De Valera, in memory of the politician. You approve? You are a hat man?'

'I like hats, and I approve!'

After he'd left, I made up a few prescriptions, answered a few letters and then I more or less forgot about the voluble but charming American author and went to have my lunch. I didn't expect to see him again, and little did I realise that Chase Anderson, the successful American author of thrillers and westerns, was destined to be the central character in a mystery of his own.

The Mystery Illness

I can remember exactly where I was, and what I was doing, when I first heard that Chase Anderson, the American author who was staying in Bilbury to write his latest book, had suddenly become seriously ill.

I was sitting in the snug at the Duck and Puddle with Thumper Robinson, Patchy Fogg and Frank Parsons.

The four of us were sitting staring at the log fire which Frank keeps alive throughout the year, even on warm days in summer. Occasionally, in July or August, a tourist who is lost and comes into the pub to ask the way will look at the fire and express surprise. Frank points out that the fire is there to provide entertainment as much as warmth. 'You can sit and watch the flames flickering and the logs turning into ash. You can lose yourself in day dreams as you see pictures forming and disappearing in the fireplace.'

The Duck and Puddle doesn't have a television set in the bar and so the fire is, as it should be, the centre of the room. (There is a television set upstairs in one of the guest bedrooms but it works only very occasionally and very few visitors bother to struggle against the constantly sliding picture. Frank did erect an aerial high on the hill behind the pub but the aerial blows down regularly and doesn't make much difference to the quality of the reception.)

But the fire isn't just a focal point for the room ('bringing things together nicely,' as interior decorators are prone to say). When the oven doesn't work for one reason or another (the power supply in North Devon is best described as intermittent) Frank cooks food over the fire. He keeps a frying pan, a set of saucepans and an old kettle in a cupboard under the dart board, all ready to be used on a metal tripod which Patchy bought in an auction in South Molton. The cooking vessels are all smoke and flame blackened; a condition which adds a vaguely smoky flavour to anything which is prepared in them. Thumper and Patchy both swear that sausages cooked in the blackened saucepan have a unique and delectable flavour and that when they are served Frank deserves three Michelin stars.

We were discussing the delightfully idiosyncratic Peter Marshall's latest campaign.

Peter, as most visitors to Bilbury are aware, runs the village shop. He is the only purveyor of any kind for some distance in all directions and is, therefore, in the position of anyone with a monopoly: he can pretty much do what he likes and never worry over much about upsetting his customers. Frank and Gilly, who run the Duck and Puddle and who are in a similar position in that there is no other pub in Bilbury, are almost invariably polite to their customers (Gilly perhaps more consistently polite than Frank) but Peter Marshall does not suffer fools, or indeed anyone else, and has a list in his shop of all the people who are banned from buying anything from him. The list, now quite long, has never been revised and still includes the name of a man who was banned from the shop in 1954 for arguing with Peter about who had been first to climb Mount Everest. Peter claimed that the first climbers to stand on top of the mountain had been George Mallory and Sandy Irvine. The customer, a bank manager from Sunderland who, together with his wife, was on a camping holiday in Devon, had claimed that Edmund Hillary and Tenzing Norgay had been the first. Neither would admit defeat. The bank manager argued that the entire world reckoned that New Zealander Sir Edmund was the first on top of Everest and that Hillary had been knighted, to some extent for arranging to reach the top of the mountain to coincide with Queen Elizabeth's coronation. Peter insisted that Mallory and Irvine had been there first, in 1924, and that their failure to return from their successful expedition merely added romance to the conquering of the mountain. The discussion ended abruptly when Peter used one of his 30 shilling mops (each one accompanied by a label claiming that the item had been 'hand-made by English artisans' and was 'guaranteed for life', though there was no mention of whether the mop was guaranteed for its own life or the life of the purchaser) to push the bank manger out of the shop. The man was told that he was banned from the shop for life and Peter wrote the man's name on a piece of paper (actually the back of an overdue invoice from a potted meat supplier) which he put by the till. At that time the piece of paper contained only the word 'BANNED' and the name of the bank manager. The next day the man's wife had turned up at the shop and asked, timidly, if she too was banned. Peter decided, after some deliberation, that the ban (and all future bans) would be individual and specific and the wife was allowed to purchase comestibles of her choice. The list, which now consists of 17 pieces of paper, stuck together with sticky tape, still has the bank manager's name at the very top. He and his wife, who now have a holiday caravan on a site nearby, still shop at Peter's store but only the wife is allowed into the shop. The banned husband, still persona non grata, sits in the car and waits. If the man's wife has any queries she has to go out to the car to consult with her husband. Peter, who is as unforgiving as he can be loyal, stands eternal guard to make sure that the banned man doesn't sneak in through the front door.

'I hear that Peter has introduced a universal ban on men wearing shorts,' said Frank, who has in the past expressed some unhappiness about allowing hikers in khaki shorts to enter the Duck and Puddle. 'He won't let adults into the shop if they are wearing shorts.'

'I heard that he had a huge row with a scoutmaster from Milton Keynes,' said Patchy. 'Peter said that the scouts could enter the shop but that his new ban covered all adult males over the age of 18 – especially if they had knobbly knees and varicose veins as the scoutmaster allegedly had.'

'Wise move to let the boys into the shop,' said Frank. 'Small boys buy large quantities of sweets – especially when they are away from home on a camping holiday.'

'The scoutmaster got red faced and very cross and asked if Peter also banned women in shorts,' said Patchy. 'Peter said that for women it wasn't a hard and fast rule as it was with men, and the scoutmaster said that was sexist behaviour, stormed out in high dudgeon and, in a parting shot, told Peter that he would be hearing from his solicitor. Peter said that no solicitor could alter the fact that the fellow had knobbly knees and varicose veins which made the wearing of shorts a visual insult.'

'What is high dudgeon?' asked Frank. 'I ask in innocence. It's just something I've always wondered.'

'Opposite of low dudgeon,' suggested Thumper helpfully.

'Offended and resentful,' said Patchy. He looked at me.

I nodded. 'It means pissed off,' I said.

'Ah,' said Frank, nodding. 'That I understand.'

'So, what happened in the end?' asked Thumper.

'The troop of small boys bought all the coconut mushrooms and liquorice sticks that Peter had in the shop, while the hapless scoutmaster, parted from his troop, waited outside and quietly fumed.'

'How do you know all this?' I asked.

'Oh, Adrienne was in the shop buying a pair of those new shoes that Peter has in stock,' explained Patchy. 'She says they're all the rage and very reasonably priced. She's bought me a pair for my birthday but she won't let me see them yet.'

I was surprised by this for I had always thought that Adrienne, who is his wife and my sister-in-law, had good taste. I found myself hoping that Patsy wouldn't buy me a pair for my birthday and wondering how well I could fake delight if she did.

'I tend to agree with Peter,' said Frank. 'I always feel worried when I agree with Peter but I don't understand why so many men wear shorts. They come in here in the pouring rain and their exposed legs are red with the cold. No one over the age of 12 should ever wear shorts unless they're actually playing tennis or they've lost their trousers in a game of poker. I lost my trousers in a game of poker once and had to catch the bus home in my underpants. I'd have been delighted to wear a pair of shorts if any had been available.' He sat thoughtfully for a moment. 'I may join Peter and have a sign made saying 'No one wearing shorts will be admitted.''

I looked at him. Frank can keep a straight face better than anyone I've ever met. You can never tell whether or not he is joking.

Just then I heard the telephone start to ring.

Frank and Gilly get very few phone calls and they now only have a phone in their living room at the back of the pub, but even through thick stone walls I can hear a telephone ringing from a quarter of a mile away. I sometimes hanker after the days when messages were delivered, Paul Revere style, by men on horseback. I rather hope I'm not still practising when, as has been forecast, they introduce portable telephones which you can carry in your pocket.

Once a month, a visitor who has stayed with them before will telephone the Duck and Puddle to book a room for a few nights. Occasionally, they'll get a wrong number or a salesman who has picked the pub out of a directory will cold call and try to sell Frank or Gilly a new variety of crisps or pork scratchings or a new brand of beer. Such attempts are rarely successful for Frank and Gilly are resistant to change.

But when I'm sitting in the snug at the Duck and Puddle and the telephone rings I start to prepare myself for an emergency. Patsy and my ever loyal receptionist Miss Johnson only ring me at the pub when there is a real emergency.

A few moments later my fears were justified. Gilly came in, apologised, as she always does, as though it is her fault that the telephone has rung, and told me that my wife was on the phone.

'Do you remember that American author you saw?' Patsy asked.

'Chase Anderson?'

'That's him.'

'He rented the cottage that the people at Bodley Hall had available.'

'He did. And Thumper's cousin took on the job as housekeeper.'

'I remember you telling me.'

'Well, Thumper's cousin just rang. She says that Mr Anderson has become quite ill and she's worried about him. Would you go and take a look at him?'

I'll go straight round there. He's probably got a hangover or eaten something that's upset him.'

I said goodbye to everyone in the Duck and Puddle, climbed into the car and drove to Bodley Hall to ask for directions to their cottage which I'd never visited before. The 'so-called' cottage turned out to be much larger than I'd expected and way larger than most cottages I'd seen. In my experience most cottages have two rooms upstairs, two rooms downstairs and, if the owners have modernised the building, a bathroom upstairs and, luxury of luxuries, an indoor lavatory. Many of the cottages in Bilbury still have an outdoor loo and to bathe they put a tin bath in front of the fire and fill it with several gallons of hot water. However, the 'cottage' that Mr Anderson was renting was huge, and very impressive by cottage standards. It turned out to have three large reception rooms, five bedrooms and several bathrooms. There were huge, fancy chimneys and even a turret. It didn't look like any cottage I'd ever seen before.

Thumper's cousin, Gladys Bunting, met me at the cottage door and led me straight upstairs to the bedroom which Mr Anderson had chosen.

The room was surprisingly small and although the house had a number of rooms downstairs, the author had clearly been pretty well living in the one room. There was a portable typewriter on a small table and there were piles of newspapers, magazines and books on just about every available flat surface and piled on the floor too. A photocopier stood on another small table. The room didn't seem to have been decorated since the 19th century. The walls were covered with dark green wallpaper which looked as if it had probably been pretty expensive when a rich Victorian had chosen it and had it hung. I could see why it had been left untouched. I was surprised it hadn't started peeling off because the room was a bit damp. The furniture was good, Victorian brown furniture – the sort that is solid, functional, reasonably pleasing to the eye and pretty well indestructible. If a bomb dropped on a house full of brown Victorian furniture the house might be flattened but the brown furniture would remain undamaged, unperturbed and covered in dust and fragments of brick or stone. It was, Gladys told me, the wallpaper which had attracted Mr Anderson to the room. A three bar electric fire was permanently switched on in order to take the edge off the damp.

When I'd last met Chase Anderson he had looked like an advertisement for good health. In the short intervening period there had been a massive deterioration and he now was lying in bed, looking worryingly close to moribund. I couldn't remember seeing such a dramatic change in anyone's appearance.

I greeted him, more cheerfully than I felt. I have never thought that it is the doctor's role to spread gloom and despondency, but, rather to radiate hope and optimism. I then sat down on a chair which Gladys had put beside the bed. 'What's been happening?' I asked him. He was shivering and there was a strange, red, pigmented rash on his skin. He was sweating and the sheets appeared to be soaked. Despite this the windows were open. I went to shut one of the windows but he stopped me. 'I hate having windows shut.'

'What's been happening to you?' I asked again.

'I think I must have a damned bug,' he said, speaking softly and slowly as though even that effort was too much for him. I had to lean closer to hear what he said. 'It's a bloody nuisance. I'd just got started on the book. It was coming along fine.'

'He's had diarrhoea and vomiting all day,' said Gladys. 'Fortunately, I found that in a cupboard,' she said, pointing to an old-fashioned bedpan with a handle; something that used to be called a gazunder because it was kept under the bed.

'I use it for the stuff coming up but I'm not so far gone that I use it for the stuff going down,' said Mr Anderson. 'It's got a picture of some scary looking bloke on the bottom.'

'The scary looking bloke is Lloyd George,' I explained. 'He was British Prime Minister fifty years ago, during and after the First World War, though they called it the Great War then, before they started numbering them. Why poor old Lloyd George became a target I can't imagine. The manufacturers used to put pictures of Hitler on the bottom of those things during World War II.'

I asked Gladys to tell me what Mr Anderson had eaten. I was hoping he'd perhaps eaten something that had upset his stomach and that, if he didn't eat it again, he'd soon recover.

But there had been absolutely nothing abnormal in his diet. He'd had a shepherd's pie with vegetables for dinner the previous evening and some ice cream and fruit for dessert. Gladys, who had prepared the meal, said she'd had the same food but that she had absolutely no symptoms and felt fine.

'Have you got any pain?' I asked Mr Anderson.

'Terrible pain in my gut,' he said. 'And my fingers and toes feel numb and sometimes they tingle – like pins and needles. I get cramps too.'

'Anything else?'

'I've had a pain my chest,' he said. 'I get these awful spasms in my calf muscles. And I've been short of breath.'

I felt his pulse. His heart was irregular. I took his blood pressure. At 110 over 75 it was a little low. 'What's your normal blood pressure?'

'It's usually 125 over 85,' he replied. 'My publisher in the States makes me have a medical once a year. They worry I'll keel over and drop dead half way through writing a book.'

'Any other symptoms?'

'A bit of a sore throat and a cough occasionally – but not as bad as the gut symptoms. It feels as if I've swallowed an octopus that's trying to get out of both ends. And however much I drink I'm thirsty. What do you think it is, doc?'

'Not sure yet,' I replied. 'It's probably a bug of some kind. Have you got any urinary symptoms?'

'No, nothing. That's just about the one part of me that's working OK. My foot pain disappeared, by the way, doc. Your advice worked. So, thank you for that.'

I smiled my appreciation. I had begun to wonder if I'd missed something and if it was possible that the pain in his foot was somehow linked to his new symptoms. As a medical student I'd always been taught to try to find a single diagnosis to explain all of a patient's symptoms – particularly for patients under the age of 70 or so. (Multiple pathology is, of course, unhappily common among older patients, whose various bits and pieces tend to begin to wear out at the same time, and whose symptoms may not, therefore, be linked.)

I thought about admitting him to hospital but, as usual, I was influenced by the difficult journey into Barnstaple. Maybe they'd have made the diagnosis quicker than I did. Or maybe they wouldn't. We'll never know.

'I'll take some blood and get some tests done,' I told him.

I took a syringe and needle out of my bag and then took out one of the little plastic bottles I use for sending blood samples to the laboratory. I collected blood and also collected a urine sample.

When I'd finished, I looked at my watch. A courier van comes from the pathology department every day to collect blood and urine samples that need testing. The van usually arrives between 4 p.m. and 4.30 p.m. It was 3.30 p.m. when I looked at my watch.

'Make sure that he has plenty of fluids,' I told Gladys. 'Are you sleeping here?'

'I've got a room along the hallway,' said Gladys. 'I don't have a car of my own.'

'Check on him before you go to bed. And ring me if you want me to come back. Meanwhile, let's see what the tests show.'

'OK, doctor.'

'I've got a bell,' said Mr Anderson. He pointed to the bedside table upon which stood what looked like an old school bell – the sort the teacher used to ring at the end of the mid-morning break.

'I found it in a cupboard in the kitchen,' explained Gladys. 'I suspect it was probably used to call in family members who were outside the house, to tell them a meal was ready.'

'Good,' I said. 'I'll have to rush off to get these samples to the hospital. I'll be back in the morning. But ring me if there's any change.'

'Sorry to be such a bother, doc,' apologised Mr Anderson.

'You'll be fine in a day or two,' I assured him, on the basis that optimism and hope are two of any doctor's most powerful weapons. I still thought that he had an infection of some kind, a gastrointestinal bug from something he'd eaten. On my way out I 'mistakenly' blundered into the kitchen and had a quick look round. Everything seemed spotless.

But the author wasn't fine the next day and when the blood test results came back they were no help at all since everything seemed perfectly fine. According to the blood tests Mr Anderson seemed to be as healthy as he had first looked when he'd come to my surgery with a pain in his foot. But, when I visited, he clearly wasn't any better. If anything he was a little worse. He still had all the same symptoms and he looked quite exhausted. The only new symptom was that his eyes kept watering though they weren't itching and he wasn't sneezing. I could think of no new explanation for his symptoms and nothing else to do, and since his vital signs were not worrying, I told Gladys to continue to make sure that he continued to rest and drank plenty of fluids.

And then the storm began.

This was not a literal storm, however, but the arrival of Mr Anderson's literary agent from London.

I would have preferred a real North Devon storm – thunder, lightning and 80 mph gales.

The agent had been telephoning him daily to see how the new book was progressing, and on hearing that he was ill (bad news) and had stopped work (terrible news) she had leapt into her Porsche and driven to Devon from London. She was waiting by Mr Anderson's bedside when I arrived on the third day of his illness.

'Why isn't he in hospital?' she demanded the minute I walked into the room. She was a small, very thin and sharp featured woman, who was wearing an elegant suit in dark grey.

'I don't want to be in hospital,' insisted Mr Anderson before I could speak. 'And don't talk about me as if I'm demented.'

'It took me hours,' to find this place, the agent complained.

'You told me to lose myself in the country,' explained Mr Anderson.

'I didn't tell you lose yourself,' she snapped back. She turned to me. 'He hasn't worked for three days, possibly four days.' She had a curious mid-Atlantic accent. 'A lot of people are waiting for pages.

He needs to get better soon. I want someone from Harley Street to see him.'

'I'll get him well as soon as I can,' I said, rather taken aback by the ferocity of the onslaught. 'I have no objection at all if you want to bring a doctor down from London. I'm always happy to have a second opinion.'

And so the very next day a consultant physician from Harley Street appeared on the scene. He arrived in a large chauffeur driven Mercedes Benz limousine (the very latest model, of course) and he brought with him an electrocardiograph machine and several other instruments which required electricity. Gladys, said that he spent an hour and a half examining Mr Anderson and took several blood samples.

When I arrived, he admitted (in a series of long and rather bewildering sentences) that he too didn't have the foggiest idea what was wrong with our patient.

Mr Anderson's agent, who had stayed the night in a smart and expensive hotel in Taunton, was not well pleased and asked him if he could recommend a third doctor who might be able to make a diagnosis. The Harley Street consultant was not well-pleased with this and climbed back into his chauffeur driven Mercedes and disappeared. He had, actually, been quite nice to me and had paused a moment to admire my elderly vehicle Rolls Royce.

That evening I sat with Patsy listening to music on the gramophone. I'd managed to get hold of a set of long playing records of an original cast recording of Gilbert and Sullivan's 'The Mikado'.

As is our custom, Patsy and I were both reading as we listened. Patsy was reading a biography of Gertrude Jekyll, the famous gardener. And, as we listened I finished reading a biography of Napoleon Bonaparte, which Patsy had given me and which I'd been reading for some time, and had started reading a magazine article about Oscar Wilde's last days in Paris.

Suddenly, I put down the magazine and jumped up out of my chair.

'I'm going to take more blood,' I told her.
'From whom?'
'From Mr Anderson.'
'Now?'

'Yes. Now. I think I might have worked out what's wrong with him. I need to get some tests done urgently.'

'What do you think it is?'

'I'll tell you when I get back. It's a completely off the wall diagnosis. But it makes sense.'

And with that I put on my coat and shoes, rushed out of the house, jumped into the car and drove out to the cottage where Mr Anderson was staying.

He was asleep when I got there and Gladys, who came to the door, told me that she'd been in the kitchen listening to music on the wireless and reading a huge novel by Barbara Taylor Bradford.

I rushed upstairs, woke Mr Anderson and took another blood sample. To his and Gladys' astonishment I also took a sample of his hair.

'Is there another bed made up?' I asked Gladys, when I'd finished doing this.

'No. But there is a spare bed in the room next door. There are clean sheets in the linen cupboard and I can make it up. Are you staying?'

'No, it's not for me. Would you show me the room please?'

She showed me the room next door. It had been recently decorated and was much larger. The walls were painted pink and the bed was a huge four poster.

I waited while she put sheets onto the new bed and then the two of us helped move Mr Anderson into the other room.

I then went home, put the blood sample into the fridge and left a telephone message on the pathology unit's answering machine asking them to send the van round to collect my samples as early as possible on the following morning. I also told them what tests I wanted them to do.

And then I explained to Patsy what I thought might be wrong with Mr Anderson.

'Can that really happen?' she asked, astonished and incredulous. 'It seems impossible.'

'It's a crazy idea,' I admitted. 'But I can't think of any other explanation.'

The next day, the head of the pathology laboratory rang me just as I finished my morning surgery. He sounded terribly excited – like someone whose horse has just come out top in a photo finish.

'This is the first time I've ever seen a positive test for arsenic.'
'Aha! So I was right.'
'Is it a poisoning? Will the police be involved?' I got the impression he hoped they would be. Maybe he saw himself giving evidence in a high profile murder case.
'No, no, nothing like that. It's just the wallpaper.'
'The wallpaper? What do you mean, the wallpaper?'
'The room the patient is in has green Victorian wallpaper. Artists used to make green paint with arsenic. It was a very fashionable colour in the 19th century, when they used the paint for toys, clothing, furniture, curtains and food. They used it on everything but they used huge amounts on wallpaper. I read that in the middle of the 19th century there were over a million square miles of arsenic soaked wallpaper on the walls of British homes and as a result, arsenic poisoning was surprisingly common. People who spent a lot of time in rooms decorated with green wallpaper often fell ill and sometimes died. I checked. And patients who had been made ill by their wallpaper developed the usual symptoms of arsenic poisoning – vomiting, diarrhoea, stomach pains, watery eyes and a skin rash. It wasn't until the end of the 19th century that they began to suspect the wallpaper, and the stuff was ripped off in many homes. They knew it was a problem when the men hired to remove the wallpaper fell ill with symptoms of arsenic poisoning.'
'But how on earth do you get poisoned by wallpaper?'
'You breathe in the poison which just leaks out of the wallpaper – especially when the room is slightly damp which this one was. And my patient had the windows open so every puff of wind that came through the window sent fragments of arsenic into the air.
'How on earth did you make such an off-the-wall- diagnosis?' He asked, then apologised for the pun.
'It was quite fortuitous. I'd never been taught about arsenic poisoning and I'd obviously never seen a case before but I'd just finished reading a biography of Napoleon Bonaparte – dealing with the years when he was imprisoned on St Helena.'
'Of course! Napoleon was poisoned with arsenic wasn't he?'
'That's what they say. And I seem to remember that they tried to kill Rasputin with the stuff – but in his case it wasn't in the wallpaper.'
'I thought it was a stomach medicine which Napoleon took which

poisoned him – something laced with arsenic.'

'That's one theory. But another theory is that he was poisoned by the wallpaper. And experts now seem to think that is probably more likely.'

'Good heavens!'

'But I only realised it could be the wallpaper when I read an article about Oscar Wilde's last days in Paris.'

'That was when he uttered the immortal line about the wallpaper – something about one or other of us having to go? But Wilde wasn't poisoned by the wallpaper, was he?'

'No, no, he died of meningo-encephalitis caused by a chronic ear infection. The poor fellow must have been in absolute agony – no real painkillers, no antibiotics, nothing much except possibly some laudanum. I think his wallpaper was just unbearably ugly. It was just the line about the wallpaper which reminded me about the wallpaper in Napoleon's room and that linked to the green wallpaper in the room where my patient is staying.'

'How long has he been there?'

'Only about a week. The house, and the room, had been empty for decades. I checked and the people who bought the house did up all the other rooms but left the one with the green wallpaper because they thought it looked rather special. I think they thought it might be something by William Morris. You wouldn't want to tear off some original William Morris wallpaper would you? I know a house in Somerset where they found original William Morris wallpaper in a pub. Posh interior decorators spent months carefully peeling it off the wall and carting it off to London.'

'Well, I'll be jiggered! I've never heard anything quite like it. Are you going to write it up for one of the journals?'

'I think I might,' I admitted. 'How quickly is he likely to recover do you think?'

'Oh, quite quickly. Arsenic gets everywhere – muscles, hair, nails, liver, intestines and almost every organ in the body, but it is expelled from the body in no time when exposure stops. It's really very nasty stuff. Just two grains can be fatal, you know. Is your patient normally in good health?'

'Fit as a fiddle, other than this.'

'Splendid. He'll be fine then. Arsenic hangs around in the hair and nails but he should be healthy again in no time if he moves out of that room. Maybe someone should take that wallpaper off. Is it like asbestos do you think? They'll probably have to bring in special teams in protective clothing.'

The pathologist sounded very excited.

As soon as I'd put the phone down, I told Patsy that my bizarre wallpaper diagnosis was right. And then I hurried off to see Mr Anderson and to give him the surprising news that he'd been poisoned by the wallpaper in his bedroom. I was relieved that as a precaution I'd persuaded him to change rooms.

The bad news was that when I arrived I saw the Porsche belonging to the author's agent parked outside. I managed to get upstairs without seeing her but she heard me and chased up the staircase after me. In one hand she was clutching a tumbler full of something that looked like water but in the other hand she held a bottle of vodka so it seemed not unreasonable to suspect that the liquid that looked like water wasn't water at all.

'He's a lot better, doctor,' said Thumper's niece who had also heard me arrive, and who followed Mr Anderson's agent up the staircase.

I knocked on the door of his room, waited for a response and when I heard the word 'Come!' bawled at full volume I felt an immense sense of relief.

The change in Mr Anderson's health was quite astonishing. He told me that his abdominal pain had gone, he was no longer vomiting and his bowel was no longer demanding a visit to the loo every twenty minutes. He was sitting at a small desk in his new bedroom, hammering away at his portable typewriter as though determined to destroy the hapless keys. On his left hand side was a box of virgin typing paper and on his right hand side a pile of paper which, I assumed, contained his new book.

That was quite definitely the good news.

'You had arsenic poisoning!' I told him.

He stared at me, disbelievingly. 'Arsenic?'

'From the green wallpaper. The same thing happened to Napoleon Bonaparte so you're in good company.'

'I've never heard anything so stupid in all my life!' said his agent, who had followed me into the room. 'Who's been poisoning him? You can't get arsenic poisoning from wallpaper.' The literary agent looked at her author. 'You haven't been eating the wallpaper, have you?' Some people might have asked that question in a way that made it clear that the query was whimsical but I suspected that she didn't do whimsical. She didn't seem to do anything very much except sharp and snappy.

He grinned at her. 'Not a nibble. Not even licked it.'

She turned to address me. 'I don't believe that nonsense about the wallpaper. What treatment does he need? I told you he should be in hospital.'

'He doesn't need any treatment,' I told her. 'And as long as he's living and sleeping in a room which doesn't have any the green wallpaper on the walls he'll recover very quickly.'

'Do you know this for certain?'

'Yes.'

'But you're just a lowly GP aren't you? How much do you make a year?'

'Very little,' I replied honestly, far too embarrassed to give her the figure.

She stormed out of the room, still carrying a glass in one hand and a bottle in the other. I've met people I would happily describe as rancid and I have met people I would describe as rabid but she was the first person I'd ever met whom I would have felt comfortable in describing as both rancid and rabid. Gladys watched her go with an open mouth.

'Was it really arsenic? Really the wallpaper?' asked Mr Anderson.

'Yes. I've done a bit of research. Back in 1775, a German chemist called Carl Wilhelm Scheele developed a new green dye for paint, using copper sulphate, sodium carbonate and arsenious oxide. His new colour was widely used in paints, dyes and pigments and used on wallpaper. Scheele was aware that the stuff was dangerous but he didn't seem to care. 'What's a little arsenic when you've got a great new colour?' he was reported to have said.

'In 1814, a new variation of the colour appeared. This was called Schweinfurt Green or Paris Green, depending on where you were at the time.'

'And it still had arsenic in it?'

'Yes, it still contained arsenic but artists loved it. Turner, Manet, Monet and Gaugin all used it. The paint was stable except in humid and damp conditions when the arsenic evaporated from the wallpaper and became dangerous. I can't help wondering if it was the arsenic in paint that sent Van Gogh rather loopy – though he did have a penchant for absinthe, of course.'

'And the room I was in had been damp for quite a while. We had an electric heater in there to dry it out.'

'Exactly. The heater dried out the room but drew the arsenic out of the wallpaper.'

'And you say that Napoleon Bonaparte was poisoned by the wallpaper in his room?'

'Yes. Almost certainly.'

'Where? On St Helena? When he was on his second exile?'

'On St Helena. He was poisoned by arsenic gas emitted from the Paris green wallpaper in his rooms. There's evidence that the wallpaper killed quite a few people. In 1862, four children were killed by arsenic fumes which came from wallpaper.'

'But they didn't ban it?'

'Oh, they did eventually ban the dye – though then they found it useful as a rat poison – but they didn't make people tear down the green wallpaper that contained arsenic. I expect most of it has been removed over the years and people gradually forgot about the danger. You've probably been sleeping in the one room in England that still has arsenic impregnated wallpaper.'

'If I wrote jolly little Miss Marple like stories I'd use all this!' said Mr Anderson. 'But I can't see any of the villains in my books using wallpaper as a murder weapon.' He paused and grinned. 'Still, who knows...'

Suddenly, his literary agent burst back into the room. 'I've called the police,' she announced loudly. 'They're coming straight away. I'm going to tell them to arrest her!'

And she pointed to Thumper's hapless niece.

And so we all had to wait for the police to arrive.

While we waited I went into the bedroom, tore off a decent sized piece of wallpaper and put it into an envelope which Thumper's niece found for me. She was terribly upset and shaking and I don't blame her. It isn't every day that one gets accused of trying to poison someone, let alone a famous American author.

'You damned idiot!' said Mr Anderson to his agent. 'Why did you do that?'

'Do what?'

'Ring the police.'

'Someone tried to poison you!' she said, her voice raising an octave and quivering in a strange, slightly hysterical way. She put her hands on her hips and glowered at him, as if he were an errant child and she an infant school headmistress.

'No one tried to poison me – unless you count the decorator who hung the wallpaper. And he's probably been dead for the best part of a century.'

It was an hour before representatives of the local constabulary arrived. I had remained in the cottage to explain precisely what had happened. I was concerned about Thumper's niece, who had managed to maintain a brave face for a few minutes, but who was now crying and inconsolable – inconsolable at least by any of those present. I didn't blame her for being upset. No one, not even most murderers, likes being accused of murder.

Eventually, the police arrived in the persons of Sergeant Carter and Constable Benson, the only two members of the local police force who ever visit Bilbury, because they are the only ones who can visit without getting lost. Sergeant Carter, who is surprisingly short for a policeman, has a head shaped like a turnip and a nose that looked more like a walnut than seems either reasonable or believable. Constable Benson, a much taller fellow, had clearly been modelled on one of the Easter Island statues.

The desk sergeants at the police station in Barnstaple would not send any substitutes to Bilbury because they were only too aware of what had happened when Constable Duckham had been sent to investigate the apparent theft of a small article of clothing from Mrs Bellamy's washing line. After Constable Duckham had been absent for four days, Constable Lloyd was sent to investigate and then, after another three days, Sergeant Miller was sent out. The missing constables were eventually found hiding in the village bus shelter and both had to take early retirement through ill health. (They were unnoticed by the villagers because there are now no buses to Bilbury and so the bus shelter is not much used.) Sergeant Miller was found in Mrs Parrot's spare bedroom. The missing item of clothing was subsequently found being used as bedding in a squirrel's dray, and the village had breathed a collective sigh of relief when it was understood that the crime wave was over.

The whole silly nonsense with Mr Anderson took much longer to sort out than it should have done because the author's literary agent continually insisted that the officers should arrest Thumper's niece for trying to murder her client.

'If you don't arrest her I'll get someone from Scotland Yard down here,' she said. 'I know important people in the Metropolitan Police and the Home Secretary is one of my authors.'

I pointed out that this was silly and quite unnecessary and suggested to the police that they too take a sample of the deadly wallpaper, and they duly did so, placing a neatly cut four inch square of wallpaper into a plastic evidence bag.

'This is all nonsense,' said Mr Anderson's agent, becoming as close to hysterical as is it possible to become without actually being hysterical. 'These country yokels are just sticking together. I wouldn't be surprised if the doctor wasn't in on it as well.'

'And why would he do that, madam?' asked Sergeant Carter.

'Oh I don't know. It's your job to find out. Look at him!' she said pointing at me. 'For someone who is supposed to be a doctor he looks thoroughly disreputable. His shoes don't look as if they've been shined for days. I bet he's got buckets full of arsenic in his consulting room.'

I thought that this was a little unfair for I have never felt that shiny shoes are an integral part of a medical practitioner's armamentarium.

'Oh do shut up,' said Mr Anderson, wearily.

His agent looked at him, surprised. 'I'm just sticking up for you!'

'No, you're not. You're being a bloody nuisance.' He paused and thought for a moment. 'In fact you're fired, so bugger off back to London and annoy someone else. Annoy one of those politicians who are always writing their memoirs.'

'You can't fire me! We have a contract.'

'No, we don't. I have a contract with Hope Springs in New York. You look after my interests in London on her behalf. I shall simply tell her to find someone else to represent me in the UK. I'm tired, I want to finish my book, I don't need this crap and you're totally, completely and finally fired.'

And that pretty well ended what was threatening to become something of a crisis.

The agent, threatening us all with lawyers ('two very eminent barristers and a judge are clients of mine') stormed out and could be heard clashing the gears of her Porsche. Thumper's niece dried her eyes, relieved that she no longer faced a lifetime on Death Row, and I breathed a sigh of relief that Bilbury's crime scandal appeared to be over.

'I'm well shot of that one,' sighed Mr Anderson. 'She's got an ego the size of a planet and a brain the size of a pea. When she signs her name, the scrawl takes up a whole page. It's a good job she doesn't write books because signing each one would use up a gallon of ink.'

'Is your agent in New York really called Hope Springs?'

'Her parents had an English sense of humour. I tell everyone that her mission in life is to find a man called Eternal so that she can marry him, adopt a hyphen and become a legend. Can I drink booze?' he asked. 'Will it mix badly with whatever arsenic is left in my system?'

'I have no idea whether or not alcohol interacts with arsenic,' I admitted. 'It would be an experiment.'

'Where would man be without experimentation?'

Thumper's niece fetched a bottle of malt whisky from the kitchen and after the two policemen had temporarily removed their helmets (thereby removing themselves from duty regulations) the five of us drank toasts to everyone and everything we could think of including Napoleon Bonaparte.

Thinking about the Future

I had been up since 6 a.m. when I'd had to visit a farm just a few hundred yards past the Duck and Puddle public house. An insomniac had got up to attend to his garden and had tripped over his excited Labrador. He had cut his head and there was blood everywhere. It looked much worse than it was, as scalp wounds often do, and cleaning the wound and putting in a few stitches had taken only minutes. Since the wound had bled profusely it seemed unlikely that infection would be a problem.

By 7.15 a.m. I was back at Bilbury Grange.

It wasn't worth going back to bed so I fed the animals (tame and wild) and made myself a cup of tea and a couple of slices of toast.

I was sitting on a chair outside the back door with my tea and toast on the table in front of me. The sun was shining and I could feel the early warmth of the day.

I was thinking about a developer's plans for a new mobile home site, to be built on the coast just a mile and a half from Bilbury Grange. The developers were applying for permission to put 500 homes on the site straight away and to expand the capacity to 1,000 or 1,500 mobile homes within two years. It takes no time at all to put hundreds of mobile homes onto a fairly flat field. The developers said they would build some simple roads, put up a shop and set up basic services such as drains, water and electricity. A whole new village would appear virtually overnight. There would be hundreds of extra vehicles crowded into our narrow lanes.

And the developers had already asked if I would provide medical services for their 'village'. They were offering a substantial fee which would be very welcome, but if I accepted it I had little doubt that I would soon be busier than ever. They had stated firmly that the rules meant that if I didn't agree to look after the holidaymakers on the site then the whole development would have to be cancelled. The problem was that I would almost certainly need an assistant. Did I want to work with another doctor? Could I work with another doctor? I had been working on my own for most of my working life and I was conscious that, like all individuals who work alone, I had become rather set in my ways.

And the developers were pushing for a quick answer.

However, before we made a decision, Patsy and I had to talk things over and make a decision in our time.

By the standards of town and city practices I have a very small practice. However, instead of being lined up in neat rows in terraced houses, semi-detached houses and blocks of flats sixteen storeys tall, my patients are spread over a number of square miles. It sometimes takes two or three hours to do the morning visits even if I only have three patients to see.

Having a small number of patients to look after meant that our income is very small, compared with that of most doctors. The rising costs of running the house and the practice mean that we are living a little more hand to mouth than I feel is entirely comfortable, and the developers had upped their offer several times. But if I could manage to deal with the larger practice it would be bound to have an effect on our lives.

I kept coming back to the thought that if I took on the extra work I'd really need to look for an assistant to work alongside me. But where could I find anyone prepared to work for the small salary I'd be able to pay? Where on earth could I find a young doctor who would want to work in a tiny village, miles from cinemas, theatres, art galleries and shops? We don't even have a supermarket in Bilbury. And where would I find a young doctor with whom I could work and feel comfortable? Doctors who work together have to trust one another's judgement completely.

Most people in the village were fighting the plans, of course, and Patsy and I supported the development's opponents though neither of us had done so publicly because of the work I'd been offered. Both Peter Marshall and Frank and Gilly at the Duck and Puddle were opposed to the work, even though they knew that they might benefit from it. Even people who might benefit in other ways were opposed, though no one in the village stood to gain as much as Patsy and me. The developer and his public relations people had responded by dismissing Bilbury as being full of selfish villagers who wanted the world to stay the same and who didn't want strangers changing the nature of our part of North Devon. No one seemed to know just who would win the argument. Medical practices in Barnstaple had looked at the possibility of working with the developers but had decided that providing night time and weekend cover would be impossible for them. It was all down to me and to Patsy.

Still, just as it is not fear but the fear of fear that kills us so it is not worrying that does the damage but the worrying about the worrying.

So I tried to put the developers to the back of my mind, nibbled at my toast, sipped my tea and watched the animals at play on the lawn.

I looked round. Patsy, in the pink quilted dressing gown I'd bought her the previous Christmas, was standing behind me.

'I didn't hear you come in!' she said. 'How long have you been back?'

'Just long enough to boil a kettle and put some bread in the toaster. Would you like a cup?'

I started to get up.

'Stay there,' said Patsy. 'Do you want a refill?'

I handed her my almost empty cup.

The telephone started to ring.

'I'll get it,' said Patsy.

I ate the rest of my toast and threw some extra nuts to a couple of late squirrels.

'It's Will!'

'Sorry to bother you so early,' he apologised. 'But it's always difficult to know when to ring you so I thought I'd telephone before you started the morning surgery.'

I asked him how he and his family were and we exchanged gossip for a few minutes. We talked about when he and his wife would come down to see us next.

'I'm sorry I haven't rung you before but I've been at a medical conference in Washington for what seemed like a lifetime and a half.'

'Was it fun?'

Will laughed derisively. 'I wanted to ask you how you got on with that student we sent you?'

'Quite well, I think. I thought she was very capable. I just hope she wasn't too bored. I gather she wants to become an orthopaedic surgeon and isn't too interested in general practice. That's a pity. The patients seemed to like her and got on well with her and as you know that's half the battle in general practice.'

'Oh, she certainly wasn't bored. Her tutor tells me that she hasn't stopped talking about her couple of days with you,' said Will. 'She says she's found her vocation and now all she needs to do is to find her Bilbury. She's told him that when she's qualified she's going to hunt around for a small rural practice – which is marvellous because most students want to work in big modern practices. She's still got a year to go before she's qualified, and then a year in house officer jobs, so she's got plenty of time to change her mind, but I think you might have succeeded in encouraging her to at least think about a career in general practice. Her tutor says she's even been talking about finding a job as the solitary GP on a small island somewhere. When on earth did you get a tractor by the way? She's bought some of your books about Bilbury and doesn't stop talking about them. I don't suppose you'd like to take 100 students next week? The world is full up with orthopaedic surgeons. We desperately need more GPs.'

I smiled to myself. Will is very much a morning person and can sometimes be unstoppable. I explained about the tractor, said how pleased I was to hear that Nancy had not been bored and told Will about the patient who had developed arsenic poisoning by breathing in the poison from his landlord's wallpaper.

Will was fascinated by my poisoning case.

'Are you going to write it up for one of the medical journals?'

'I'm thinking about it,' I said, though to be honest I hadn't been thinking about it very much.

We then said our goodbyes and promised to speak again before long.

When I'd put the phone down I told Patsy that Nancy seemed to have enjoyed her stay with us. Patsy was as pleased as I was, of course.

And then the telephone went again.

'I expect that's Will who has remembered something he forgot to tell you,' I said, wishing that someone would invent a telephone that didn't have to be fixed to a wire coming out of the wall. I'd heard of people developing telephones which could be carried from one room to another but thought it would be a long time before we'd be able to afford one, even if they ever became widely available.

But it wasn't Will.

It was Chase Anderson, the American author.

'Just wanted to say thank you for saving my life,' he said. 'I've finished my book so I'm driving to Heathrow and back off to the States sometime this afternoon.'

'Crumbs that was quick! You write fast. It was good to meet you! I hope you're feeling better.'

'Oh, I'm feeling fine thanks. I just wanted to say that if you ever get to the States make sure you two come and visit me. I'd love to see you. And don't worry about getting tickets I'll send the plane for you.'

'Thank you! What time does your plane leave today?'

'Oh, when I get there,' he said. And I smiled as I remembered the story he had told me when we first met. 'The damned plane's been sitting at Heathrow since I got here. It's about time the crew earned their living. I rang them up yesterday and told them to fuel it and stock the bar. They've been living in my Suite at the Ritz.'

'You have a Suite there?'

'Yes.'

'Permanently?'

'Yes, I keep one in London and one at the Ritz in Paris. It makes travel more comfortable. Your C.S.Forester, the doctor who wrote those Hornblower books, kept a permanent Suite at the Savoy Hotel so that he knew he had somewhere to stay in London. I thought it was a great idea.'

We said our goodbyes and I put the phone down and smiled at the idea of someone being so rich that they could keep Suites at two expensive hotels and have a plane and crew sitting on the tarmac for weeks at a time.

I told Patsy about Chase Anderson's kind invitation.

'We'd need a babysitter for the practice,' she said.

'I think they prefer to use the word 'locum',' I said, laughing. 'But babysitter is fine.'

I think we both knew we'd never take up the invitation – however attractive the idea might seem.

And suddenly I knew, too, that I didn't have to wonder about the future anymore. Nothing fundamental was ever going to change because we wouldn't let it change.

For us, Bilbury is a way of life and a state of mind.

'I don't want to take this job with the mobile home development,'

I suddenly blurted out.

'Splendid!' said Patsy.

'You don't mind?'

'Of course not! I don't want our lives to change any more than I think you do. If you took on a huge clump of patients in a mobile home park, everything would change. And I don't want anything to change.'

And it was as simply as that.

There and then, I scribbled a note to the developers and put it in the tray where our mail goes, for the postman to pick up. Twenty acres of beautiful countryside in and around Bilbury would remain unspoilt. The mobile home park would not go ahead. I wouldn't need an assistant and my working day would remain unchanged.

Patsy and I celebrated the decision by having more tea and more toast. And I put extra marmalade on my toast. It wasn't champagne and caviar but for us it was better. We're toast and tea people – not champagne and caviar people.

A week later I received a parcel, delivered not by our usual postman but by an international courier company.

'Open it!' cried Patsy, who has even less patience than I have.

The parcel contained a hat box and in the box there was a hat. Tucked inside the hat was a note. 'This is a Gambler's hat, from the same store which sold me the one you admired. But now that it's in England, you may call it a 'Chesterton'.'

I tried it on. It was a perfect fit.

'Are you going to wear it in public?' asked Patsy, who appeared to be having trouble not laughing.

'You can laugh as much as you like but I shall not remove it until I go to bed,' I told her firmly.

Appendix One
Freedom of Bilbury

Readers of The Young Country doctor books are entitled to hold the Freedom of Bilbury, North Devon, England and are, in recognition of this honour, entitled to:

Graze up to 12 sheep or goats on Bilbury Common for up to 60 days a year.

Be an honorary Life Vice President of Bilbury Cricket Club. Vice Presidents are guaranteed a deckchair at all home matches and unlimited supplies of tea, sandwiches and cake. They are also entitled to describe themselves (on CVs, biographies, etc.) as being a Life Vice President of Bilbury Cricket Club.

Hold honorary life membership of Peter Marshall's Vegetable of the Month Club (for rules of membership and discount details please see the notice at the back of the shop).

Vote in all elections held in Bilbury.

Enjoy a guaranteed reserved seat in Bilbury Church on the occasions of both the Harvest Festival and the Christmas Carol Service.

Appendix Two
The Author

Vernon Coleman qualified as a doctor and practised as a GP. He is a Sunday Times bestselling author who has written over 100 books which have been translated into 26 languages and sold in over 50 countries. His books have sold over three million copies in the UK alone, though no one is sure whether three million people each bought one book or one person has a very large bookcase. Vernon Coleman is also a qualified doctor. He and his wife (whose real name is Antoinette) live in Bilbury, Devon, England. Vernon is an accomplished bar billiards player (three times runner up in the Duck and Puddle Christmas competition), a keen but surprisingly dangerous skittles player and an accomplished maker of paper aeroplanes. He once had a certificate proving that he once swam a mile for charity and this may well still be in that box in the attic that contains all those bits of old rubbish (keys that don't fit anything, broken padlocks, pens which don't work and so on) which ought to be thrown away but which have managed to hang around until the next spring clean. He was, at some point in the early 1960s, second in the Walsall Boys Golf Championship and was awarded with three brand new golf balls which were wrapped in cellophane and presented in a smart, cardboard box. He claims to be one of the best stone skimmers in North Devon. (Nine bounces are by no means unheard of and he has a personal best of 12 bounces.) He is a long-term member of the Desperate Dan Pie-Eater's Club (vegetarian section) and although he can juggle three balls at once he cannot knit. He can fly a two string kite without mixing up the strings but cannot stand on one leg without toppling over. He can ride a bicycle without holding the handlebars but cannot write a note of music or hum the simplest tune. He has never jumped out of an aeroplane (with or without a parachute) but he has, on several occasions, lit bonfires in the rain and is particularly proud of the fact that he once managed to light one in a snowstorm. He has not yet availed himself of the extensive opportunities apparently offered by social media (he says he is waiting to see if the idea catches on) but notices about important events are pinned on the noticeboard outside Peter Marshall's shop in the village and he has had a website (www.vernoncoleman.com) since the day after King Alfred burnt the cakes. Entrance to the website is free of charge and there is ample parking space. Visitors to the site are requested to wash their hands before entering and to wipe their feet before leaving. Sadly, there are no advertisements or refreshment facilities. The Author is registered as an Ancient Monument and selected parts of him are Grade II listed.

Vernon Coleman's novels include: Mrs Caldicot's Cabbage War, Mrs Caldicot's Knickerbocker Glory, Mrs Caldicot's Easter Parade and Mrs Caldicot's Turkish Delight. All these books are, oddly enough, about a character called Mrs Caldicot. Other novels, which are not about Mrs Caldicot, include: Mr Henry Mulligan, The Truth Kills, Second Chance, Paris in my Springtime, It's Never Too Late, The Hotel Doctor, My Secret Years with Elvis and many others. He is also the author of three books under the pen name 'Edward Vernon'. All of these books are available as e-books on Amazon as are the 15 other volumes in 'The Young Country Doctor' series. There is a fairly full list of other books available as hard cover books, paperbacks, and eBooks on Vernon Coleman's biography page on Amazon.

Appendix Three
In December 2024 Vernon Coleman was interviewed for 'Unbekoming on Substack'.

The writer of the popular 'Unbekoming on Substack' sent Vernon Coleman 15 interview questions. Here are the questions and his answers:

You've had quite an unconventional career path – from magician's assistant to police surgeon. Which of these diverse roles has most shaped your perspective on medicine and society?

Between leaving grammar school and starting medical school I chose to spend a year as a Community Service Volunteer in a new town called Kirkby, just outside Liverpool. It was, to say the least, an eye opening experience. I suddenly found myself living and working as a catalyst in an area where the police station was barricaded and covered with razor wire and where the buses were always followed by a police car to give protection to the driver and conductor. Largely through naivety I wandered untouched like a white faced clown through the town and recruited a sizeable army of teenagers to help decorate old people's flats and do their shopping for them. The more the unions and the council protested the easier I found it to recruit kids. No one ever threatened me, bricked me or knifed me, and before I left I was made an honorary member of one of the gangs. That year changed my life. When I started medical school I opened a discotheque in the city centre because there was absolutely nothing else available at the time. We couldn't afford a glitter ball so I 'borrowed' an epidiascope and a projector from the medical school and showed coloured histology slides and old black and white films on the ceiling. The club was popular with several knife carrying gangs with whom I became good friends – mainly, I suspect, because I carried a Victorian sword stick and my blade was definitely bigger than anyone else's. Idiotically, I described the club on national radio and the Dean of the Medical School heard the broadcast. That was the end of the epidiascope and the projector (which had always been returned the following morning) but the club continued until the council closed it when it was accurately reported that there were beds around the edge of the dance floor. The beds were rescued junk and were there because I couldn't afford to buy or hire any chairs. It was all completely innocent. I was a GP Principal for ten years but I was never going to have an orthodox career. (I resigned when the NHS tried to force me to put private health information about my patients onto sick notes, something which I refused to do because I felt it was wrong). They fined me and threatened to keep fining me so I quit. I seem to have resigned a lot in my life.)

In your biographical notes, you describe yourself evolving from an 'angry young man' to 'an angry old man'. What continues to fuel this sense of righteous indignation after all these years?

I cannot abide injustice or a lack of freedom. I won't allow myself to be bullied and I don't like seeing other people bullied. When I was about 12 I remember seeing a beloved aunt and uncle cry because the local Gas Board was bullying them. I always think of my Aunt Alice when I'm fighting bureaucrats. When I became a GP I spent much of my life fighting health service administrators on behalf of my patients. I discovered quite early on that all bureaucrats are terrified of higher authority, and so when fighting some senseless rule which endangered a patient's life (and that happens more often than you'd think possible) I would point out that if my patient died as a result of their nonsense I would put their name on the death certificate as the cause of death. This never failed. I don't use death certificates as weapons any more but I'm still soaked to the bone in righteous indignation. This may well be why I am now banned by just about everyone.

Your early warnings about benzodiazepine tranquillisers led to stricter government controls. What initially drew your attention to this issue, and how did you persist with that campaign for 15 years?

I first became aware of the benzodiazepine problem in the 1960s and was writing articles about it throughout the 1970s and onwards. (I still am). The British Government changed the law in the 1980s, and the Health Secretary admitted in the Commons that they'd done it because of my campaign. I wrote a book called 'The Benzos Story' which contains some of the research material I used. Sadly, doctors ignore the law and still over-prescribe the darned things. Sadly, as I had warned, the drug companies replaced the benzodiazepines with useless and dangerous anti-depressants.

You've written over 100 books that have sold more than three million copies in the UK alone and been translated into 26 languages. Which book do you feel has had the most significant impact, and why?

This is like asking a parent to name their favourite child but I suppose the book which has had the most impact is 'Bodypower' which I wrote in 1983 and which was my first big international bestseller. It is still one of my bestselling books. It is, in a way, a very simple book which describes the self-healing properties of the human body but it has changed the way quite a lot of people think. It also influenced a number of other authors. I made several TV series based on the book though all my old programmes have been removed from YouTube. The basic principle is that if left alone the body can heal itself in many ways – and potentially dangerous drugs aren't always necessary.

Mrs Caldicot's Cabbage War was adapted into a film. What inspired that story, and how did you feel seeing your characters brought to life on screen?

When I first started writing Mrs Caldicot's Cabbage War the book was going to be something entirely different. I started to write a book about old people who rebel and rob a bank. (It's been done several times since then, but it wasn't a cliché when I started the book.) However, Mrs Caldicot took over (as I find that fictional characters often do) and the book developed along entirely different lines with Mrs Caldicot becoming a 'voice' for an oppressed group of nursing home residents. Antoinette and I bought tickets and watched the film at a large cinema, and at the end the entire audience stood up and applauded Mrs Caldicot. It was rather touching. I've since written another three novels about Mrs Caldicot and her chums and I'm terribly fond of them all. They're a feisty and fearless bunch who look after one another and stand up to officialdom. In 'Mrs Caldicot's Easter Parade' they end up broke in Paris and earn money for food by performing old music hall songs in the street. In 'Mrs Caldicot's Turkish Delight' they inherit a broken down old pier and have all sorts of fun. As I wander further into the foothills approaching middle age my affection for Mrs Caldicot grows.

You've mentioned giving evidence to committees in both the House of Commons and the House of Lords. What were these experiences like, and did you see tangible results from your testimonies?

I gave evidence to both Houses about the pointlessness and danger of using animals in medical research. It was, I'm afraid, a complete waste of time. When I spoke to a House of Lords committee one eminent member of the committee slept through the whole of my evidence. When speaking to both Houses, I pointed out that a good many drugs which are prescribed for humans are known to cause cancer or other serious health problems when tested on animals. The drug companies say this doesn't matter because animals are different to people. On the other hand, if a drug doesn't kill an animal the drug companies say this proves the drug is safe for people. I find this illogical as well as immoral. Unfortunately, the drug companies own the medical establishment and so campaigning against animal experiments has been a struggle. I have been opposed to animal experimentation since I was a medical student (I refused to perform required experiments on animals, and persuaded one or two other students to abstain with me) and this has always made me unpopular with people who have a lot of power and money. Animal experiments enable drug companies to launch new products without testing them properly on human patients.

Your list of favourite historical figures includes quite an eclectic mix, from W.G.Grace to Che Guevera. What common thread do you see connecting these diverse personalities?

Freedom and independence. I admire people who stand up for what they believe and don't give a damn for the consequences. W.G was the best known Victorian after the Queen herself, and he didn't lead any revolutions or die in a hail of bullets but he changed his world by being himself. He could be a bit naughty but was so popular that cricket grounds put up notices saying 'Admission 6d or 1 shilling if WG plays'. Che cared and was a professional rebel. Even when he was a Minister he still worked in the docks on Saturdays.

You've been consistently critical of the relationship between the medical establishment and pharmaceutical industry since your 1975 book 'The Medicine Men'. How has this relationship evolved over the decades?

I'm not sure there is a relationship. I loathe and despise the medical establishment and the pharmaceutical industry and they hate me. Between them they've bullied, threatened, sued and tried to bribe me. They've stopped me speaking and got me fired. I don't know who it was but someone tried to kill us during the covid fraud. 'I'll rest when they bury me,' as Clarence Darrow said.

You resigned from your newspaper column over the Iraq War coverage. Could you tell us about that decision and the principles that guided it?

It was an easy decision but it was a hard decision too. I've spent most of my life writing at least one column a week (at one point I had weekly columns in four national newspapers in the UK and half a dozen other columns in newspapers and magazines) and resigning from The Sunday People was hard because I had a lot of lovely readers (and, to be blunt, they paid me a great deal of money). I wrote a column criticising the Iraq War and the editor refused to print it. That was it. I have never allowed editors to decide what I should write and I always wrote articles and columns according to what I believed in. I've always been a fan of the newspaper editor you see in cowboy films – the one who prints editorials criticising the bad guy who is tormenting the town. I miss having a column but I now try to put new material on my website every weekday (except for a two week break at Christmas). I never accept advertising or sponsors for the website (and I never allowed my videos to be monetised). My income comes from selling books which I now self-publish since, after I exposed the covid fraud at the start of 2020, most of my publishers and agents abandoned me.

Your work has often challenged conventional medical wisdom. What gives you the confidence to maintain your positions in the face of establishment opposition?

I spent a lot of time (and money) on research. For my first book I spent more on research than I received as an advance or as royalties, even though the book did very well. My wife, Antoinette, the most compassionate and caring person I've ever met, shares my passion for truth, justice and fairness and is a brilliant and tireless researcher who can follow a complex trail with great skill and unwavering determination.

You've expressed strong views about the European Union. How has your perspective on global versus local governance been influenced by your observations in medicine?

I first became really interested in the EU in the late 1990s when I realised that national campaigns were ultimately always dependent on EU law and that there was very little point in fighting to change a law within, say, the UK unless the EU was also targeted. For example, when fighting against the use of animal experiments I found that the EU was the ultimate source of evil and legislators, administrators, drug companies, etc., would disclaim responsibility and blame the EU for every law and rule.

Your interest in Napoleon Bonaparte is well documented. What lessons do you think modern medical and political leaders could learn from his era?

It isn't widely known but when Napoleon was imprisoned on the Island of Elba and was planning to escape and return to France, the entire French army was sent to capture him. Napoleon, riding a white horse as usual, had a small faithful platoon of bodyguards with him but he rode ahead, alone and the entire French army, instead of capturing or killing him, circled round behind him as he led them to Paris. I have a copy of the leaflet his men distributed to the soldiers. It is one of the most powerful and moving documents ever published.

Your book 'The Dementia Myth' challenges common assumptions about cognitive decline. What motivated you to explore this particular topic?

When my mother fell ill with what appeared to be dementia, my wife researched her symptoms and concluded that my mother's symptoms were most likely a result of normal pressure hydrocephalus. We arranged for a total of nine neurologists to examine my mum. They were all dismissive, and even with the diagnosis handed to them on a plate they refused to accept it. When doctors finally accepted that they were wrong and that she did have normal pressure hydrocephalus, it was too late to repair the damage that had been done. The more I investigated the more I realised that many patients with alleged dementia have been misdiagnosed. There are several reasons for this. First, for some inexplicable but doubtless malign reason, doctors in the UK receive a cash bonus every time they diagnose dementia. Second, drug companies work hand in hand with charities to promote dementia in general and Alzheimer's disease in particular. I wrote 'The Dementia Myth' to draw attention to the commonest, easily cured diagnoses which are overlooked in favour of the default diagnosis of dementia.

You've been critical of medical screening programmes. Could you elaborate on why you believe they benefit doctors more than patients?

I never really saw the point of screening programmes. Having an annual medical check-up is like getting an annual bank statement. It tells you what your health is like on a particular day but it doesn't tell you what your health is going to be like in three months' time. Medical screening is a hugely profitable industry which has been shown, time and time again, to benefit no one but doctors and screening programme companies.

For readers who want to engage with your work and ideas, what's the best way to follow your current writing and activities?

Prior to February 2020 I didn't have any social media accounts. However, I was so horrified by the way the covid pandemic was promoted, that I tried to open accounts in the usual places. Even then I warned that compulsory vaccination programmes would be introduced and that, when it came, the vaccine would be dangerous. However, the censors were quickly into action. Facebook told me that I would be a danger to their community. Linkedin let me open an account and then closed it. The rest all refused to let me onto their sites. YouTube let me put up a few videos (some of which were viewed millions of times) and then expelled me for sharing too many truths. And so I am now left with the website www.vernoncoleman.com which I started in 1990. Since I am now also banned from all mainstream media, my website is the only place where my work appears. Details of new books and videos always appear on that website. Ironically, although I am banned from all social media (for the curious modern crime of telling the truth) I'm told that there are a number of fake sites using my name. When I first became aware of this I asked the platforms involved to remove the fake sites but nothing happened. So for readers who want to follow my current writing, I suggest that they visit my website which has new articles and details of campaigns posted every weekday. I am always grateful when people share the articles on my website because I am totally banned from all social media.

Appendix 4: What the papers say

(These quotes are included to balance the abuse and lies which are now littered throughout the internet.)

'Vernon Coleman writes as a general practitioner who has become disquieted by the all-pervasive influence of the pharmaceutical industry in modern medicine...He describes, with a wealth of illustrations, the phenomena of modern iatrogenesis; but he is also concerned about the wider harm which can result from doctors' and patients' preoccupation with medication instead of with the prevention of disease. He demonstrates, all the more effectively because he writes in a sober, matter-of-fact style, the immense influence exercised by the drug industry on doctors' prescribing habits...He writes as a family doctor who is keenly aware of the social dimensions of medical practice. He ends his book with practical suggestions as to how medical care – in the developing countries as well as in the West – can best be freed from this unhealthy pharmaceutical predominance.' – G.M.Carstairs, The Times Literary Supplement (1975)

'What he says of the present is true: and it is the great merit of the book that he says it from the viewpoint of a practising general practitioner, who sees from the inside what is going on, and is appalled by the consequences to the profession, and to the public.' – Brian Inglis, Punch (1975)

'Dr Coleman writes with more sense than bias. Required reading for any Minister of Health' – Daily Express

'I hope this book becomes a bestseller among doctors, nurses and the wider public…' – Nursing Times

'Few would disagree with Dr Coleman that more should be done about prevention.' – The Lancet

'This short but very readable book has a message that is timely. Vernon Coleman's point is that much of the medical research into which money and expertise are poured is useless. At the same time, remedial conditions of mind and body which cause the most distress are largely neglected. This is true.' – Daily Telegraph

'If you believe Dr Vernon Coleman, the main beneficiaries of the hundred million pounds worth of research done in this country each year are certainly not the patients. The research benefits mostly the medical place seekers, who use their academic investigations as rungs on the promotional ladder, or drug companies with an eye for the latest market opening…The future may hold bionic superman but all a nation's physic cannot significantly change the basic mortality statistics except sometimes, to make them worse.' – The Guardian

'Dr Coleman's well-coordinated book could not be more timely.' – Yorkshire Post

'The Medicine Men is well worth reading' – Times Educational Supplement

'Dr Vernon Coleman…is not a mine of information – he is a fountain. It pours out of him, mixed with opinions which have an attractive common sense ring about them.' – Coventry Evening Telegraph

'When the children have finished playing the games on your Sinclair or Commodore Vic 20 computer, you can turn it to more practical purposes. For what is probably Britain's first home doctor programme for computers is now available. Dr Vernon Coleman, one of the country's leading medical authors, has prepared the text for a remarkable series of six cassettes called The Home Doctor Series. Dr Coleman, author of the new book 'Bodypower'…has turned his attention to computers.' – The Times 1983

'The Medicine Men' by Dr Vernon Coleman, was the subject of a 14 minute 'commercial' on the BBC's Nationwide television programme recently. Industry doctors and general practitioners come in for a severe drubbing: two down and several more to go because the targets for Dr Coleman's pen are many, varied and, to say the least, surprising. Take the physicians who carry out clinical trials: many of those, claims the author, have sold themselves to the industry and agreed to do research for rewards of one kind or another, whether that reward be a trip abroad, a piece of equipment, a few dinners, a series of published papers or simply money.' – The Pharmaceutical Journal

'By the year 2020 there will be a holocaust, not caused by a plutonium plume but by greed, medical ambition and political opportunism. This is the latest vision of Vernon Coleman, an articulate and prolific medical author…this disturbing book detects diseases in the whole way we deliver health care.' – Sunday Times (1988)

'…the issues explores he explores are central to the health of the nation.' – Nursing Times

'It is not necessary to accept his conclusion to be able to savour his decidedly trenchant comments on today's medicine…a book to stimulate and to make one argue.' – British Medical Journal

'As a writer of medical bestsellers, Dr Vernon Coleman's aim is to shock us out of our complacency…it's impossible not to be impressed by some of his arguments.' – Western Daily Press

'Controversial and devastating' – Publishing News

'Dr Coleman produces mountains of evidence to justify his outrageous claims.' – Edinburgh Evening News

'Dr Coleman lays about him with an uncompromising verbal scalpel, dipped in vitriol, against all sorts of sacred medical cows.' – Exeter Express and Echo

'Vernon Coleman writes brilliant books.' – The Good Book Guide

'No thinking person can ignore him. This is why he has been for over 20 years one of the world's leading advocates on human and animal rights in relation to health. Long may it continue.' – The Ecologist

'The calmest voice of reason comes from Dr Vernon Coleman.' – The Observer

'A godsend.' – Daily Telegraph

'Dr Vernon Coleman has justifiably acquired a reputation for being controversial, iconoclastic and influential.' – General Practitioner

'Superstar.' – Independent on Sunday

'Brilliant!' – The People

'Compulsive reading.' – The Guardian

'His message is important.' – The Economist

'He's the Lone Ranger, Robin Hood and the Equalizer rolled into one.' – Glasgow Evening Times

'The man is a national treasure.' – What Doctors Don't Tell You

'His advice is optimistic and enthusiastic.' – British Medical Journal

'Revered guru of medicine.' – Nursing Times

'Gentle, kind and caring' – Western Daily Press

'His trademark is that he doesn't mince words. Far funnier than the usual tone of soupy piety you get from his colleagues.' – The Guardian

'Dr Coleman is one of our most enlightened, trenchant and sensitive dispensers of medical advice.' – The Observer

'Vernon Coleman is a leading medical authority and known to millions through his writing, broadcasting and bestselling books.' – Woman's Own

'His book Bodypower is one of the most sensible treatises on personal survival that has ever been published.' – Yorkshire Evening Post

'One of the country's top health experts.' – Woman's Journal

'Dr Coleman is crusading for a more complete awareness of what is good and bad for our bodies. In the course of that he has made many friends and some powerful enemies.' – Western Morning News

'Brilliant.' – The People

'Dr Vernon Coleman is one of our most enlightened, trenchant and sensible dispensers of medical advice.' – The Observer

'The most influential medical writer in Britain. There can be little doubt that Vernon Coleman is the people's doctor.' – Devon Life

'The medical expert you can't ignore.' – Sunday Independent

'A literary genius.' – HSL Newsletter

'I would much rather spend an evening in his company than be trapped for five minutes in a radio commentary box with Mr Geoffrey Boycott.' – Peter Tinniswood, Punch

'Hard hitting...inimitably forthright.' – Hull Daily Mail

'Refreshingly forthright.' – Liverpool Daily Post

'Outspoken and alert.' – Sunday Express

'The man with a mission.' – Morning News

'A good read…very funny and packed with interesting and useful advice.' – The Big Issue

'Dr Coleman gains in stature with successive books' – Coventry Evening Telegraph

'Dr Coleman made me think again.' – BBC World Service

'Marvellously succinct, refreshingly sensible.' – The Spectator

'The living terror of the British medical establishment. A doctor of science as well as a medical graduate. Dr Coleman is probably one of the most brilliant men alive today. His extensive medical knowledge renders him fearless.' – Irish Times

'His future as King of the media docs is assured.' – The Independent

'Britain's leading medical author.' – The Star

'His advice is practical and readable.' – Northern Echo

'The layman's champion.' –Evening Herald

'All commonsense and no nonsense.' – Health Services Management

'One of Britain's leading experts.' – Slimmer Magazine

'The only three things I always read before the programme are Andrew Rawnsley in the Observer, Peter Hitchens in the Mail and Dr Vernon Coleman in The People. Or, if I'm really up against it, just Vernon Coleman.' – Eddie Mair, Presenter on BBC's Radio Four

'Dr Coleman is more illuminating than the proverbial lady with the lamp' – Company Magazine

'Britain's leading health care campaigner.' – The Sun

'What he says is true.' – Punch

'Perhaps the best known health writer for the general public in the world today.' – The Therapist

'The patient's champion. The doctor with the common touch.' – Birmingham Post

'A persuasive writer whose arguments, based on research and experience, are sound.' – Nursing Standard

'Coleman is controversial but respected and has been described in the British press as `the sharpest mind in medial journalism' and `the calmest voice of reason'. – Animals Today

'Vernon Coleman…rebel with a cause.' – Belfast Newsletter

'…presents the arguments against drug based medicine so well, and disturbs a harmful complacency so entertainingly.' – Alternative News

'He is certainly someone whose views are impossible to ignore, with his passionate advocacy of human and animal rights.' – International Journal of Alternative and Complementary Medicine

'The doctor who dares to speak his mind.' – Oxford Mail

'Dr Coleman speaks openly and reassuringly.' – Oxford Times

'He writes lucidly and wittily.' – Good Housekeeping

Printed in Great Britain
by Amazon